Surgeon in Borneo

Priest in St Helena

Surgeon in BORNEO

Priest in ST. HELENA

Michael Crook

The Book Guild Ltd.
Sussex, England

The Book Guild Ltd.
25 High Street,
Lewes, Sussex.

First published 1992
© Michael Crook 1992
Set in Baskerville
Typesetting by APS,
Salisbury, Wiltshire.
Printed in Great Britain by
Antony Rowe Ltd.,
Chippenham, Wiltshire.

A catalogue record for this book is
available from the British Library

ISBN 0 86332 775 3

To
VERNON PENNELL,
Who made me a Surgeon

and to
Bishops EDWARD CANNAN and JAMES JOHNSON,
Who made me a Priest.

How far is St Helena from a little child at play?
What makes you want to wander there, with all the world between?

How far from St Helena to the Gate of Heaven's Grace?
That no one knows, that no one knows, and no one ever will.

Kipling

CONTENTS

PREFACE

Few books need a preface and most would be better without one. Sometimes it is necessary to explain what the book is about, but in an autobiography this is evident from the title. In other cases though, it is wise to say a little about the author, his life and work: but again there is no excuse for that here, as it is the whole subject of the book. Most of what I am saying here I had intended to reserve for the final chapter, but I feel the need to say it now, otherwise, I suspect that many readers who might enjoy the book would never get beyond the first page.

A Physician has a quite different outlook upon the world. To him nobody, and no part of anybody, is completely healthy or (unless dead) hopelessly unhealthy. He thus sees everything in shades of grey: nothing is black or white. He is educated as a gentleman and his attitude is one of understanding, tolerance for the imperfect, and Christian charity. To the Surgeon everything is either right or wrong, healthy or diseased, good or bad; and his life is dedicated to defining the boundary between what is wanted and what is not, cutting out the bad, and stitching the good parts together to close the defect. He is unstinting in his praise for what he sees as right and good, but reacts savagely to anything which does not please and satisfy him. Tolerance and charity are to him but other names for spinelessness and licence. It is no coincidence that although many Physicians take Holy Orders when they retire, a Surgeon-priest is almost as rare as a pregnant Archbishop.

For this reason if for no other my life has been an unusual one, and I hope very much that some people will find it interesting and entertaining: though I hardly dare hope that any will feel inspired to go and do likewise.

1

THE FAMILY

My paternal grandmother was one of the two nastiest women I have met anywhere in the world. The other was an Anglo-Kadazan who was beaten to death by her English husband, and who richly deserved it.

Grandma was born Helen Warwick Wood, the daughter of Alderman Warwick Wood, Mayor of Southport in 1908. Her husband Frederick Arthur Crook described himself as a fishmonger. His father may have had some claim to the title since he owned a chain of fish shops, but Grandpa had none. He had the misfortune to inherit thirty thousand pounds at the age of nineteen and it destroyed him. He was a musical performer of unusual ability who might have gone far; but who on the strength of his newly acquired wealth (and it was wealth in 1889), quarrelled with his professor and left Oxford without a degree. With the exception of a few days conducting D'Oyley Cart during the Great War, he did not do a single honest day's work in his life and lived to the age of eighty-six in misery, bitterness, and, it has to be admitted, squalor. His wife confided to me after his death that she had not known a day's happiness since her wedding day. I was surprised she knew the word. She certainly could never have had any use for it. I am sure neither she nor her husband ever caused or enjoyed a moment's happiness in the whole of their long lives.

My father was born into this menage before his mother was twenty: a very undesired encumbrance to two young people determined on a life of entertainment if not of enjoyment. For five years he virtually never saw his parents, being farmed out with the local milkman and his wife, while Grandma and Grandpa toured the country on bicycles. Progress must have

11

been slow, at least in the early stages, because Grandpa is known to have explored the Lake District on his honeymoon accompanied not only by his wife and luggage, but by a wet-plate camera and the portable darkroom-laboratory that went with it; all presumably carried on the two bicycles.

The house in Birkdale, then a town quite distinct from Southport, was reputedly built for his father to be born in which would date it about 1850, but the name 'Hougoumont' suggests a date a generation earlier. Any family connection with the battle of Waterloo had long since been forgotten or, as a result of the same inverted snobbery which caused Grandpa to call himself a fishmonger, deliberately suppressed. Grandpa had a brother and a sister but of course quarrelled with them and my father was quite unaware of the existence of a charming very aged maiden aunt until he was in his sixties.

From the age of five until the Great War when he was twenty, my father lived with his parents in that house in Liverpool Road and appears to have been treated like a dog and a good deal worse than a cat, as the family were cat lovers as well as cat purloiners. They never bought one; but any neighbour's cat that was found attractive would be enticed with food and milk and its feet smeared with butter to make it stay, as it always did. It was not a policy calculated to make them popular with the neighbours, nor did it. They were certainly the richest couple in the area and this was sympto-matic not of miserliness so much as an extraordinary contempt for ordinary standards of behaviour and honesty. During the last war Grandma used to put flowers every day before a Shrine in the memory of one of these stolen cats. My mother, who had a suspicious mind and remembered what the ill-tempered creature looked like, once opened the silver frame containing the photograph said to be of the dear departed, and found it was a commercially produced postcard of a different cat altogether.

Daddy was sent to the local elementary school and won a scholarship to Manchester Grammar. For a few years they provided him with a train ticket, though not with food or lunch money, but as soon as he was fifteen they refused to provide even that, and put him to work as an office boy in the local branch of the Midland Bank. He carried on at night school, passed all his banking examinations, and ultimately rose to be

Superintendent for the whole of South Wales at Head Office by the time I was a small child. He never rose any further as he became almost stone deaf by the time he was forty. Almost until he reached retiring age, by which time it was too late, he refused to admit the fact and use a hearing aid. After the Great War, as an external student, he took two degrees in Economics at London University, and was the first honours graduate to obtain the degree of Bachelor of Commerce. Grandpa was a weak man, but not I think essentially evil. These things were entirely the doings of his wife whom he was too spineless to oppose.

I had almost written that he was a stupid man, but we all do occasional foolish things, and possibly he repented bitterly such stupidities as leaving Oxford and marrying Grandma. Had he not inherited money he could have been a great man in any one of several fields. He was one of the earliest experimenters in wireless, and perhaps the only man in the country legally to use a television set after the last war when television licences came in, without having to have a licence. Sometime in the very early years of the century he was granted a licence for wireless transmission and reception that lasted for life; and it was held that this covered receiving television transmissions for all kinds including colour. He had one of the very first rotating disc receivers for the experimental transmissions from Manchester before Baird moved his station to one of the towers at the Crystal Palace and many years before the BBC started up at Aly Paly in 1935.

He was moreover a scientist, or at least a successful experimenter in his own right. He wrote a paper in Wireless World about 1914 describing how amplification could be obtained from a germanium crystal by using a second 'catswhisker'. He never claimed any credit for it and never even ordered any reprints of the paper: but he showed me a cutting and I had a transistor radio driving a loudspeaker in the physics laboratory at Monkton Combe School in 1943 some ten years before the two Americans won the Nobel Prize for its invention. He was also probably the only man to build the 'Flying Flea' and live to tell the tale. He only discovered after completing it in the cellar that it was too big to get out, and by this time having largely lost interest in the project, was just too lazy to take it to pieces and reassemble it somewhere else, where it would certainly have killed him.

His eccentricities sometimes reached a point where they might be called by an unkinder name. Sometime before the Great War he bought the superb Willis tracker-type organ from Holy Trinity Church, when they had the funds to buy a new electro-pneumatic one. It was almost as large as a cathedral organ, and far too big to go into the house, so he rebuilt the house around it. It was installed in what had been an outside courtyard with the consul projecting into the music room, which already contained a Steinway Grand. This blocked the only way into the dining room, which ever after had to be approached via the servants' sitting room, kitchen, scullery, and a surviving part of the former courtyard. Still it was a very fine organ.

This is not the end of the story. This organ was originally powered by a gas engine; but when he installed the engine in his cellar he converted it to water power. The idea was a sound one (he did not tell the water authority and continued to pay the standard water rate) except for one small point. The water-table in Birkdale is about six inches below ground level, and it was impossible to get rid of the effluent except by very slow seepage. He therefore had to build a huge static water tank, about half the size of the house, for the water engine to discharge into. There was a very fine fountain in the centre, but made simply from a bare pipe. He would not pay for any sort of ornamentation as he maintained, not unreasonably, that he would never see it working. The fountain after all only played when he was away playing the organ.

This is still not the end of the story. On a visit to the Southport Flower Show one year he was attracted by one of the ornamental water gardens on display. He could well have afforded to buy it, but that was not Grandpa's way. He photographed it from every angle and then paid a down-and-out odd job man to build him an exact copy. He then arranged for the water to be supplied by the overflow from the static water tank. I have already mentioned that he was a very gifted musician. One day shortly before he died, he played for me two and a half Bach Fugues. In the third he stopped suddenly in the middle of a bar, and hastily screwed down a valve projecting from the floor alongside the consul, saying 'I shall have to stop now or it will syphon and I shall loose my

14

goldfish.'

☆ ☆ ☆

In the early days of the Great War Daddy went to London with a friend from the choir, and they applied together for commissions in the Artists Rifles. The friend, who did the talking, said that he was educated at St Paul's (actually he had spent one term only at St Paul's Choir School), indeed that they had both been educated at St Paul's, and my father said nothing to correct him. They both got their commissions, and my father, although he appears on the Roll of the Artists Rifles, at once transferred to the Royal Artillery and rose to Field Rank. He served at Ypres and Passchendaele and got through the war without a scratch, although he was twice gassed. My mother always maintained that his deafness was the result of the concussion of artillery fire, although I suspect that it was really otosclerosis from which I suffer as did his father, though to a lesser degree.

After the war and after about a year in the army of occupation, he rejoined the Bank and spent what were probably the happiest few months of his life in charge of the branches on the Great Cunarders, first *Mauritania* and then *Berengaria*, making in all twenty-four double crossings of the Atlantic. Those were the days of prohibition, and they were able literally to do anything they wanted on the American side, as all the senior police and customs officers used to make use of the bank when it was closed in port as a private bar for their own refreshment and that of their important friends. Curiously nobody ever told me that prohibition was over and I suffered much inconvenience as well as ridicule when I first visited the United States in 1963, quite unaware that it was then legal to ask for a drink.

His great friend at Manchester Grammar School (I think his only friend as he made very few in his life and there was not one he could ask to be Best Man at his wedding) was a boy of the same age named John Hayes Fearnhead (Jack) with whom he travelled on the same trains every day. He visited his home in Southport and was dimly aware that he had a sister two years younger: but respectable boys of that age did not have girlfriends, mainly perhaps because respectable girls did not

15

have boyfriends. Be that as it may he claimed, I think rightly, that she would not look at him until she saw him in uniform. Even that is understating the case because they did not marry until 1924; which is why unlike most of the sons of those few who served throughout that war, I was too young to be killed in the next. Jack died on the Somme in 1916.

My father's parents were not present at his wedding. They had chosen for him a different girl altogether, though I have never been able to discover what they saw in her as she had neither rank nor money. They refused to recognize my mother for another fourteen years. At the time of the wedding reception they gave a rival party with this girl and her parents as guests of honour. When I visited them in the later days of the last war they constantly referred to her as their daughter and her offspring as 'Our other grandson'. They ultimately dropped them both in exactly the same way they had acquired them, when the boy refused to marry the girl they had chosen for him. Having lived in the East I think arranged marriages are a very good thing, but not with those two doing the arranging.

My mother's grandfather was always right. Indeed everyone in my mother's family was always right, but William Fearnhead was exceptionally right even by the family standard. He was a master builder in Manchester and Swinton, and built half the ugly little railway stations in Lancashire. He married an Elizabeth Blair and was soon so right that all his brothers, and all but one of his children, emigrated to South Africa to start a new life as far away from him as possible. The same thing had happened in the previous generation and I have thus far more living relatives in South Africa than in England, but as they took the family traditions with them few of them are on speaking terms with one another, and many of the present generation are unaware of each other's existence. Three of them died fighting for their King at Delville Wood, but left children who with the grandchildren have now been deprived of their status as subjects of their king's grand-daughter.

They are of course little worse off than the children and grandchildren of my mother's two half-brothers who died

16

fighting with the Canadians and Australians respectively, who cannot get permits to work in or even to stay in England: due to the congestion caused, amongst other things, by allowing the Germans to come in without restriction. I have a nasty feeling that if the people of the New Elizabethan England should ever need help, the Bosch might not be all that willing to give it, and that the betrayed peoples of the Empire will probably say they would see them in hell first. This is after all essentially what happened in the Falklands War and probably the reason for our spinelessness over the rape of Grenada.

My mother's father was one of the very few who remained at home and he took over the family business. He married young and raised five children by his first wife. Two of these were very young when he became a widower, and being at the time a member of the Plymouth Brethren, he had little difficulty in finding a new young wife from among the faithful.

If my paternal grandmother tended to leave a smell of brimstone behind her wherever she went, my mother's mother had at least some claim to be described as 'Saintly'. She inherited five of the most unlovable children east of the Altantic Ocean, and brought them up with a degree of love and devotion almost unknown in late Victorian England. 'Nanor' as I have always called her (and shall continue to do so to avoid the overtones always associated in my mind with the word 'Grandma') was one of thirteen children of John Hayes, a technician at Pilkingtons: a man definitely of the artisan class but who nevertheless taught himself Greek in his old age, the better to understand the New Testament. She brought up the five Fearnhead children, added two of her own, and found time to lecture three or four times a week on behalf of the women's Liberals and the Southport Women's Temperance Association, of which she was president for twenty years. Needless to say the association had as little to do with genuine temperance as the Women's Liberals (always referred to as 'Women's Lib.') had to do with the teaching or morals of the movement which today bears that name.

[There is something odd about this John Hayes which I have not yet fully investigated. He appears to have been a member of the Church of England who, as a result of having to shelter from a storm one Sunday afternoon in a Plymouth Brethren meeting house, joined that sect and remained a member for

17

life. I have a Bible which belonged to him and which is illuminated with some hundreds of exquisite miniature water-colours and annotated on every page in miniature writing that requires a powerful magnifying glass to read it. This writing, mainly in English but with many Greek and Hebrew quotations, is indicative of a degree of High Churchmanship which surpasses that of the Tractarian Movement and suggests a degree of mysticism positively Germanic. I find it quite incredible that such a man should have converted to any form of Low church protestantism, let along to the sect he is said to have joined.]

I have never been able to find out how or exactly when the entire family left the Plymouth Brethren and changed to Methodism. It must have been at a very early stage in his second marriage, because by my mother's early childhood, her father had already quarrelled with the local Methodists and been expelled from the Church. There was never any question of moral turpitude or heresy; they just couldn't stand a member who was always right and who always saw it his duty to point out where they were wrong. Right or wrong however, it provided Grandpa with the most satisfying and enjoyable occupation of his life. Pamphlets were printed giving a blow by blow account of all the wrongs that had been done him by the church worthies and they were distributed by his multitudinous children outside all the local Wesleyan Churches every Sunday. 'The Cause' or 'My case' provided work for the whole family all through my mother's childhood and right up to the Great War.

'The Cause' may actually have provided the children with welcome interest and entertainment: precious little else was permitted especially on Sunday which had to be devoted otherwise to Church, Sunday school, Pilgrims Progress, and Fox's Book of Martyrs. Anything to do with the theatre was of course of the Devil, and even at the age of seventeen and studying for her exams, my mother was not permitted to read Shakespeare. Fortunately John Wesley had never said anything about the Music Hall, and at least once a month Grandpa would regale himself at this entertainment which at that time in Manchester achieved a degree of licence unknown at any time in any civilized country until the permissiveness of the New Elizabethan England.

18

Southport is, I suppose, the Family Home, though on my mother's side only for her generation. I have visited there regularly since the war and until recently largely to see family friends, including for some years one named Valerie whom I was hoping would become more than a friend. I now go to visit the family graves, and because it has one of my sort of hotels and one of my sort of bookshops.

The Prince of Wales Hotel was at one time a 'Hydropathic' institution and had probably the best Turkish Bath in Lancashire. In my time all that remained of this was the magnificent equipment of the ordinary public bathrooms. Private baths only became universal in English hotels in the past quarter century, and even in an otherwise excellent hotel one would normally be expected to share a bathroom with four or five other rooms. Even so it remained and still remains a very pleasant and comfortable hotel and I frequently stay there for a week or so, although there is little else attractive in the town itself. Southport used, long after the last war, to be a place where Sunday was Sunday, where Lord Street was what Vauxhall Gardens used to be, and where the police use to take care it remained so. Today Sunday football, bingo halls, and filthy postcards are the least of its attractions to the worst of the young New Elizabethans. One will not walk far down Lord Street at night without being solicited by Irish prostitutes; and if one remains out for long there will be offered drugs, sodomy, and a variety of other entertainments unknown in the cities of the plain, and perhaps even in Port Said and Marseilles.

Even so, if one remains indoors and does not use the 'Late night Channel' on the local television network, The Prince of Wales remains a little oasis of clean, comfortable, respectable, Christian civilization. Nothing is perfect though. The food in the hotel dining room used to be superb as was the service. This dining room has now gone and been replaced by what must be the Southport equivalent of the 'Coffee Shop' of one of the International hotels, though it does not remain open at all hours and the food is much better. In addition, however, half the frontage where the Turkish Bath used to be has been converted into an immensely successful 'International Restaurant' where the cuisine embraces everything to be found between Cherbourg and Istanbul, and the same old Lancastrian waiters have been trained to speak with various continental

19

accents. This is not quite my cup of tea, but the quite exorbitant price was justified the only time I have dined there by a remark by one of these pseudo-garcons. I asked, as I always do, for my Cauliflower au gratin to be prepared without cheese. He gave me a look of withering scorn and announced in a loud voice 'Au Gratin, Monsieur, is French for with cheese sauce.'

It is not quite impossible that I have some close relatives in Southport of my mother's family, not of necessity arising on the wrong side of the blanket. Very recently when I remarked that a passing small boy showed a remarkable family likeness, she told me of an incident after the Great War when one of her father's managers became ill while winding up his business, or at least one of the builder's yards, and she took over for a few days. Apparently the driver of a brick-cart came in for his wages, smelling strongly of his horse, and while waiting for his money remarked in a friendly fashion ''appen as 'ow arm thi coosen'. My mother gave two weeks pay and indicated that if she ever saw him again she would set the dog on him. She apparently never had any interest in finding out what it meant.

At the very end of his life Grandpa appears to have mellowed. A few months before his death, and in Paris of all places, he announced that he really ought to see something of the theatre against which he had been inveighing for so long, and instructed his daughter to book three tickets for the opera. Knowing nothing of the subject my mother made some discreet enquiries as to which operas had unexceptional plots, and as a result the poor old man sat through six hours of Parsifal in French. He remarked afterwards that he did not think John Wesley would have minded.

He died one month before I was born. I am said to be very like him.

2

BEGINNINGS, SCHOOLDAYS AND THE WAR

It is surprising how little the average man remembers of his own childhood, and this I think explains how little most adults understand children. It is often said, particularly by psychiatrists (a psychiatrist is a man who devotes his life to proving that a child gets the same pleasure from childhood that an adult does from adultery), that in the past the mistake was made of regarding children as miniature and rather wayward adults, whereas in reality the child is a totally different organism, reacting and thinking in a way of its own.

Nothing could be further from the truth; at least assuming that I and the children I have known, have grown up into what can be regarded as adults. The boy is not even Father to the Man. The adult man IS the boy, grown larger, more experienced, and perhaps more disillusioned. I am quite sure that I have the same character in all its essentials as I had at the age of six. I may weep less often and seldom become physically violent, but the stimuli which produced these reactions half a century ago, are still the same stimuli which move me to the verge of tears (and sometimes over the verge) or produce the outbursts of temper which before I took orders were more often expressed in insult and abuse, and now simply by a rise in blood pressure and a certain degree of Clerical Choler.

Many writers of detailed and frank autobiographies will claim that they have no memories at all for events before the age of nine or even twelve. I find this incredible. I am able to fix certain dates with absolute accuracy, such as all the events on the day we moved house one month before my eighth birthday, and am quite certain I could fill a book this size with detailed recollections of events which happened before that. I think it is for this reason that I am able to get on with and understand as well as obtain the trust of small children much more than most men including those who have brought up large families.

[Perhaps a factor that prevents many adults identifying with and sympathizing with the attitude and problems of a child, is that although they do in fact remember their own sensations, emotions and reactions in a similar situation, they were told at the time what the proper adult attitude was considered to be, were laughed at or otherwise shamed; and the shame persists. They are thus strongly inhibited from seeing things from the child's point of view, which once was their point of view, and thus not only lose the chance of making a trusting friend for life, but possibly the chance of ending an injustice which recurs from generation to generation.]

What is possibly my earliest clear memory must date from the age of three or less as there was an infant type pram in the hall, which was replaced by a push-chair as soon as I was big enough. It is not, as is usual in such cases a purely photographic memory but visual and olfactory. I can remember very clearly coming downstairs with the sun shining in through the hall window and a strong and pleasing smell of buttered toast. Furthermore I can remember thinking that it was not a new experience, but that every day seemed to begin the same way.

There is one other clear recollection though which could be from much earlier as it must be of a visit to Southport. From the family photograph albums I see that my parents went there in the spring of 1928 and again in 1929 when I was two. It is just possible that there may have been a visit the following year although I can find no record of it, but certainly no more until the first year of the war as thereafter summer holidays were always spent at Bournemouth or Eastbourne. I am sure that before the spring of 1931, from which time at the age of four my memories are very complete, holidays at Southport were regularly talked about and I remember wishing I could remember at least something of Grandpa and his wonderful house and garden. The photographs of myself in that summer of 1929 show me as a very well developed and mature child for that age, and I really think that this memory must date from then, at the age of only a few months over two.

This incident is a very clear memory, my great grandmother, the widow of Alderman Warwick Wood. She was a dear old lady of immense age, certainly in her late nineties, sitting in a highbacked padded chair reading a very large Bible with a big brass and ebony Regency reading glass, which I have beside me as I write this. It probably began life in Warwick Castle. In the best Victorian tradition she was dressed in widow's weeds for her husband who could not have been dead less than ten years and probably twenty. [This was not unusual in Southport even ten years later as in the early days of the war I met many elderly ladies, not all of them widows, still in deepest mourning for sons who had died in the previous war.] I suspect that I was taken to see her more than once as I can remember her kindness and almost hear her voice. I can see her now, seen looking up from about the level of her knees, just the height of a two year old. I most certainly do not confuse her with Queen Victoria. The Great Queen may have looked very much the same but was someone I only knew from photographs and who did not belong to me personally, which Great Grandma definitely did.

She was the only person who had ever been kind to my father in his childhood, and certainly the only relative for whom he had any love and affection. She spent the last few years of her life at Liverpool Road with his parents, and they did not even bother to tell him of her death until she had been lying for five weeks in an unmarked grave. I have no proof of a story of a suppressed will, though she had told my father repeatedly that he was her heir, and I have never wanted to go to Somerset House to learn the truth.

I have very extensive memories for the weeks and days leading up to my fourth birthday. For some reason I had got it into my head that it was to be a vital milestone in my life: indeed that it would be the dividing line between childhood and manhood. I pictured myself as suddenly in a single night, transformed from a little boy in a white blouse and coloured shorts into a man in a dark suit expected to make my own way in the world. The conviction must have persisted for a period of weeks at least, as I can remember lying awake night after night, proud of what was coming, but dreading the responsibility that I was sure was going to be forced upon me. The excitement of a birthday morning must have driven the matter from my mind as I cannot remember any feeling of let-down or relief when the day dawned and I found myself still a little boy; though I can remember marvelling that night that the dreaded day had passed and that things were as they always had been. It was a curious obsession and has never recurred.

Several months before I turned five I had a brief glimpse of the cinema. The reason was peculiar and characteristic of the attitude to children in the early thirties. The local 'Astoria' had a floor show between films and it was decided to take me in to see twenty minutes of ballet. As exact timing was impossible and my mother was afraid that I might be frightened by the darkness and the 'Moving pictures' (though I had already been to the pantomime), it was arranged that I should go in for a few minutes that morning while a projector was being tested. The film was curiously unsuitable. It was a scene from a Laurel and Hardy film where the thin one (Laurel I think) was giving an arm to arm blood transfusion to the fat one. The equipment jammed so that the transfer could not be stopped before the donor had passed out. The nurse in charge rushed out to ask the doctor what to do and received the cross reply 'reverse the operation of course'. Some fifty years later I chanced to see the whole film on television in Hong Kong, and was gratified to find that every detail was as I remembered it. I sometimes wonder though if it had anything to do with my quite pathological horror of spilled blood throughout my childhood and adolescence.

The events of my fifth birthday had a profound influence on my future. I had been told in advance that it would be celebrated by a visit to the science museum, and I can remember the mental picture conjured up by the descriptions. I was expecting to find a darkened room like the theatre or cinema, and in it two or three little machines like the slot-machines in a fairground. The reality of course exceeded a million times my wildest expectations, and for the next ten years a visit to the Science Museum was the automatic and invariable choice for the last day of the holidays or for any other treat. Actually I was lucky to survive to get there at all. We went to South Kensington by tram, which involved a change at the Streatham Hill tram station with its wonderful roomful of switches and relays, which was almost a Birthday treat in itself. Unfortunately the refrigerator at the large fish shop next door exploded, and we were enveloped in a deadly cloud of ammonia gas. Several people were dragged away unconscious, and I would certainly have been killed had I already become an asthmatic. The science museum though made up for everything.

I started school at the age of five and a quarter, but before that I had been taught my tables up to twelve times and to write after a fashion, but was quite unable to read. I don't think reading was a skill acquired gradually over a period of months and years. I already knew my letters of course, but in my first term at school I simply gazed at the reading book for what seemed years but was probably only a few weeks, and then found suddenly in a single day that I could read it all. Within a matter of months I was reading children's books for pleasure and well within a year was struggling with *Treasure Island* and of all things, *The Swiss Family Robinson*. I have never learned to spell and no-one ever tried to find out why I couldn't. Actually I have no doubt at all that I suffered from a quite severe form of 'word blindness' but things like that were never considered.

A terrible thing happened on my first day at school and its consequences plagued me all my schooldays and will continue to do so until the day I die. It involved me in a lie that I never admitted to until I was over fifty. In all fairness I cannot remember that I was talked into it. ('I knew you would and you did didn't you?') although I think it very probable. I was after all a rather honest child. Nevertheless, however it happened, happen it did. I simply said that I had enjoyed my first morning at school. Before the day was out, the family and all our friends were rejoicing in the fact that I loved school. How wonderful it was, and how convenient too, that an only child with so few friends was happy at school. Indeed more than happy. He hated the holidays and counted the days until he could get back to the school he loved. Count the days I certainly did, especially the days from the first day of term to the next brief respite of comparative freedom. The truth is that with the exception of my last two terms at my Public School, I loathed and detested every day, every hour and every minute of my schooling; loathed it with a loathing I think far greater than that of anyone of my acquaintance who has had the honesty to admit such an attitude.

For some reason, and after going to inspect all the infants

schools for miles around, it was decided to send me to a school which was known to be closing down after one term. Streatham College was a sizable, and I suspect very good, girls school with a kindergarten section under one very competent young mistress. It is possible that my mother knew that she would be opening her own school on Tooting Common when the bigger one was pulled down as part of a rebuilding scheme, and regarded this just as a way into the new one. I am ashamed to say that I cannot remember her name, though I do remember her voice and appearance and her almost childlike agility. I don't think she could have been much over twenty. It seems incredible that she should have been able to set up and run a school for girls of all ages as well as for infants and, as far as I know, run it most successfully.

For the first few days at Streatham College, my mother took me there by tram, involving at least a half-mile walk to Norbury High Street to catch it, and then usually standing in the crowded vehicle for about twenty minutes. She soon realized this would not do, and after a very few days driving lessons (there was no driving test then) bought a Standard Nine to drive me to school. Due to his horrendous upbringing my father was always plagued by a reverse Oedipus complex, and though I now know he loved me very dearly, he was never able to avoid jealousy of the ordinary acts of maternal affection shown me which he had never experienced in his own childhood. The result was that he insisted that the car was also used to take him every morning, and bring him back every evening to and from Trinity Road tube station. To this day I cannot see what the advantage was to him. There was an excellent first class service between London Bridge and Norbury, and even if that part of the District Line had first class carriages, as many did up to the war, they could not have been anything like as comfortable. He may have saved a few pence on the fare, but it would be nothing to the cost of the petrol. However he had to pay his own fares but the car had been bought by Nanor, and the petrol either came from the housekeeping or from the £100/ year allowance which he more than half suspected my mother was getting from her. The new school was on the way to Trinity Road.

I think I am only just beginning to understand my father's attitude towards me at this age and indeed throughout my childhood. At the time I am sure my mother believed it to be one of indifference almost amounting to dislike, and I am afraid I assumed the same as I grew older. I think now that it was the exact opposite and that he loved me very dearly, but shyness and the consciousness that his own childhood had been so loveless and abnormal made him afraid to show it. Very seldom did he manage to establish any sort of rapport with me, but one such success was occasioned by a book of popular science called *The World of Wonder*. This was in three volumes published in weekly parts over a period of a year or more starting sometime early in 1934. He would buy each part on Thursday or Friday but keep the fact secret until Saturday evening when he would take me on his knee for an hour or so while we went through it together page by page and line by line.

For as long as I can remember I have been mechanically minded, but I cannot decide whether my quite remarkable grasp of physical science from a very early age is the result of this, or the reason why for so many months this was the joy of my life and the focal point of my week. In either case this book and the use Daddy made of it must have been the most important formative influence in my life. Subconsciously I must have yearned for a normal relationship with him, and in providing the means to know and love him it may also have given me a lasting love and knowledge of what he was teaching me. I am almost sure these were the only occasions when I ever sat on his knee. From my experience with other small boys since then I know that I would have loved and understood him far better if he had occasionally put me across it.

This lack of understanding lasted to the very end. When he was dying and my mother told him that hearing he was ill I had flown home from Borneo overnight and would be at his bedside in an hour, he at first refused to believe it; and then almost in tears said 'I would never have believed he cared for me like that.' Considering that only a dozen years before he had sat by the deathbed of his own worthless father for ten nights, this degree of humility was pathetic.

We moved house from Norbury to Purley in April 1935, four weeks to the day before the Silver Jubilee. The little semi-detached house in which I had been born was considered to be too small for the family, and the neighbourhood undoubtedly went down after the Second War, but I think at the time we left it was still a pleasant and respectable middle-middle class area. The little house had a small but attractive front garden, two nice reception rooms, one with a French window giving onto a sizable back garden, two large bedrooms, and a maid's room. The hall, kitchen and only bathroom were rather small but larger and much better finished than most postwar houses I have seen. Every room had proper ornamental plaster finishings to the ceiling, and of course every room was papered including kitchen, bathroom, and loo. In the entrance hall was a circular stained glass window which I think today would cost at least half of what we got for the whole house. I suspect my father had bought the house eleven years before for about a thousand pounds and he sold it for seven hundred, which in those days was just the cost of a standard Rolls Royce.

'Manor Side' in Woodcote Valley Road Purley, was a different proposition, and cost my father the enormous sum of £3,200. It had a quarter of an acre of land, but only a year before the owner had refused to buy for three hundred pounds a further adjoining quarter acre. When I remarked after the war that it was a pity, my father told me that had the price been three hundred pounds more, he could never have considered buying.

For this, my father got what I still regard as the most beautiful, if not the largest house and garden in Purley, a place renowned for the beauty of its homes, as well as perhaps being the most fashionable of the southern suburbs. It was a detached corner house built on the side of a steep hill so that the garden was a series of terraces. The front garden, about four feet above the road was on the first level, the house on the second, a small lawn, beneath which was later built an air raid shelter the third. Above this was a well fenced and superbly maintained grass tennis court, and higher still another small lawn. It was one of the very few houses of that period which had an internal garage opening off the entrance hall. There were five bedrooms, one of which my father furnished as a study. Even in those days it must have been incredibly good value for money. He sold it for seven thousand in 1963 having refused to let me buy it as an investment as he was quite sure it was not worth the money. It would fetch well over two hundred thousand today.

28

I did not actually see the Silver Jubilee procession but the dress rehearsal the previous Sunday morning. The event was well publicized and large crowds lined the route. Orders had been given that nobody was to be admitted to the stands, but the bureaucrats had reckoned without my mother. I overheard a whispered conversation with one of the workmen putting the finishing touches to a stand, and the magic words 'would ten shillings be any use to you?' A ten shilling note was pushed through the barrier for the four of them and immediately returned as each was unable to divide it. My mother produced ten shillings in silver and we were admitted to see the procession in style. I am not proud of the incident and mention it only to show the detail which a child under eight can remember all his life. Ten shillings was to me of course a vast sum of money.

A few months is a long time to a child, and it seems incredible that it was less than a year later that the whole world sat glued to the wireless that terrible night that George V died. My father was almost the same age when Queen Victoria died and apparently exclaimed in disbelief that he didn't know a queen could die. I knew full well, and it was like losing a member of the family. In fact I shed more tears over him than over anyone since or even over my great Grandmother Warwick Wood who had died when I was four and whose reading glass, it will be remembered, I have on the desk beside me as I write, for use whenever I lose my glasses. With the cinema, newspaper photographs, and above all by his Christmas broadcasts, he had made himself a deeply loved Father figure to all his peoples and especially to the children. We had also come to know the Prince of Wales in a similar way, and his weak face and insincere manner were just as familiar to us. Children have an instinctive judgement of character, and perhaps even at that age we subconsciously feared the loss of his father because we knew that he was a rotter.

As in most schools, if weather conditions made afternoon games impossible the whole school would go on an organized walk. I hated walking almost as much as football, but not quite, and it was a relief to me when on rare occasions games were cancelled and the walk substituted as a collective punishment for the whole school. I don't think though that it was for either reason that this happened on 10 December 1936. The whole Nation was hushed and horrified at what everyone knew was about to happen. It was a sad and almost silent walk, though we did exchange views on the enormity of what we saw as a betrayal by a man who almost by definition could not betray. We all knew the Ten Commandments, though in those days very few boys of that age knew the real meaning of the word 'Adultery'. It may have been made worse for us by the fact that we had been taught it meant 'Stealing another man's wife'. We all knew of the American woman (and each one of us would willingly have killed her if given the chance), that she already had a husband and was living with another man, and that she wanted our King. I have since heard of people who sympathized with him and thought he should have been allowed a morganatic marriage, but I think they wisely kept very silent at the time. The masters told us nothing, and we knew it would be indecent to ask.

When I got home that evening, the wireless was silent except for a brief announcement every half hour. I can remember much of it word for word:

> 'This is the National Programme. Here is a special News Bulletin. At four o'clock the Prime Minister walked to the Bar of the House and addressing the Speaker said "A message from the King Sire".'

The wording of the announcement was too formal for a nine year old but its meaning was clear. I remember the recurring words 'this instrument of abdication' and the incredible finish by the man who no longer ruled over us. 'God Save the King.' I would have been allowed to stay up to hear his farewell broadcast that night but I was too disgusted to listen. By morning he had left the land he had betrayed; our only quitter.

I saw the Coronation procession from the upstairs window of the Midland Bank on the north side of Piccadilly. One of the General Managers had taken the whole floor to stage a party for the senior head office staff and my father and mother were invited. In some way Daddy managed to get me there in his place, while he stayed at home to potter round the garden. Incredibly he managed to get away with the same trick sixteen years later for the Coronation of Queen Elizabeth. On both occasions the magnificent spread included Beluga Caviar to which I formed a lifelong attachment, but which otherwise never tasted until I started regular air travel. I think I am right in saying that on both occasions what we did not see through the windows we watched on television, though in 1937 the cameras were not allowed inside the Abbey so we did not actually see the King crowned. Three days later, on my tenth birthday I was given a real stamp album (my previous one had cost sixpence at Woolworths) and one stamp; a mint three-halfpenny brown, commemorating the Coronation.

In the summer of 1937 I had my first brief holiday abroad; two weeks in Paris to see the Paris Exhibition. We went by sea and rail, third class in England and second class on the ship and in France, and stayed in a little hotel in the Rue Cambon. Curiously I remember much more about Paris (the Invalides, the Opera, the Arc de Triomphe, Notre Dame and the Sacre Coeur, and especially the Louvre and the Winged Victory) than the exhibition we had gone to see. Although I have travelled widely I have only been to Paris once since then, when I saw nothing, and all my memories date from this visit at the age of ten. I remember particularly my disappointment at the Eiffel Tower, and my joy at the ancient and magnificently finished railway carriage in the garden of the Invalides where the German surrender was signed.

The exhibition itself was a disappointment. In fact I believe that not only through the eyes of a ten year old it was a flop. Except for the British effort which was contemptible, huge sums had been spent by every nation to produce a magnificent spectacle but obviously only with a view to political prestige. Perhaps it was the last manifestation of Britain's conviction of her own self-evident superiority to everything foreign, that we just did not bother. The only previous comparable function had been our own at Wembley in 1924 when we obviously had to give of our best: but this foreign imitation was childish and unworthy of our serious attention.

The German pavilion was impressive, but in spite of having for the first time had explained to me, the enormity of Communism and Stalin's Russia, I could not help but realize that the Russian exhibits completely outclassed everything else; and this was less than twenty years since they had started from nothing after the revolution. The most impressive were the magnificent farming and other agricultural machines. The British pavilion (they were in fact huge concrete buildings but ours was the smallest) also had the whole downstairs floor (there were only two) devoted to country life and pursuits. There were farm carts of timber with wheels of wood and brass, scythes, cast-iron horse ploughs, and a dramatic if crudely made river scene with a two-dimensional life-size cardboard cut-out of Baldwin fishing. It was all most impressive to a boy of ten (and possibly to others), and I gained the childish impression that Russia might have a future.

But I anticipate. 8 April 1935 was not long before the beginning of the schools summer term, and I was entered for the small pre-preparatory school attached to and adjoining 'Downside' prep school. I cannot be certain but I suspect that this little school was owned by its headmaster and his wife and was really completely independent of the prep school itself. In spite of the fact that I refer to him later in this narrative as 'Stupid' (which he was) this headmaster was hard working and dedicated, and had at least the sense to recognize in his wife a person who could run the school and make it a success, while always paying lip service to the myth that he was in charge. Small boys are not taken in by this sort of thing, even if their elders are.

Teaching was good and I was able to move up to the prep school proper after only two terms, curiously at Christmas rather than at the beginning of the school year, and into the second form where I was introduced for the first time to Geometry and Latin. Geometry I found easy and very enjoyable but of Latin I learned very little, then or at any time during the next seven years until I gave it up on going to Monkton. I still do not know enough to read a tombstone, and although I can understand the Latin Mass (as I understand every line of Wagner without having learned German) I have only picked it up by using a line by line translation. For the first few weeks I did well by treating the grammar as a form of mathematics, but then the rot set in as with any language and I allowed myself to be overwhelmed by the hopelessness of learning the massive vocabulary. I always came bottom of the class.

Downside Preparatory School in Purley had nothing to do with the great Roman Catholic Public School of the same name, and was owned and run by an elderly and very competent Head Master named 'Dodd'. There were a handful of borders but most of the boys came from the prosperous professional class families in the neighbourhood and were destined for one of the five or six second rank Public Schools.

By the third form we were doing Algebra, and rapidly reached a remarkably high level. Algebra as well as Divinity was taught by the Head Master, a very kindly and understanding man with a real gift for teaching very small boys, or at least those who were capable of being taught and who wanted to be; but who like every schoolmaster I have known, never considered trying to find out why a boy was not learning and what particular method of learning was best for him. It is much easier to report 'He could do much better if he tried' and genuinely believe it to be true. Having heard this said so often of myself, I gained the lifelong love and respect of one of my godsons by refusing to accept it when it was said to him. Like me he was a very late starter, though I fear in his case he was also an early finisher, but for him as for me it was certainly not a case of 'If he tried'. We were both trying desperately hard but did not know how to set about it, and nobody thought it his duty to find out and tell us.

I still have not made up my mind about compulsory school games. On the whole I think they are a good thing, not as a means of inculcating the team spirit (they don't) but as a form of discipline. It is a good thing to learn from an early age to accept having to do something one dislikes, and to strive to do it well. If this is the object though, it is unfortunate that the vast majority of boys thoroughly enjoy it; and as I was definitely one of the minority, it is difficult for me to form an opinion not biased one way or the other. At Downside discipline was reasonably strict but to avoid excessive whackings one of the methods used was a system of black marks, freely given for very minor offences, of which if one got more than four in a week one missed a 'Free period' given up to cricket or football according to season. I frequently deliberately acquired extra black marks by 'forgetting' to bring a book into class or something similar in order to spend these free periods in the comparative luxury of sitting in comfort in a warm classroom doing extra work in Latin or, if I was very lucky, mathematics.

The reason why mathematics often featured on these occasions, was that the extra classes were taken by a retired Naval Officer always known as 'Commander Turtle', who I am sure detested getting out onto the football field as much as I did. He taught arithmetic and geometry very well, but his knowledge of Latin was little better than mine, and I suspect his attitude to the subject much the same. He was a charming character and a good teacher, as they all were, but affected the air of a tough old sea dog. He was constantly maintaining that we all needed the discipline of a training ship and that he was going to introduce it next week, but he never did. Indeed whenever the Head was sick and as deputy he took over, he simply did not get round to punishing anybody. The only other master I remember at all well was a youngish man named 'Mills'. His name was his only claim to fame as it resulted in our singing Blake's *Jerusalem* whenever any boy was given the privilege of choosing a hymn. To small boys a joke never palls, and we derived great joy from singing 'Dark Satanic Mills'.

History, or what passes for history as a school subject, was as badly taught as at any of my schools, and for that matter as I know it to be taught at schools today. It consisted of a detailed study of uninteresting events during very brief periods of the history of England from 1066 to 1812. I doubt if any of us knew that Britain had ever been a Roman Colony, or a single fact or name before the arrival of William I. I was being given history lessons two or three times a week (I avoid saying learning or even being taught) from the age of six to fourteen, but I left school not knowing whether the Armada came before or after the beheading of Charles I, whether the French, Spanish, or Russians had any history at all apart from what we inflicted on them, or of course what happened to Napoleon after the retreat from Moscow. Modern history which starts in 1453 (I never knew why and had not heard of Mahomed II) ended in 1812. In 'Current Affairs', which is not history, I learned a bit about the Battles of Waterloo and Zeebruger but not of the Somme or Sevastapol. Of the teaching of geography, there as elsewhere, it is best to say nothing.

It was only long after leaving school that I discovered from my own reading what a fascinating subject history can be. Unlike geography, I think it is one that could and should be taught in schools, but it should not be remotely the subject that is taught now. There is no merit at all in teaching minute details of the history of one country for scattered periods, without having a general framework on which to hang these

34

isolated facts.

Children need to be given a comprehensive picture of the whole of history in the Western World from the first Dynasty of Egypt to 1952. Once the New Elizabethan age is past this too needs to be included, as it then can be without treason, as it will be seen to have been as important as the whole of British achievement since the fourteenth century, all of which has been thrown away. New World history can be taught in a few days, but the history of China, India, and the Middle East together need at least as much study as that of Britain.

Because of the huge canvas on which the picture needs to be painted, there will be no time for the minutae of any one national history, and certainly none for learning vast numbers of dates, though a rough chronology is important as one should know that Tutankhamen was probably later than Abraham but earlier than Moses, that King David and the Yellow Emperor reigned about five centuries before the flowering of Athens and ten before the death of Caesar, and that Jericho had been a city for about 3,500 years before Joshua destroyed it 3,500 years ago. If they can also be taught that St Augustine arrived in England in the sixth century to be met by Bishops and Priests of an ancient Celtic Church which possibly ante-dated Rome and who refused to recognize the Pope, so much the better. Any schoolboy who did not know the date of the Battle of Hastings but could tell me that the king killed there was Harold II, and that there had then been kings of all England for more than 200 years would become my friend for life.

It would be absurd to pretend that I enjoyed my time at Downside, any more than I enjoyed any of my schooldays; but I think it was a well-managed, civilized, and efficient prep school run on good Christian principles. If I had a son I would wish to send him to one very similar.

There now follows a brief chapter in my schooldays and relationship with my father which I find difficult to explain; indeed of which I am still quite uncertain of the true meaning. On the face of it, it looks very much as though he had abandoned any hope of turning me into an educated useful member of society, and was proposing to treat me much as his parents treated him; and cast me out to a future as a local tradesman. Even had this been so (and I cannot say with certainty that it was not) he would have had much more excuse than his father had. Unlike Grandpa he was very far from being a rich man, he had already done enormously more for me than had ever been done for him, and I had never had a school report which was anything but bad. The wicked comment 'Could do better if he tried', common though it may be among incompetent schoolmasters, suggests a degree of ingratitude which tests the charity of any man who is paying for a boy's education. (Even today though it is a really no judgement on the boy, but a confession of incompetence and laziness by the man who is paid to teach. Birch twigs can be gathered freely in any public park, and if the responsible master honestly believes this to be true, the remedy is in his own hands. Perhaps he cannot make a boy do better, but he can most certainly make him try.) There was never any question of my winning a scholarship as he did, nor had he expected it. He was eager and willing to keep me and provide me with transport to a Grammar school, which was what his very rich father refused him when he had obtained a scholarship. What he apparently decided (and later events suggest that it is just possible he did not intend it to be a final decision) was that I should go to a grammar school until I reached school leaving age, which was then fourteen, and then be put in the best job I was able to get.

No Downside boy had ever failed to go to a Public School, and it is very much to Mr Dodd's credit that he agreed to keep me on, if he genuinely believed I was destined for such a future. He was though a very perspicacious as well as a very good man, and it is not impossible that he saw through my father as he saw through so many small boys who were boasting of the terrible things they were about to do without any real intention of doing them. He was also certainly aware that with the pressure from brilliant scholarship boys, the standard required in the entrance exam to Whitgift Grammar School was enormously higher than Common Entrance, and that to get me through would be a private triumph, even if he did not want it made public knowledge.

Be that as it may, my last year at Downside, when I ought to have been taking advantage of the only opportunity I have ever had of learning Greek (a lack which has enormously diminished what I have got out of life and now sorely hampers my work as a priest) was spent in intensive study of mathematics and other subjects (excluding, I remember, French and Latin) which I was required to offer to get into Whitgift. In the event, of the whole day's examination I only remember papers in Arithmetic and English and how angry I was not to be able to show my knowledge of Algebra and Geometry. In the English papers I wrote two long essays, one on the ARP and the other on the Thetis disaster. I passed so well that my father was recommended to enter me for a scholarship the following year, even though I should already be in the school.

My father was delighted, but all my mother told me was that he was so pleased that he had decided to let me go on to university, if I worked hard at Whitgift. Nobody seemed to consider that I had shown myself to be as worthy as my schoolfellows of the normal education of my class. What my father really intended to do with me I have never been sure, but Hitler took the matter out of his hands.

My father was one of the very few people I have known who really saw Hitler's war coming. Reading the histories and autobiographies of the years just before the Great War, there seems no doubt that right up to July 1914 nobody outside Germany considered war remotely possible; but if the people I met and talked with in my childhood were in any way typical, things were just as bad during the rise of Hitler. However, the day after the invasion of Austria my father was quite certain that war was coming, and at a few hours notice packed me off in the care of my grandmother ('Nanor' the good one) to stay in a little lodging house (it must, I am sure have gloried in the name of 'Private Hotel') in Southport. To what extent I really understood what he was trying to save me from and what the full implications of a new war would be I cannot say, but I was quite sure he was right and everybody else just stupidly ignorant. I can remember very well the maid coming in with my morning tea the day after the Munich agreement, and the tremendous relief of hearing that there was to be no war and that the Prime Minister had promised that there was to be

'Peace in our time'.

Within two days I was back at school, subject to a certain amount of ridicule for having run away thinking that there was going to be a war. Possibly my father also suffered some chaff at the bank, but he knew he had been right, that it had been a very near thing, and was not in the least put out at having jumped the gun. As a result he did exactly the same thing early in August 1939, still somewhat prematurely, but then absolutely right. This time we went to stay for nearly a month in the Palace Hotel, and before the month was out my mother was sent to join us. All-in charges at this, probably the second most select hotel in Southport were then a stupendous three guineas a week, and I have never discovered how long he had intended to keep the three of us there.

However the thing was taken out of our hands by the evacuation plans. His mother (the one I call 'Grandma') arrived one morning nearly hysterical, having been served a notice that five evacuees were to be billeted on her. Within hours we had moved into my grandparents' house (although they had long sworn that no-one of my mother's family should ever cross their threshold) together with two extra servants, one a mere child herself, recruited solely to block the available rooms and beds and so avoid their being compelled to do their humanitarian and patriotic duty. It was hard on us but, had the unfortunate children known it, a wonderful reprieve for them. The arrangement did not last long. As soon as the authorities had been satisfied that the house was now so crowded that it should have excited the interest of the medical officer of health, Grandma announced that she 'was being made a convenience of' (the only time I have heard the expression) and threw us all out again. I think the Palace Hotel had been requisition for some government purpose, and we went to live in an annex, which was in fact a makeshift lodging house but staffed with some of the more elderly servants from the hotel who hadn't been able to join up.

Once we were properly, if temporarily, installed in Liverpool Road, it became necessary to see to my schooling. To this day I do not know why my own prep school which had been evacuated to Bedford was not even considered. Admittedly I had officially left, but my mother knew that we would probably only be in Southport to the end of the year and I certainly would have had the chance of a reasonable continuation of my education. Instead I was sent for but a single term as a dayboy to a little prep school on the outskirts of Southport (whose very name I cannot now remember though there is plenty about it I shall never be able to forget) that was in many ways like something out of Dickens. Like many, probably most small preparatory schools it was privately run by one man, who had the capital and a fondness for children but in general no profound learning himself and almost certainly no training for the job. I do not remember him very well but in all fairness I think he was probably a nice chap and in spite of the severity he had to exert at the request of his staff, was almost certainly neither perverted nor sadistic.

Prep schools originally grew out of the sort of small school (including the Dame's School) where one teacher had to cope with every subject, and the system had persisted there if nowhere else. It was not that there was insufficient staff, there were at least five forms, but each form was in the care of a form master or mistress who taught them everything. Such a system also dates from the days of teaching by chastisement, which too had become obsolete elsewhere but was retained in this school. In any good school where it is intended the boys will get on, punishment needs to be applied to blatant slackers; but there must have been very few left at that time, and even fewer today, where it was used freely on those who made minor mistakes in a single lesson or who failed to attain the required standard in the regular tests which came several times a day. I now realize that it was only the unwonted privacy of living in a hotel which prevented my mother seeing evidence of this, when she would certainly have removed me, particularly as it was obvious I was learning nothing.

I think I was probably lucky, although I did not see it at the time, in being allocated to a class taken by an elderly lady who probably had a vast store of knowledge on every subject, or at least a hundred per cent knowledge of the school book account of the subjects she was supposed to teach to her ever-changing flock. She had however no idea at all of how to teach, and made no attempt to do so. Her method (and aided by the headmaster's strong right arm it was said to be highly success-ful as no boy had ever failed to pass the Common Entrance exam) was in every class and for every prep to set a portion of the textbook, be it Euclid, history, Latin, geography, or Bible study (which that term meant twenty verses at a time of the Acts of the Apostles), and the following day to conduct a detailed test on it. This would comprise a regular series of twenty questions on the passage, covering it in the minutest detail. Failure to secure a satisfactory mark in such a test meant an hour and a half detention working on the same passage, the last few minutes being spent on a new viva-voce test which if not passed meant a repeat of the whole proceeding.

The only fault in the scheme was that there were only three detention periods available in a week, and once a boy had been booked for all these (which many of us had by Monday evening) all further failures had to be made up by a visit to the headmaster for chastisement.

I don't think the good man enjoyed these demands on his time, though he was in splendid physical shape for his age and this appeared to be his only source of exercise; but he too obviously regarded it as a normal and essential part of the running of a school. He was however very merciful in one respect. These incidents were so frequent that had he used a cane, few if any of his pupils would ever have been able to sit down from beginning to end of the term. A cane is a savage weapon in that not only can it hurt very severely at the time, but it inevitably causes deep bruising which goes on hurting for hours afterwards and leaves the part tender for days. Punishment was administered on the bare skin with a thin black switch, possibly made of whalebone. It stung like blazes at every stroke, but the moment the whipping was over the pain began to go, and by the time we had listened to the head's comforting assurance that all was forgiven and that we had been very plucky (even if we hadn't) the sting had diminished to a mild and insignificant warmness.

My remark about healthy exercise was intended to be humorous, but it has just occurred to me it could be true. With nearly 200 boys almost all of whom got at least six strokes not less than once in a six-day week, with an eight hour working day this works out at a minimum striking rate of twenty-five per hour; by no means a sedentary occupation. I imagine he was as unmoved by the operation as a Chicago pork butcher killing piglets.

Had I remained at that school for any length of time I

cannot honestly hazard an opinion on what might have been my state of knowledge, or my psyche. I certainly learned nothing. As will appear later I have never been able to learn by conventional methods, and I might have been their first scholastic failure. Whether I would have been a much more humane person or a sexual pervert it is hard to say. Just possibly I might have been both. As it was I was taken away to go to live in Bath a few days before the end of term. The only reaction of the good dame to hearing that I was leaving to go to Bath was to ask whether there was not enough water for me at Southport. I am not sure that my reply was born of quite so much precocious wit as might be thought, but I was bright enough to say 'Yes but I prefer fresh water.'

We were going to Bath because my father was there, and likely to remain there 'for the duration'. After Munich, possibly I suspect as a result at least in part of his advice, the Midland Bank decided to make contingency plans for evacuation of its Head Office provincial departments, to places where German bombing was unlikely. One would have thought that each department would be quartered in one of the safer parts of the area it served, but this was not so. In most cases they were about as far away from the branches they were running as if they had stayed in London. Perhaps at that time the possibility of invasion had not been considered by anybody, but when the danger arose it was obvious that a Head Office department cut off from its branches by a German army would have been as useless as if it had stayed in London and been bombed.

Whatever the logic behind it, the South Wales department was to be moved, and in due course was moved, to Milsom Street Bath. A possible reason in this case was that there were two disused upper floors above the Bath branch, and my father was sent early in 1939 to plan their conversion to the offices of his department and to find accommodation for the staff somewhere in the vicinity. I cannot imagine why he was chosen for the job, unless he had played at least a major part in planning the whole operation. The staff accommodation he found was in a rather scruffy hydropathic hotel at Limpley Stoke, about five miles outside the city.

It must have been only a few days before Christmas that the rest of us arrived in Bath. Accommodation was almost unobtainable in the town following the arrival not only of the Bank but of the very much larger pay department of the Admiralty. My father had given up trying, but Mummy drove down and found an ideal place within a few hours.

It was a late-Victorian semi-detached house on the outskirts, with three storeys and extensive kitchens and outhouses, owned by a lady of a type which is probably now extinct, and even then was very nearly so. She was the last survivor of an ancient family, paintings of whose members in Bishop's gaiters or the sash of the Garter adorned every wall. In a glass case in the hall was the sword of her only son, a regular officer in the 24th Punjabis killed in the previous war, and behind the garage about two thousand empty quarter-size whisky bottles. There were only twelve books in the house, including of course the *Army and Navy catalogue*, but also two genealogies of her family showing how both sides were descended from Edward III. She had recently had a stroke and gone into a nursing home from which she never emerged; and her nearest relative, a Bishop's wife of course, had arranged the renting on condition that we retained the only servant, an excellent cook general who worshipped everything to do with the family and if she touched nothing else carefully dusted the genealogies and family portraits every morning.

Our next door neighbour was a woman doctor, Clara Cross MD, MRCP; formally a pathologist at Bristol University. She was married with two young children but at the beginning of the war took over the running of the military hospital which sprang up in the grounds of the nearby St Martin's Workhouse and which has since become one of the best known hospitals in Somerset. She worked there full time as a physician but still found time to act as Coroner's pathologist for the whole of Bath, and Blood Transfusion Officer for the whole area, as well as for some private practice. Her third child was born early in the war. She finished her Saturday morning clinics, admitted herself to have the baby, and was back at work on Monday morning.

Her husband was an engineer who had a small factory or workshop opposite the hospital in which he manufactured prototypes of some of the weirder inventions which people

42

devised to aid the war effort. They had a gentleman's agreement that neither would interfere in the others work even if this endangered the home or family. Clara believed that there was an advantage in using children's blood in babies, and used on occasion to bleed their own children nearly white: while he had no scruples in starting up half-size aero-engines in the sitting room. I only knew her once to protest, when her husband and friends cleaned a piece of equipment with petrol and dried it in her new electric cooker. The resulting explosion drove the remains of the cooker through the kitchen wall and over a fence into our garden. I think her influence played a large part in guiding me to each of my professions.

It was of course too late for me to go back to school for that term (did my mother suspect something of the one at Southport? else why was I not left there as a border for the last week or so?) and I have regarded it to the everlasting credit of my father that he tried at once to get me into Monkton Combe. Otherwise I should have said that the war was my salvation as without it I should have finished up as a Whitgift Grammar School boy, probably to be a bank clerk or a prominent local tradesman. Many parents, I think quite wisely, decided during the war that their children should be at schools near at hand. As it was I was just too young for Monkton and rather than send me to the Junior School I was sent for two years to the superb Edward VI Grammar school, then still in its ancient buildings. I thus got the best possible of both worlds, learning enough in two years to see me through School Certificate and as regards Physics and Chemistry all I was ever actually taught for Higher Certificate, and then going on to a Public School to be educated.

For the amassing of knowledge, nothing can possibly touch a Grammar School, but this of course has little or nothing to do with education. KES was one of the very best, perhaps not even second to Manchester Grammar. The standard and competition were astoundingly high, due to the method of selection. All but a handful of the boys had passed two separate scholarship exams and were the cream of the state schools in an area of many hundreds of square miles. Physics was in the hands of a Mr Langley, a brilliant scholar and teacher as well as a devout Christian who took prayers every morning and was a lover of Gilbert and Sullivan. I may have learned a little myself from the books but nobody else taught me a single fact in the subject, and it was his teaching entirely that carried me through School Certificate and Higher Certificate years after I had left the school. Indeed at Monkton I was employed to teach physics to the lower forms.

The class I entered in January 1940 and was then the second form (we moved up almost automatically year by year) contained about thirty boys, but for some reason three of us formed a little solid group. I don't think it was a matter of class and it was certainly not that we were of similar ability or even interested in the same school subjects. David Coombe, who wore powerful spectacles and was known as 'Goggles' was far and away the most brilliant boy in the school, and always the top in every subject until I began to surpass him in physics, although I remained almost bottom in everything else. David Griffiths was the son of a dentist who had been a friend of Goggles' father in the Great War and was living with the Coombe family 'for the duration'. I was the duffer of the three and I have never known what the two Davids saw in me. Had anyone said that we might among us produce a parson we would have laughed the idea to scorn, though if pressed we might have admitted that Goggles might finish up that way. He is in fact a Fellow of Christ's and a specialist in an obscure field of Botany who has barely set foot outside the College since he went there from school. David Griffiths and I are in Holy Orders, he after a chequered career in Cocoa and then in Lloyds is an Archdeacon in Reading, and I after a lifetime in Surgery, a Curate in an isolated outpost of the Empire.

It was only in my last year that I joined the JTC and got just a little bit of experience of things military. We held parades almost every week, marching through the town with a band playing and drilled at the Bath football stadium. I left King Edward's just too soon to take Certificate A and was only able to do one term in the corps at Monkton as my health limited my activities, and the 'Commander', an ex-private of the Medical Corps, was not interested in a boy who was unfit. He could however have been kinder in the terms he used in pointing out that I was unsuitable. He may have thought I was shamming, but with his limited knowledge and intelligence he was hardly justified in telling me that I was 'Rotten to the core'. It enabled me though to leave with the magnificent rejoiner 'Well sir, the Corps has always been pretty rotten to me.' I think he was reasonably popular among the lower forms where he taught arithmetic, but even so, much joy was caused when in his temporary absence his photograph was accidentally printed in the local paper with the caption 'Bath Handbag thief gets three months'. It was exhibited on the school notice board for several days.

It was through David Griffiths that I was introduced to one of the most amazing families I have known. In an ancient house on Combe Down lived a lady of unbelievable age with her three maiden daughters (the youngest about seventy) whom she ruled with a rod of iron. They were the survivors of a family which had served India since the days of Clive, and India was their only interest in life and almost their sole topic of conversation. It was only after one had known them for some time though that one began to realize that they had lived their lives almost in Purdah and that their ideas were derived from their long dead men-folk. Their India was not the Indian Empire, which they all regarded as the apotheosis of decadence. The old mother who still went about the garden on two sticks had been a young woman, not a child, at the seige of Lucknow and their India was the Company's India before the Queen declared herself Empress in 1858.

I have come across similar cases of active but very aged people. The last time I attended a Monkton Combe Old Boys' dinner at the St Ermine's Hotel in Buckingham Palace Road, the guest of honour was a retired Head Master then aged 101 who was still working part time as a locum priest. He had come up that afternoon from Bath driving a pre-war Austin Ten and about eleven o'clock, after having made a long and racy speech and been the life and soul of the party, he apologized for having to leave early but said that he had to drive back to Bath and did not want to be too late to bed. A certain amount of pressure was brought to bear on the old man to persuade him to stay the night in the hotel and return home at his leisure the following day. He replied 'Oh no, I must not give way to my age. My young brother took to his chair when he was ninety-three and that was the end of him.'

While I was a house surgeon at Cambridge in 1951 the Master of a certain college died at a similar age. For many years he had not been known to say anything at the High

Table, and the Fellows on entering would simply bow, say 'Good evening Master' and then talk across him as though he had been part of the furniture. One evening someone said something about the war. The old man's eyes lighted up and he said 'Oh, I remember the war.' There was a respectful pause while everybody tried to work out whether it was going to be the Boer War or the Crimea. The registrar I was working with who was present claims he then went on 'I was in the republic at the time, I met Lincoln, he seemed a nice young man.' On my last visit to Capetown in 1986 there died a man aged 108 who had been at the Cenotaph service the previous November and had been a young officer in the force that relieved Mafeking. During my childhood in Purley there lived in the adjoining suburb of Wallington a lady whose father had been a young man in Paris during the French Revolution.

About the end of 1940 the old woman who owned the house died, and the Bishop's wife arranged the sale of almost all the contents so that we could get our furniture out of store in Croydon and have our own home about us again. Although only semi-detached, it was in fact a larger house than Manor Side, and my mother was able to lay in a very fine collection of the Regency furniture which was freely available in Bath at ludicrously low prices. Air raids were a distraction rather than a nuisance, though in the early summer after the fall of France it was distressing to see the perfect formations of German bombers flying on their way to and from Bristol without any opposition. The Battle of Britain was fought in the south, and we saw no signs of the RAF during the weeks of massed daylight raids. The boys at KES were divided into 'Funk Squads' and whenever the sirens sounded we were supposed to go to relatively safe places in the vicinity to take cover. My destination was at first the packing room of a dairy, which would have collapsed like a house of cards had there been a bomb anywhere near (it did two years later, during the Blitz) and later the cellars of an ancient wine merchant, which was probably better. (The wine merchants had the superbly appropriate name of 'Fuller and Hicks'. When I was a baby and on the verge of starvation from failure of the natural supply of nutriment, Nanor brought home for me a tin of 'Cow & Gate' and a book of instructions. The whole idea of artificial feeding was so contrary to family traditions that almost certainly all would have been lost had it not been for a picture on the cover of a bouncing well-nourished child with the caption 'Baby Hicks'. My father at once exclaimed 'So does ours' and I was saved.)

Air raids at night were not much of a problem in the early days, as all we had to do was move to our own Funk Hole and sleep there. There was a theory that the space under the stairs was the safest place in any house (ours was a commodious butler's pantry) and that if the house collapsed, this space would remain. Often it did, with the debris of the house on top of it, but it did not necessarily follow that one would be dug out. Rescue squads seldom had a plan of what the house had been like when it was a house, and nobody would know where the staircase (staff and family) in these old houses would be. On the first night of the Bath Blitz I watched a young nurse (she was a fulltime worker in hospital but spent her nights off as a volunteer at our First Aid post) crawl twenty yards in a tunnel which had formed under the debris, and at the height of the bombing, to give morphine to dying casualties who couldn't be released from the masonry pinning them down. This was certainly service in the face of the enemy, and I cannot see why she did not get the VC.

There is perhaps little point in narrating the reactions of a fourteen year old to the shattering events of December 1941, but I do so because my recollection of people's reactions at the time and the account which can with difficulty be extracted from the records differs so much from what is being said today and taught in the schools. That the American Navy was completely unprepared is of course true, but there was no possible excuse for their being so, and it is nonsense to say that this was the beginning of the war in the Pacific. Japan had already invaded Malaya and Borneo. Admittedly it was only a matter of a few hours, but knowing (as they certainly should have known) that the Japs had already made a murderous attack on us, it is quite absurd that no preparations were made for a surprise attack, that the ships' officers were ashore for the day, and that when the Japanese aircraft were seen on the radar screens they were assumed to be friendly.

Even Lord Moran writing in 1966 states of Pearl Harbor that 'This act of pure aggression brought the United States into the War'. Nothing 'Brought' the United States into the war, and probably nothing ever would have done so. Not only Japan but Germany, Italy, and even Thailand themselves declared war on the USA before that country had decided how to react to the attack. Roosevelt had said to the American people a few months before 'I give you one more assurance. I have said this before, but I say it again and again and again. Your boys are not going to be sent into any foreign wars.' (At the time this was a relief to many people. After the fall of France there had been a real danger, discussed in all seriousness in the press and elsewhere, that Roosevelt would repeat the mistake of President Madison in 1812 when he thought Napoleon had got us down, and join in on the other side to share in the loot of the British Empire.) It is difficult to see how he could ever have gone back on this pledge.

What is astonishing to me now, is that in everyone's conversation and as far as I remember the newspaper reports and comments, all the emphasis was on the attack on Hawaii and little if anything said about the much more significant attacks on our own Eastern Empire and the Philippines. Whether the American Navy would have paid any greater part in the war than it did may be uncertain, but situated where it was and with their armies completely unprepared, they could have done nothing to prevent the Japanese conquest at that time even if they had wanted to. What is more, had Japan left the American fleet alone they would have been left free to pursue their conquest of SE Asia and Australia; and when they had established bases in North Borneo, no effective resistance could have been made to their occupation of the Philippines.

Nobody would dispute that the American forces played a major part in the fighting at the end of the war, but it is very questionable whether the war against Germany would not have been won much sooner if both Japan and the USA had remained neutral. Our losses in the Far East would have to be balanced against the advantage of having American forces fighting with us, and the complication we suffered of having our own forces under the command of men who had never heard a shot fired in anger. It is generally accepted that Hitler had no hope of winning after the end of 1940.

☆   ☆   ☆

One boon that came from going to King Edward's was that I

48

was able to join the Civil Defence, a thing which would never have been permitted at Monkton though incredibly my Housemaster allowed me to remain a member as I was already in, and I thus managed a tiny bit of war service and earned the Defence Medal which meant everything to me. I think there had been a talk given to the older boys, and a boy in my form at least a year older took me with him to apply to become a messenger at a first-aid post. His name was Alan Barnard. I never heard what happened to him after he joined the Fleet Air Arm where there was said then to be a mean survival time of fourteen days after completing training. We both lied about our ages of course and were both accepted. After a period of training the only duties were to sleep there one night a week, and be prepared in an air raid if communications failed, to ride out with messages. Even so this was adventure enough for a fourteen year old who had never before escaped from maternal supervision. I see from my diary for 1942, which is one of the very few completed even in part which has survived from my schooldays, that it was on 16 March that I spent a first trial night on duty at the Beechen Cliff FAP, and the 19th that I did my first regular night duty alone. There was only five weeks to go before the first night of the Bath Blitz.

Like everything ignoble the Germans did in this war, the Baedeker Raids were blamed on Hitler; just as all atrocities were on the Kaiser in the previous war. Actually it could be argued that Bath, with a vital branch of the Admiralty in its exact centre, was a legitimate target; but this cannot be said of York, Exeter, or Norwich, and to send the whole might of the Luftwaffe to destroy a beautiful and ancient city was characteristic of the mind of a Prussian, not that of Hitler who was an Austrian. In any case with the city completely undefended it would have taken but a single plane to destroy the Admiralty buildings at the top of Combe Down and the majestic pile of the Empire Hotel which was their office immediately opposite the Abbey, each of which stood out in daylight like a sore thumb and in the event neither of which was significantly damaged.

I cannot remember what time it was that the sirens sounded but the warning came very late and within half an hour it was clear from the sound of bombs and the flames lighting up the sky that Bath was at least a major target, and that the Casualty

Service was going to need every man, woman, and boy it could muster. As I started off on my bicycle on what should have been an easy ten minute down-hill journey, there was a temporary lull and the whole valley was lighted up by the fires started by the first incendiary bombs. However no sooner had I turned the corner into Wellsway, a magnificent modern road sweeping down into the town from the south, than a straggler unloaded its supply of High Explosive somewhere over the other side of the city and then flew immediately overhead. There was no opposition then or at any time in the two nights, and the rear gunner, presumably feeling that up to then he had not been doing much for the war effort, sprayed the road from side to side as he went. For no obvious reason the aircraft then turned and drove back exactly the same way, again with only the rear gunner firing, turned over the blazing city, and repeated the performance for the third time.

I have since considered that, not knowing that the RAF was never going to show up, it is hardly possible that a crafty Bosch would risk a valuable aircraft simply to let his friend in the rear amuse himself shooting at a small boy on a bicycle; but it certainly seemed like that at the time.

There is however one very significant aspect of this matter. I have always had a profound fear of injury and death, and as a child and adult have been almost morbidly careful in crossing a busy street or avoiding getting dangerously far out in swimming; but on this occasion I had no fear at all. I was quite sure I was going to be killed, and I could, without grave dereliction of duty, have abandoned my bicycle and taken cover in one of the regular stone recesses on the paths up to the houses. Fear of death is one of the most valuable instincts for the survival of mankind, but it is suppressed automatically when a man feels he is dying for his country, his tribe, or his family; which is of far greater evolutionary value to the species than survival of the individual. Over the centuries, fighting 'men' have been what we now consider young boys. The average age of Napoleon's troops and of those of the armies fighting against him was about fourteen, and this instinct is most highly developed at this age. I am sure not one of those last few to die at Thermopyloe would have wished to be anywhere else.

I don't think this instinct (or rather this inhibition of an instinct) is developed in a girl, but it is replaced by a willingness to die in defence of her young and just possibly of her mate. It is for this reason that I would hold more highly the sacrifice of Nurse Edith Cavell or the heroism of that other nurse this same night, than I would the bravery of Boy Cornwall VC, the numerous continental Boy Scouts rounded up and shot by the Germans in 1940, or the members of the Hitler Youth who made their last desperate stand in 1945.

Although the London Blitz went on continuously every night for months at a time, there were occasional remissions of a week or two, and during one of these, I think in August 1942, my parents went up to Town and stayed at the Strand Palace Hotel. So quiet was it that when my mother left, Daddy stayed on and I went up on my own to join him there for three nights. Unfortunately the Hun started his frightfulness again that very night but we were able to go to a prom and to see the revival of Chu Chin Chow. My mother was quite unworried as the BBC had just stopped referring to specific towns as targets (presumably in the hope that the Luftwaffe did not know where they had been) and only reported 'enemy air activity against Southern England'. Unless we had had a good night's shooting, the scale of an attack was always played down. I think these three raids were directed at the East End and Docklands anyway, and nothing came at all close. The hotel was never damaged at any time, but I have heard that it suffered in reputation and that there was a proposal afterwards to erect a plaque to the numerous young women who fell there during the war.

I have already mentioned one profound effect on my life of a book called *The World of Wonder* which my father and I read together when I was very small, and the arrival of his books from storage when we got the house to ourselves revealed an even more momentous work *The Science of Life* by Wells and Huxley. I have bought this, usually in three volumes instead of the one large one we had, for each of my godchildren; and although dated I still think it is probably the most useful gift one can buy for a growing boy. I find it hard to see why my father did not make use of it in the same way and can only suppose he was terrified at the possibility of my asking questions on the subject of reproduction which was very lightly and delicately touched upon. I have had no such reservations with my godsons who rightly or wrongly (I think wrongly) have since the age of eight been taught at school more about what are called 'The facts of life' than would have been found in any book which could have been published legally at that time. I started reading this when I was nearly fifteen and for the very first time began to learn something of biology and get some confirmation of my suspicions that babies were not just 'sent by God', which was all I had ever been able to learn at home or in school. It was more than a year later that I happened upon a book on contraception hidden away behind a bookshop shelf. I have not yet got over the sheer horror of realizing that there were people (and I never related it to the sort of people I knew) who would deliberately prevent a baby being born. Even as a Medical Student I was not the only one of my year who on seeing a condom auctioned by one of the ex-service seniors in the dissecting room, had no idea what it was or how it was to be used.

I had already spent more time than planned as a dayboy at King Edward's, and this year was admitted to the fifth form at Monkton. I fear this delay must to some extent have been partly at least a result of my own instinctive opposition to change, and ought to have been harmful: as certainly no boy should enter a Public School one day later than the earliest possible if he is to obtain the full benefit of the finest system of education yet evolved. On the other hand had I gone there a year earlier I should have made no contribution at all to the war effort, which would have been a profound blow to me and surely affected my future outlook on life adversely. Those who did in fact enter a year or more younger though would say that this was a trivial advantage and that I would have benefited enormously more by having had to go through all the trials of a junior fag and ultimately risen to become a school prefect. They could be right.

Monkton Combe was (and pray heaven will once more become) a most remarkable Public School. Indeed it was unique: but at the time I was far from being in sympathy with the extraordinary situation. There are many schools with a profound Christian dedication and some where this is the dominating feature of life; but in all of these it is jealously guarded and maintained by the staff as being the very purpose for which the school exists. Monkton must surely have been the only school in which such an atmosphere of Christian conviction, dedication, morality and ethics was transcendent but where this did not come from above but from below. It was not imposed by the staff but arose spontaneously from the boys, with the youngest and most junior being in the vanguard. I know now that had I been receptive, I would have become there and then a much better man than I shall ever be. As it was, rebel as I have ever been though convinced Christian as I was, I found the religious atmosphere oppressive and not to be tolerated.

All this is not to say that we did not at times permit ourselves the most monstrous irreverencies. There was no real harm in remarking that the quite revolting school fish always appeared just after our future doctors had thrown away their dissected and long pickled dogfish: but in many a less religious school it would have been regarded as improper to refer to it as 'The piece of cod which passeth all understanding'.

My entry into Monkton was delayed and mared by a sudden and lasting impairment of my health. I had long suffered from mild attacks of asthma, but this summer I had three very severe bouts of status asthmaticus each lasting three weeks and with only about ten days remission in between. They were destined to be repeated in exactly the same form the following two years. I thus began the term late, with the School Certificate class well started when I joined them. I made a real effort, as I always had done if anyone would believe it, but the odds were very much against me. I was exempted from Games and the JTC as I was still very weak, and was allowed to spend the time, three hours every afternoon, working alone in the library trying to catch up on what I had missed and also to learn some biology, which as a school subject was entirely new to me. As a member of the fifth I was only required to do two terms' fagging and this was made very easy for me, which may not have been a good thing. In short, I was regarded by myself and everybody else during the rest of my schooldays as a chronic invalid. Then an incident occurred which completely altered my life.

My mother telephoned the Head to ask if he did not think that under the circumstances I should go down a form and work for School Certificate the following year. He apparently answered that I was doing all right and had a good chance of success: and then he said something which may only have been a casual or chance remark but which when I heard of it changed the direction of my whole life. He said 'You know Mrs Crook, he is a tremendous worker.' Whether it was a considered opinion, or he was thinking of another boy altogether, or simply said it to all mothers, I shall never know. Certainly the effect on me was devastating. Nobody in my whole life had ever suggested that I was anything but bone idle, and only a very few that 'he could probably do better if he tried'. I had never considered Ted Hayward as anything more than another bothersome person in authority, but from that day I worshipped him and worked myself to the bone to live up to the absurd opinion that he claimed to have formed of me. I do not think we, any of us ever know or consider the profound effect even a chance remark may have on the entire life of someone else.

It happened that I had already discovered for myself the secret of the only way I have ever been able to learn. I do not think teaching at Monkton, at least on the modern side, was anything but mediocre, with the exception of Biology and English Literature which were taught in a way that fitted in very well with my own method, and consisted largely of the dictating of notes on the part of the subject we were studying, and then leaving us to read up the subject and add such details as we found necessary. It is possible that teaching was better on the classical side as the English Literature (Macbeth and Chaucer) was taught us by the classics master who inspired in us a real love of what he was teaching. This is never easy and in the case of the set books for an exam of this sort I would have thought well-nigh impossible. Everyone I know from elsewhere who has 'done' a Shakespeare play at school has finished up with a hatred at least of that work, and frequently of the whole of Elizabethan drama.

[For the sake of completeness I should perhaps mention what my own method of study has been, which has taken me through every examination from School Certificates to at least the Primary examination for the FRCS, and provided me with the factual knowledge for the final part of that exam. It consisted of arming myself with a syllabus or else a series of books said to contain everything that was necessary, and slowly and laboriously writing a detailed precis of the whole subject. It is of course a terribly time-consuming method but is all that has ever worked with me. It is easier and quicker today when one can use a computer as an electronic notebook and add to, update, and revise one's notes so easily. Fortunately few if any others need to resort to this, but it should be suggested as a possible way for any man, woman, or child who wants to pass an exam and has not yet found a satisfactory way of learning. It was my own discovery, and indeed nobody even at Monkton ever tried to find out the best method for me or for any other boy. I think this is far and away the most important service a schoolmaster can ever give to a child, but I have never heard of one attempting it.]

'The Basher', a little round man with short stumpy legs and an honours degree in mathematics, was my Housemaster. He knew and understood every boy in his house and was a perfect 'father figure'; in other words a perfect housemaster. He did nothing to live up to his nickname.

Up to that time it was unheard of for a woman, let alone an attractive young woman, to teach at any respectable boys' school; but this was total war and worse things happen at sea. Biology was in the hands of a Vicar's daughter of about twenty-two named 'Miss G.M. Trevaldwin' (GMT is never fast) but universally known as 'Twiddles'. She was an excellent teacher and, to use her own expression (not original – she got it from St Peter), was no respecter of persons. As I have said, her method of teaching fitted in with my method of learning.

The only other extraordinary character at Monkton was 'Kitch'. He had been Chemistry master since 1910 and had retired early in 1939, presumably not younger than the age of sixty. He returned at the outbreak of war, as did so many to release younger men for the forces, and stayed on for some time after, until demobilization was complete. He then took Holy Orders and worked as a curate (like me he refused a Vicarage) until the eighties. It is difficult to see how he could have been younger than about 103 when he died.

As a by-product of the Bath Blitz, I became seriously concerned that I had never been baptized. Everything had been arranged, a Christening robe made, and Christening presents received, when for some reason my father announced that he was not coming. The Christening never took place but at the age of sixteen I went to see the very elderly vicar at Southstoke Church and arranged the thing for myself. Daddy again did not turn up. He was as good a church-goer as any of us and I never knew why, and only my mother and Nanor were present.

I sat the School Certificate examination in July 1943. In those days one had to obtain at least a pass in five subjects including English language and elementary mathematics in order to get a certificate at all. This after all is surely essential if it is to be evidence of any sort of education; and the present idiotic rule that a boy can get into a university with but a single subject followed by two or three at advanced level had never been thought of.

It was only about February that it was discovered that I had entered for one more subject than the conditions permitted. This was because on the strength of all I had learned at King Edward's, I had insisted on taking Physics, Chemistry, and Biology as separate subjects instead of 'general science'. On being sent for by Ted Hayward I did a very foolish and unkind thing. In spite of all he had done for me, I elected to omit Divinity. True the subject as it had to be taught for exam purposes had nothing devout or even religious about it, but I should have considered what he would think. I am sure that he took me in those days for a godless little savage with a bent towards the sciences. He was such a sound man that it is just possible he realized the truth more than I did, but I doubt he ever thought that I would eventually take Holy Orders. Had he lived to see it I know he would have been delighted as well probably as being amazed. He would have known that his influence played a major part in preparing me to meet the call when it came. What I should have done was to have left out Geography, a useless subject as taught then and now, and one in which I failed and deserved to fail as I did in French.

In the event I passed with three distinctions, in English, Elementary Maths, and Physics; and with credits in Advanced Mathematics, Chemistry and English Literature. My only ordinary pass was in Biology, which considering I had only been at it less than a year was not really a disgrace. I turned it into a credit at Christmas, which was less than I had hoped for, and also managed to scrape a pass in French. I have never been

56

able to learn even the rudiments of any language, even of Malay which is the lingua franca of the country where I have spent half my life. Probably the reason is the impossibility of completeness. One cannot get hold of a syllabus or textbook to be learned my way, and I have always felt overwhelmed by the vast amount I don't know and the conviction that the next sentence will contain words I have never met before.

This second French exam was the culmination of my having studied the subject as traditionally taught for some eleven years, and I entered conscious that I did not know enough to call a taxi in Paris. I still don't know enough Malay to call one in Kuala Lumpur. Actually I almost gave up. My excellent coach who had been sweating blood over me, advised me to scratch on the evening before the paper. I said I might as well go down with flying colours but he said getting a result as bad as I should would not be flying colours but dragging the school's name (by which he meant his own) into the dust. I passed, having got very low marks throughout but one hundred per cent for unseen translation. I had just been reading Dumas in English, and the rather obscure passage was not unseen. My coach, an excitable Roman Catholic who subsequently went to work at Downside, thereupon went around all the junior forms saying that Crook's success in French showed what an intelligent boy could do without the slightest knowledge of the language. I took it as a compliment.

I was in fact working flat out from before the summer results came out to try to get Higher Certificate in one year instead of the usual two, in Physics, Chemistry, and Biology. When I got back after the holidays, Ted Hayward characteristically gave me every encouragement as did 'The Basher' (Wicks, my Housemaster). The latter did however rather plaintively say it was a pity I was giving up Mathematics, and so, as it was his subject and solely to please him, I agreed to try 'Subsidiary' mathematics as well. Fairly common though it was in some schools, nobody had ever taken less than two years over the course at Monkton, and Kitch was livid that anybody should be so presumptuous as to try. His principle in life, stated daily at least somewhere in the school, was 'You can't run before you can walk' which being interpreted meant that nobody should be allowed to try to run until the most backward boy in the class had learned to walk.

Even so to attempt three main subjects plus a subsidiary in one year showed a degree of self-confidence amounting to arrogance. My only excuse was that I knew no better, that I wanted to get into the Fleet Air Arm at the earliest possible moment, and that neither my Housemaster nor the Head did anything to dissuade me. Kitch however did, and when he heard that I considered the Chemistry paper difficult, announced cheerfully and repeatedly 'Crook has bitten off more than he can chew'. I will admit however that when I had passed in all four subjects including his own (for which he had refused to give me extra tuition on the grounds that it was useless) he made an ample and public recantation. In those days, with conscription at the age of seventeen and four months, and the chance of volunteering for various services about a year earlier, there were only about ten boys in the upper sixth sitting Higher Certificate. They had of course all taken two years over it, and something of a sensation was created by the discovery that I had not only for the first time in the school's history passed in one year, but got a better pass than any of them and won the school's prize for the year's best Higher Certificate. 'Could do better if he tried' forsooth.

Not for the last time I suffered as a result of ignorance of what was the traditional thing to do; in this case what to do with a money prize. It was the considerable sum of ten pounds 'to be spent on books'. What I should have done, what Ted Hayward or the Basher should have advised me to do as my father didn't, was to order some worthwhile sets of books in presentation bindings with the School Crest embossed on them. Instead I ordered about twenty books I wanted, largely of ephemeral interest, but including second hand finely bound sets of Shakespeare and Yarrell's British Fishes. Both these have crests on them, but they are not mine.

I said of Downside Prep School 'It would be absurd to pretend that I enjoyed my time at Downside, any more than I enjoyed any of my schooldays; but . . . If I had a son I would wish to send him to one very similar.' It would be equally absurd to pretend that I enjoyed Monkton, except perhaps for my last two terms: but if the Monkton I knew still existed and I had a son I would move heaven and earth to send him there and nowhere else. Many things have changed though in the last forty-five years and Monkton no less than any. I believe that it is still a very good Christian School, almost certainly achieving higher technical standards than it did in my day, and although neither the Head, nor as far as I know any other master, is in orders, they claim to have made up for it like many schools by appointing a school chaplain. There are many such schools though, several of which have not become co-educational and not abolished traditional discipline. Did Monkton still produce essentially doctors, clergy, and missionaries I might even now consider it as a first choice. Otherwise I fear I should choose a school which teaches boys (and only boys) to fear God, honour the Queen, read, write, and count as well as gaining some knowledge of classical learning, how to accept discipline (and administer it) and which does not send its boys to Henley to take part in rowing matches on Sunday.

However, to return to the 1940s: my own hopes of military service came to nought. When at sixteen I volunteered for the Fleet Air Arm, I was put in medical grade two which should have meant easy acceptance for any other service except fighter command: but when I got my ordinary call-up papers, and lied just as hard, I was put in grade four which meant that they did not propose to send for me again as I was hardly likely to live until the next batch were examined.

By this time I had become a workaholic, in fact a beastly little swot. I had never really failed an examination, and I deluded myself I liked them. Again before the results were out I had started working for First MB (The First Examination for Medical Degrees). This was of course a university exam and from most schools boys would go to university for the beginning of the medical course. There was a tradition at Monkton though that at least those going to London University took the first exam from School as external students, and very few had ever failed. Furthermore as the three parts of the exam were Physics, Chemistry and Biology, and the standard demanded in the first two was much lower than in Higher Certificate, boys always worked for all three subjects from the beginning. Having passed all three in Higher Certificate I was exempt from having to do Physics and Chemistry again, and even Ted Hayward saw no objection to my sitting Biology at Christmas. Neither he nor I, nor even the Basher, considered for a moment that I had only started Biology since I came to Monkton, and my passing in Higher may have been something of a fluke. The fact that I had only managed to improve my results to a credit at my second attempt at School Certificate in this subject only six months before, suggest that it was. Also I suspect that with the approaching end of the war in Europe, the standard may have been drastically raised to eliminate some of those recently demobilized elderly candidates who wanted to use their gratuity to become doctors.

There was another factor though that was decisive. Twiddles had been sacked (or forced into resignation) and replaced by a master who, whatever his other qualifications and merits, at that time knew nothing of teaching embryo Medical Students, and appeared to care less. He did not even bother to provide himself with a syllabus, or to read it when I lent him mine. He wasted hours and days of my time on animal types which were not required and in dictating notes and drawing diagrams of such things as the detailed neurology of the dog. Either this differs profoundly from that of man as described in Grays Anatomy, or his notes were hopelessly inaccurate or out of date. Certainly he no longer understood them himself (if they were in fact his notes) and if questioned on a point would look it up in an obscure textbook and fail to find it. Left to myself I might have had some faint chance of passing. As it was I failed twice running, lost my chance of ever getting honours, and got so discouraged I almost gave up.

Conditions were not good in any case for my first attempt. All candidates had to attend at the Imperial Institute, and I stayed at a small private house in the Cromwell Road. Flying bombs were still coming over and there was no lessening of the V2 attacks. These latter, although one of the great technological advances of the age, were one of Hitler's worst psychological blunders. Even the Londoner would have become worn down in time by the Buzz-bomb with the nerve wracking wait after the engine cut before one knew who was going to cop it; but the V2 left everybody completely cold. In spite of all the noise, the fact that it travelled faster than sound and that hence the first thing one heard was the bang, meant that one knew nothing until it was all over, and nobody bothered about them in the least.

Or at least almost nobody. The last part of the exam was a six hour practical involving biochemistry. For some reason the big laboratories at the Imperial Institute did not have a gas supply for Bunsen Burners, and every candidate's bench was provided with a spirit lamp. Methylated spirit was at that time one of the things completely unobtainable like bananas and number eight batteries, so these lamps were filled with petrol. Shortly after one rocket had landed uncomfortably near, the man at the bench behind mine managed to get his lamp to explode. There was a colossal bang and a sheet of flame up to the ceiling. We all thought we had been hit, and it was a long time before we stopped shaking and could get on with our work again.

I think it was going home that same day, as I was passing the Exhibition Road entrance to the Victoria and Albert Museum (I was lying flat on the pavement at the very bottom of the steps with my hands pressed to the back of my neck) when the V1 landed on the row of houses on the opposite side of the Cromwell Road. The gashes made by the bomb splinters in the door pillars are to be seen to this day, and my godsons refuse to believe the story as it has to be admitted that if my rear end was then anything like its present size, it is impossible to see how I got it away unscathed. The only other one of these things that unnerved me cut out while I was crossing Picadilly Circus. Londoners were quite uninhibited about casting themselves to the ground on these occasions; but for a country boy who had just stepped off the pavement into what even in wartime was still the worst bit of traffic in the world, it was a difficult decision to make. It was impossible to know how far these things would go on after the engine had cut out and this one went on so far that I never heard where it finished up. In carrying on to the central island I thus proved my superiority over those who flung themselves almost under the wheels of the traffic.

VE Day came while I was working flat out for my second attempt, and although almost unrestricted leave was given to go to London for the celebrations, I rather foolishly decided not to. Those who did, had a wonderful time, several of my friends riding on the roof of a car immediately behind that of Winston Churchill. Almost all were late back and, in the best public school tradition, Ted Hayward organized a special detention for about three quarters of the school in consequence, including all the prefects.

VJ Day was in the summer holidays after I had left school,

and I did even less. I well remember the evening nine days before when we learned from the nine o'clock news of the first atomic bomb on Hiroshima. The factual news announcement was followed by a recorded message from Churchill (who was of course no longer Prime Minister) and a rather well expressed brief statement of the scientific explanation of how the thing worked. I was passing through a phase of questioning all the basic mathematical theory of matter and the atom, and had recently come to the conclusion that all talk of energy locked up in the atom was nonsense. David Coombe had never really followed my reasoning (which was entirely spurious), and triumphantly rang me up a few minutes later to ask what I thought now. I had to admit that my theory had disintegrated as completely as Hiroshima, with the reservation that it might only be a propaganda story and a bloody big bomb. I wish to heaven I had been right.

I bought my first .22 rifle during the summer holidays while waiting for the exam results, being on this occasion reasonably if mistakenly certain that I had passed and having given up working for the first and last time in many years. It was a Remington bolt-action magazine repeater, a delightful little thing that I wish I had not had to sell when hard up working for the Fellowship. I got my firearm certificate on the strength of taking it down a few times to shoot on the outdoor range at Monkton. Insofar as I really used it at all, and I doubt I fired two hundred rounds through it in ten years, it was for potting at rooks and rabbits in the farmlands of my friends and I regret to say in the back garden, which was of questionable legality. These little guns are fun to use but quite useless for target shooting as they will not consistently even put every shot in the scoring area at twenty-five yards and seldom one into the bull. Perhaps most men shoot from the standing position as inaccurately as this, but if one is going to shoot small game standing one would do better using a shotgun. Ugly, clumsy and heavy as it would be, if I wanted go go out after rabbits with a .22 I would prefer to use one of the standard post-war target rifles (not one of the present-day monstrosities) with a heavy barrel and a sling. Such a barrel does not flip, so it is completely silent out of doors (one hears nothing but the click of the action) and it will put every shot onto a sixpence at normal ranges. Even a magazine is unnecessary and if one really wanted speed one could have a quick loader screwed to the side of the Martini action.

My other sporting interest at that time, as ever since, was fishing. I had tried course fishing in the days of the long country walks when we first came to Bath, which sometimes took us to Bradford-on-Avon and back along the canal bank from Limpley Stoke. After sounding out the market, I was able to buy, from my carefully hoarded Christmas and Birthday monies, a rod (which I still have), a brass reel, a line, casts, hooks to gut, float, leads, and a packet of bait, for a total of seven and sixpence, or thirty-seven and a half new pence. It would not pay for the float today, but my father was disgusted and said they had seen me coming and that I would never learn the value of money. Somehow in spite of the vast numbers of roach one could see in the canal, I never caught anything in many hours and days of effort. Then one day I saw a man spinning for pike in the river, and nothing would satisfy me but a set of spinning tackle. Somehow over a period of months I managed to scrape together the huge sum of two pounds. For thirty shillings I could have bought a beautiful Alcocks 'Light Caster' split-cane rod, but this was clearly outside my budget. (I have regretted the fact ever since and managed to buy a second-hand one forty years later for thirty pounds.) Instead I spent twenty-two shillings on just as fine a rod, with agate rings throughout, but made in Greenheart, seven and six on a plastic Nottingham reel called 'The Aerialite' and five shillings on a 'Black Spider' spinning line. For the remaining five shillings I managed to get a steel trace, one spoon bait and a small Devon Minnow. My mother bought me a year's membership of the Bath Anglers' Association, so I had access to all the best fishing in the area.

Spinning was more fun and marginally more rewarding than float fishing, and even a small pike is a more worthy prey than other course fish: but I still had more blank days than successes. Isaak Walton's recipe for roasting a pike, which he says makes a dish too good for any but anglers or very honest men, provides a superb meal which was very welcome in wartime. One had of course to modify it slightly. It was not feasible to use a pound of butter ('or if your pike be more than a yard long use more than a pound'), not that it ever was a yard long, but it always turned out very well.

But after a few weeks I happened to see a man dry fly fishing, and at once knew that was for me. There was no question of my being able to afford a special fly-fishing outfit, but I bought a few casts at Woolworths, and dry flies which were 3d. to 4d. each. Some of the wet flies at three half-pence were usable dry with care and plenty of paraffin. Nobody told me, and it was months before I found out, that a flyline must be stiff, heavy, tapered, and in those days greased. I started with my spinning rod, reel and line with a fly cast tied on the end, and incredibly at once started catching fish in quantity. The Dace is a small fish but rises very well to the dry fly: and there were few days when I did not get three or four. I even took my first trout in this way, a nice little fish of well over half a pound. My casting was quite extraordinary, and always resulted in a zigzag line on the water, but I learned to get surprising accuracy and to recover line rapidly before the fly floated over my fish. Once I was able to buy a proper flyline, I was already an expert at stalking and hooking the little Dace which abounded in the Avon and its tributaries. Only once did I take a Roach on the dry fly, and once a Chub. Trout were few and far between, but I never minded. It was the fishing I enjoyed; and I was always quite pleased when a worthwhile fish could be put back because it was unwanted.

Apart from stamp collecting, my only other hobby in my schooldays was building model aeroplanes, and this had to be abandoned early in the war as petrol models were banned in 1940 and rubber for the elastic motors became unobtainable little more than a year later. I had read in 1939 an article in the *Boy's Own Paper* on building and flying petrol models and bought a copy of a book on the subject. Both recommended learning first on rubber powered machines, and as the cost of a petrol engine (about six pounds) was well beyond my means, I bought a kit for a scale model Hawker Hurricane for two shillings. It was quite unsuitable for a beginner, but at least it did fly. Then the war came, and for my first Christmas in Bath I was given a kit for a proper flying model, and then never looked back. There was a firm in Bristol which sold kits for ten or twelve different models, and over the next year or so I built them all. I could never afford another kit, but they sold the blueprint of each (and they really were blue prints, made in the traditional way) for about two shillings, and I bought the materials as and when I needed them and had a few pence to spare. Towards the end I had mastered enough simple aerodynamics to be designing them myself. My pocket money was still 3d. a week, as it remained to the end of the war, and I had not yet resigned myself to giving up my two weekly papers which yielded another 4d. How I managed to get *The Aeromodeler* as well I simply do not know, but of course I was helped out with small gifts all the time.

I have never understood the reason for this unsatisfactory arrangement over pocket money. If 3d. a week was considered enough when I was five, it could not possibly have been so thirteen years later. Whenever I asked for an increase, I was told that I was really getting 7d., as I could always give up my two papers. Perhaps one of these could be considered a 'comic', but the other was a quite serious, instructive, and morally instructive magazine called *Modern Boy*. I missed it very much when it had to be sacrificed to earn me another 2d., and I still treasure and re-read a few dozen old copies from about the time of Munich. Its theology was good, and I get some useful sermon material from it. Admittedly some of my friends were not getting much more but they were allowed and encouraged to earn small sums by genuine hard work in the house or garden, or even by doing newspaper rounds, which I personally still consider a good thing. Whenever I suggested this I was told that Daddy and Mummy did everything for me and provided me with food, clothing, schooling, and holidays, so that anything I could do for them must be done from a sense of duty, not for money; and that as for earning money this way from the neighbours, that would be turning myself into a tradesman. I had always accepted that my parents were right in everything, and hence, that however attractive it seemed, other parents must be wrong in this. Fortunately it was many years before I learned that it was certainly not the rule when either of them were young, and that my father earned quite large sums this way by which he had built up his very fine stamp collection. I never went without anything reasonable that I really wanted, but I never had any money to buy it for myself. Among the things which were not considered reasonable were a microphone and a real fly-rod, for each for which I saved up my threepences or sevenpences for many months.

It is to my shame that I have done little better where my godchildren were concerned, though I have given them many times as much in real terms allowing for inflation. Even so there must be a limit to the fixed 'allowance' as it is called today, and a boy who wants to build model aeroplanes, wireless sets, or today computers, has to think in tens if not hundreds of pounds instead of shillings and pence as we did. Perhaps this is one of the few occasions where there is a genuine 'generation gap'. If they always wanted to buy the same sort of things I yearned for at their age, I am sure I would willingly provide a regular income for them to do so, but they don't: any more than I wanted to buy the things on which my father spent his hard-earned pennies. To him fishing meant a bent pin and a worm; and if he could afford a real hook he tied it to a hair from the tail of a passing horse as did Isaak Walton. A child who wanted a built-cane rod and dry flies was to him as thriftless as one is to me who wants a machine to plug into the family television set and several pounds a time for tapes to play at Star Wars.

Stamp collecting is a hobby which has interested me at intervals since I was about five. My father had a fine collection which fascinated me when I was very small, and at an early age I was given a remarkably neat and well-bound album from Woolworths and a big packet of foreign stamps. I still have the packet, with some of the original stamps still in it, for many were duplicates. My first serious album came on my tenth birthday as I have said, and soon after going to Bath I was given a loose-leaf album to which I soon added a second volume in red to hold the British Empire pages. From then on I rather specialized in Empire issues and before the war was over considered myself a Great Britain specialist.

It is hard to remember when exactly I determined to become a doctor, and equally hard to think of a boy who would appear less suitable or even of a less suitable career for a boy such as myself. I had no family background, which in those days was almost a sine qua non, I regularly fainted at the sight of blood, and the only subjects I had ever been any good at before going to Monkton were Physics and Maths, neither of them of much help in Medicine or Surgery. Certainly I had never suggested such a possibility until going to talk to Ted Hayward after

66

passing School Certificate, but I must presumably have been thinking about it then for some time.

Early in 1945 a notice appeared in the Biology Lab at Monkton advertising scholarships at St Mary's Hospital, and without much hope I applied and was called to London for an interview. The Head must have given me a splendid testimonial because I afterwards realized that these scholarships are only awarded to outstanding Rugger players, and they could not really have been interested in me at all. I don't remember a thing about the interview except that nobody except Lord Moran who was Dean asked me a single question; and he kept the thing going for twenty minutes or so. I do however remember being shown round the Medical School including the very modern dissecting room, where I saw fluorescent lighting for the first time. Also for the first time, at the age of eighteen, I saw a naked female body, in fact several of them. Until then my knowledge of what the pudendum and breast looked like was dependent entirely on the copy of *Gray's Anatomy* I had bought about a year before. This must sound incredible to the youngsters of the New Elizabethan age, but it was perfectly normal then. They were of course dead bodies and none was younger than about eighty, so it probably did my morals no lasting harm. Outside this dissecting room and apart from patients I never saw another, alive or dead, young or old, for a further ten years, by which time I had been a qualified doctor for five.

As soon as I received the polite notice informing me that I had not been awarded a scholarship, I wrote asking for admission as a paying student. Again I had no idea that I was asking the impossible, that not one applicant in fifty was admitted, and that even he was likely to have two generations of Mary's men behind him. The Secretary must have been so astonished at my presumption that he referred that matter direct to Lord Moran, and I received a reply saying 'The Dean is very interested in your case and has agreed to offer you a place in October.' At that time I fully expected to have passed First MB by then, but when I did not I was with several others permitted to start the Second MB course and continue working for the Biology exam at Christmas.

3

MEDICAL STUDENT

Although I had been granted a place at St Mary's, it was by no means certain that I was going to be able to get there. My father had declared in terms of ridicule that he was certainly not going to pay for me to go to a Medical School to take First MB. In fairness it must be said that I don't think he had any more idea than I had of what an incredible privilege it was for me to have been offered a place at all, and that if I did not take it up at once there could be no possible chance of my getting another. It is possible that he soon found out and for that reason relented.

Shortly after VJ Day the Bank returned to London and he had to go to live in a service flat. Purley was in 'Bomb Alley' and Manor Side had been commandeered by the local authority during the early flying-bomb attacks for the storage of furniture from bombed houses. In a sense this was a blessing as the roof was replaced and the whole house weather-proofed. In the preceding few days the front door had been blown off five times and replaced each time by our elderly gardener 'Surrage'. After that he gave up, disappeared into the country somewhere, and was never heard of again. Just about the last possible moment before I should have had to admit to St Mary's that I had not the means to live in London and take up their offer (and how very like my father's experience with his family it would have been) he telephoned to say that he had heard that the house was to be released very shortly (it wasn't) and that I could start by living in digs, as of course nine students out of ten had to do. I booked in the same private hotel in South Kensington where I had stayed while sitting for First MB during the war, though this soon proved too far from the hospital, and then moved into another in Lancaster Gate, within easy walking distance.

The sudden transition from a schoolboy to a London Medical Student living in lodgings and being treated as a man is a traumatic one, and has proved disastrous for many. At least I had a father living in London who called on me every evening and took me out to dinner; always the 'Salad Bowl' at the Coventry Street Corner House where one got a plate of soup, as many helpings as one could hold of an enormous cold buffet, a huge slice of Gateau with ice cream, and coffee, all for two shillings and fourpence. We always wore white shirts, bow ties and dark three-piece suits, and I once heard a man in the queue behind remark to his mate 'I do like the way they run this place for the working classes.' I was on a bed and breakfast basis at my hotel and had a set lunch at the Medical School for 1/3d. including coffee. My total daily expenses including a cup of morning coffee and afternoon tea were about half-a-crown; for which I submitted a detailed account to Daddy at the end of the week. My pocket money was still 7d. a week, which left me little for drink, tobacco and dissipation.

During the four or five months before the house at Purley became available, I used to go home to Bath on Friday evenings for alternate weekends, my fares being paid by Mummy out of her very meagre income. The closeness of the medical school to Paddington enabled me to start back early on Monday and be there in time for the nine thirty am lecture.

After some weeks, my father set out to find me cheaper lodgings, as my hotel was charging two pounds ten a week including lunch on Sundays, but with a one hundred per cent discount for any night I was away. He was a man of fifty who had been an army officer and served in the Merchant Marine and in New York, but his innocence and naivety were unbelievable. He selected as a convenient site the Sussex Gardens complex near the Hospital, the biggest and best brothel area in London. He reported to me in absolute seriousness that evening that he had only visited one 'Lodging House' as the prices were outrageous. Apparently when he asked the Madam her weekly rates she had replied, 'Well I don't rightly know. It's five pounds a night, but nobody has ever asked for a whole week before.'

Actually my hotel was not a good one and probably not

good value for money by the standards of the day. Nobody else there was under the age of sixty, and many of the permanent guests (who may have been paying less of course) had been there for thirty years or more. There was a retired Bishop and his wife and a group of four elderly widows of excellent breeding but who played Bridge very badly every evening in the sitting room where I had a desk for my studies. Every hand was followed by a post-mortem when they frequently became white with anger at each other and sometimes appeared to be on the verge of coming to blows. After some time one of them spoke to me about my 'Friend' who came every night to take me out to dinner, and they were all horrified when I replied 'He's no friend of mine – he's my father.'

These were the days when London was flooded with American service men, and the hall-porter used to make money by letting out rooms by the hour while their proper occupants were out. He would also for an added fee provide the girl but they usually brought one with them. The only other thing I remember about the place is the occasion when I asked if I could have hot buttered toast for breakfast and was told by the slatternly manageress 'No, but you can have hot toast and butter it yourself.' There was another similar hotel in Bloomsbury under the same management where I stayed for one night some years later and was put in the squalid staff quarters. I was apparently mistaken for a new Head Waiter or something similar, and my morning tea was brought by an unwashed tweeny in bare feet and a nightgown. I was only too relieved that she had not visited me earlier.

I went up to London the last day of September to start at St Mary's the following day, and took a taxi to the 'Imperial Hotel' in the Cromwell Road. It was a long time before I realized that this was not the world famous commercial hotel of the same name in Southampton Row, and much confusion was caused to my friends and correspondents as a consequence. My father called that evening to take me out to the Corner House and, welcoming me as at last a fellow Londoner, took it upon himself to give me a fatherly talk on the dangers and vices of the New Babylon. I remember only the expression 'Loose women' which was new to me (it may have been new to him; I cannot think he can ever had a use for it before) and I don't think there can have been much more as he became so pink and embarrassed that he stopped short and for the first and last time suggested a drink before dinner. He needed it.

The next morning I set out by tube from South Kensington, walking past the crater opposite the Natural History museum of the Buzz-bang which had so nearly ended my career only a year or so before, and passing a stationers in Praed Street, recollected that I had no means of recording any words of wisdom which might come my way, so bought the two thick firm-bound foolscap notebooks in which I entered my lecture notes for several years. As it happened there were no bona-fide lectures that day. We queued to sign on and receive our locker keys, and then found that there was nothing else all day except an introductory address by the Dean and a so-called 'anatomy lecture'. Both were momentous, but the Dean's address came first.

Lord Moran had retired and been replaced by Dr Dennis Brinton, a very able Neurologist who also dabbled in psychiatry and was said to have got more men out of the RAF than Hitler did. The official consultant in psychiatry was a man always known as 'Brigadier James' who had certainly done as much in the Army. There were at that time in the medical school, men who had been there since before the war without having passed Second MB. They were staunch pillars of the Rugger Club and thus protected from conscription and the dangers which might well have followed therefrom. The true perpetual Medical Student was still not extinct: young men with money (or men with money who had been young when they first came) who enjoyed the life, paid their fees regularly, but could not face the life and responsibilities of being a doctor, and had no more desire to qualify than they had any chance of doing so.

Dennis Brinton's speech was a bombshell. Almost his first words were 'The curtain has fallen on the unlimited chance.' Anyone who failed First MB once, or any other exam for a second or third time (irrespective of when he last got round to presenting himself) was out, and would not come back while he remained Dean. There was a certain movement afoot in the rear seats to take steps to see that he did not remain Dean, or anything else for that matter, for more than a few more minutes, but it died down for want of support among the younger element.

He then went on to tell us another horrifying piece of news, but this time he made it quite clear that he was one of us and was as angry and resentful as anybody. The Labour Government had ordered that Medical Education must be co-educational as was the teaching in the board schools where they had been dragged up. (The words are not mine, I remember the Dean's speech very well.) Guy's and Mary's were to lose their status as all-male schools and have two women students wished on them the very next year and, horror of horrors, two unfortunate young men were to have to go to The Royal Free Hospital for Women. Tyrants never make a request without a threat, and Bevan had said that if we did not comply we would be allowed to carry on for a time without our grant; but that it was unlikely that it would be acceptable for long to the godless little savage who had mocked the dying words from the Cross and who had boasted 'We are the masters now'.

I think many of the younger of us, not knowing the traditions of Medical School parlance, were startled to hear a man dressed in a Saville Row suit and whom we knew to be one of the princes of the profession speaking in a way suggestive of an angry Covent Garden porter: but now he went on to say something which left us speechless, as it did our seniors of the hospital staff even though they too had been students long ago. The arrival of women would necessitate the building of toilet facilities for them and, if we wanted to retain any male preserves at all, the construction of their own common room. He went on to say that he had planned to have it in the garden space outside the library, but had now been told that in the summer this space was used for outdoor study and recreation. However provision had to be made, and we would have to decide whether we 'wanted to have an erection out there, or a sprinkling of women in our own common-room'.

There was a dead silence for perhaps ten seconds. Then the newly arrived Australian assistant Professor of Anatomy threw back his head and laughed loud and coarsely 'Haw, Haw, Haw, Haw, Haw'. The meeting broke up in disorder. It was years before some of us were quite sure what he had really meant to say.

The so-called Anatomy Lecture was, unknown to most of us, the last full blooded presentation of a traditional 'Rag' dating from the earliest days of the Medical School. It had to be toned down considerably the following year when there were two girls present, and thereafter fell into abeyance. As in all lectures the first year students assembled with those who had completed a year and were due to take the exam in another eight months. The 'lecturer' was one of the seniors dressed in a white coat and deliberately arrived late. This enabled the other seniors to introduce us to the traditional ritual used if any lecturer (not excluding the Dean) should be late. After singing 'why are we waiting' there follows an obscene chant whose only point is in its obscenity.

'We won't, We won't, We won't be buggered about.
We absolutely bloody refuse,
We won't be buggered unless we choose,
We won't, We won't, We won't be buggered about.'

[A few days later we had occasion to use it in earnest when Dr Greenfield, the superbly gifted Assistant Professor of Physiology, was a few minutes late. He waited discreetly at the door until we had finished and then with the utmost politeness entered and turned to us saying 'Gentlemen, I assure you that is the very last thing I shall want to do to you'.]

The lecture was then announced to be on the surface anatomy of the arm and shoulder and one of the newcomers having been informed that he had volunteered as a model, he removed his jacket and shirt and stood on the lecture table to have various deep structures painted onto him with coloured chalks. Only then was the lecturer told that half the class were dissecting the leg and buttock. Once the victim had been deprived of the rest of his clothing, a messenger arrived to say that 'Dr X' was urgently required in the operating theatre. He withdrew, followed by the senior students murmuring that they were not going to wait for ever, and the rest of us waited patiently with the naked victim until it was obviously tea time, when we left him. It was all very childish but surely better than the savage initiation rites of American universities and even of their High Schools.

Teaching started seriously the next day with a physiology lecture by Professor St George Hugget who had the distinction not only of being a distinguished member of the Communist party but also of being married to the professor of physiology at the Royal Free. He was thus a traitor both ways to everything St Mary's stood for, but everybody loved him. On the morning of the Derby Dr Greenfield came in rather after the last minute to stand in for him, announcing that the Professor was ill. It was the year Airborne won at thirty-three to one and the next day Hugget gave the whole show away by calling our three ex-parachutists up and handing them thirty-four pounds each. Medical students forgive this sort of thing very readily.

That first afternoon was given up, as were three out of four in the next twenty months, to 'Practical Anatomy', that is corpse carving. After his first year of Physics, Chemistry, and Biology (which most Monkton boys spent at school), the embryo doctor is required to spend eighteen months or more, before he is ever allowed into the hospital to see anyone who is sick, learning about the human body not in sickness but in health. This involves a considerable period of study of normal physiology and biochemistry, but pride of place goes, or ought to go, to Anatomy. We were required during this period to dissect the whole of the human body at least once 'to the satisfaction of our teachers'. This in itself would have been a mammoth task if 'satisfaction' had merely meant showing them that we had carried out the instructions and demonstrated every structure we were required to. It meant more than this though. After completing the dissection of each region, and there were eight or ten each in the arm and the leg, we had to get a 'sign up' from one of the staff to say we had done it and mastered it. This involved a viva voce examination on what we had done as well as what we should have learned about it not only from the dissecting manual but also from *Gray's Anatomy* and other textbooks. With over sixty students it was impossible for us all to be examined for a hour or so every few days by one of the senior staff, so much of this had to be done by 'Anatomy Demonstrators', junior qualified doctors who were working for the primary FRCS. I became one myself in due course but at that time they were all recently demobbed ex-service men who were hoping to use their gratuities to become surgeons. Some were nearer sixty than forty, and all had forgotten so much of their student anatomy that they knew little if anything more than we did. The difficulty of a sign up thus depended entirely on whom one asked for it. Those who wanted an easy time went to one of these. Those who intended to get on went to the

74

Professor and were frequently told to go away for a day or two and read it up.

Perhaps here is the place to say something about the whole plan and structure of medical education, both then and now. It is traditionally based on the training of the true General Practitioner, who has nothing in common with the Family Doctor of the Health Service. The General Practitioner who was the salt of the earth, survived at least in country districts until after the last war but is now, in Britain at least, as dead as the Dodo. He still exists in a few isolated overseas areas as the General Duties Medical Officer.

When I was young the good GP, using when necessary the facilities of a small Cottage Hospital, expected to treat pneumonia, fractures, ingrowing toenail, varicose veins, diphtheria, heart disease, VD, anaemia, tetanus, and a hundred other conditions as well as all normal and abnormal obstetrics. He would stabilize a diabetic as readily as he would remove an appendix, conduct a forceps delivery, or perhaps even do a Caesarean Section. The Cottage Hospital was for him and for him alone, and if on rare occasions a specialist was sent for it would be for a single consultation, conducted with a rigid protocol designed to impress on the patient that the great man was there solely to give a 'Second Opinion' and offer his advice to the GP who was always the doctor in charge of the case. A hospital specialist who saw a patient and treated him without the active collaboration of the patient's own doctor would have been struck off the register, and rightly so. The idea of a 'Consultant' seeing someone in his outpatients on his own responsibility, treating him, referring him to other consultants, perhaps admitting him for treatment or operation, and then sending him home, all without a word to his own doctor or at the most with a letter from the house officer a few days later, would have been quite inconceivable.

The training course for doctors was designed, and very largely remains, for the production of men like this. Unfortunately, for I still consider this the ideal way for the sick to be catered for, the enormous advances in all branches of medical science in recent years makes this impossible if training is to be completed in time for a young man to have any useful life left after qualification. The time has come when a complete re-appraisal needs to be made of the whole system of medical education and with it, unhappily, the structure and divisions of what are now the medical and surgical professions. In theory even today a man having completed the basic medical course and done two six-month house appointments in hospital is registered and qualified to practice all or any of the specialities from Cardiology to Brain Surgery, from Tropical Diseases to Heart Transplants. Nothing can be done to stop him, unless and until he kills or injuries someone from his own ignorance or lack of skill; when very rarely disciplinary action is taken on the grounds of 'Malpraxis'. This word has nothing in common with the 'Malpractice' of American Lawyers, a word that is seeping into the English language and means simply professional negligence. Malpraxis is tackling something that one knows, or ought to know, one lacks the skill, knowledge, or experience to deal with properly.

We have got to a stage where it is absurd to spend years trying to train one man to do everything, and then putting him in a job where not one tenth of what he has been taught will ever be of any use to him. However much men of my generation will regret it, we must accept the concept of training men for one particular task in health care, and awarding them qualifications to practice in that one branch only. The ENT Surgeon who works in an area as restricted as that of the dentist, the Ophthalmologist whose field is even smaller, will have to be trained and qualified in that speciality alone. Such training will of course involve the recognition and provisional diagnosis of conditions outside their own field of practice which they are especially likely to notice and will need to refer to another specialist. The expert on Tonsils needs to recognize when one of them is the site of a Syphilitic lesion although he will not treat it, and when a chronic lesion of the nose is evidence of generalized allergic disease which requires investigation by someone else; but he will not spend months and years learning the anatomy of the hand, the abnormal positions of the foetal head, or the changes in the electrocardiogram produced by beri-beri or even by a coronary thrombosis.

The problem of the Family Doctor is of course a political as well as an emotional one. Whatever we would like him to be, we have to accept the fact that he is most definitely not a General Practitioner. At best, at the very best, he is a specialist in triviality. Almost all his work (quite all the work of many

who are willing to have it so) and unhappily the only important part of his work, is sorting, making appointments, filling
up forms, and signing certificates. One would like to think of
him at least as a man who decides whether a patient really is ill
and whether it is necessary to send him to a hospital department already so overburdened that patients are dying from
want of care while they remain weeks, months, or even years to
be investigated and treated; but he is not. No Family Doctor in
the NHS will ever stand out against a patient who demands to
be sent to a 'Specialist', nor does it matter what specialist he is
sent to. The hospital will pass him on to the right department.
There is no inducement even for a doctor to take a history or
examine. What is wanted, and what is given, is a piece of
paper, it need be no more than a visiting card with a few words
scrawled on the back, which will get him onto the conveyor
belt of the hospital service. A few years ago there was a nation-
wide scandal over a patient whose tracheotomy tube had fallen
out and who died while waiting several hours for the ambulance which his doctor had called. It was a difficult problem for
the Ministry as it was of course necessary to pin the blame on
someone who was not a member of a Trade Union. Even so,
nobody considered for an instant blaming a man who called
himself a doctor and who was not able and willing, if not to
repeat the tracheotomy, at least to hold the breathing hole
open until better qualified help was available.

However, unless and until there is a complete revision or
collapse of the present Health Service these people are necessary, and the work they are doing (yes, what they are doing) is
necessary. But they are not working as doctors and do not need
to be trained as doctors. The country and the world simply
cannot continue to afford that they should be. Not only is their
present training unnecessary: it is useless. The state recognizes
this by requiring that however highly trained a man may be,
even if he has had to give up specialist practice with triple
higher qualifications in Medicine, Surgery, and Gynaecology,
he cannot have an NHS practice until he has had a further two
year period of training in the non-medical work that he will
have to do.

Doubtless a day will come when the idea is abandoned that
everyone should have his own doctor, but until it does there is a
system of training elsewhere in the world that will meet the case

far better than what we have at present. In Africa, but much better in the Far East, we have courses of training for what are called 'Medical Assistants', probably not unlike though one hopes better than Mao's 'Barefoot Doctors'. It is based on and run pari passu with the nursing training course, and the men emerge as fully trained male nurses: but as a rule it lasts longer and they are taught not just nursing but essentially everything of clinical medicine and surgery that a Medical Student learns in his three years of clinical study. In the past, Singapore-trained 'Dressers' or 'Medical Assistants' were much better at the day to day care of patients in clinics and tiny hospitals than a newly qualified doctor; and for a very good reason. They knew nothing of theory and had not wasted years learning Physics, Chemistry, Biology, Anatomy, Physiology, Pharmacology, and Pathology. Their training was entirely empirical and they could only recognize symptoms and carry out treatment; but they had five years of such training behind them as against three for the young doctor.

The man who is to provide first call in the Health Service needs much less training in clinical practice than these men receive, and like them none at all in basic science; so a year of more of his time can be spent in learning the other trades which go to make up doctoring today. It can be argued that many men do not know what branch of the profession is best for them when they start training, but as about eighty per cent are going to finish up this way it is surely necessary to accept that they have got to know, and not waste their time and the country's money training for work they will never do. Similarly those destined for a specialist career will have to decide early and be trained for what they are to do, rather than be trained expensively for everything and inadequately for anything before they start on their specialist courses.

There is however a small and rapidly diminishing group of people for whom this sort of comprehensive course is necessary. The Colonies and developing countries, and such groups as mission stations and oil installations in isolated and inaccessible places, still have a need for the General Duties Medical Officer. The normal course of medical training in UK today falls between two stools as it does not really provide all he needs, any more than it provides for the needs of Family Doctors or future specialists. In recent years, only in Holland has there been any proper provision for him.

Holland like Britain was an Imperial Power. I have no qualifications to form an opinion of Dutch standards of Medicine, but as I shall mention later I believe that their standards in Surgery and all related disciplines are, compared with ours, poor. As a consequence I have no great respect for their hospital services, though I wish we could equal their standard of respect and courtesy towards foreign visitors. It would be unkind and possibly unjust to suggest that awareness of this poor standard of their overseas hospitals is the reason why they provide so much better than we do for the training of their GDMOs. I suspect that Dutch medical education is good. Certainly the basic course for qualifying as a doctor extends nearly three years longer than ours. That their ideas and principles differ so much from our own can only justly be judged by results. In the matter of the management of sick children in the tropics, I have presumed on the basis of their results to judge them rather harshly in a later chapter; but in other respects I think a newly qualified Dutch doctor has been trained at least as well as our own.

Unlike our own newly registered young men and women, he is not however judged fit to be sent to an outpost of the Empire to provide for the natives all the medical care they will ever get. Dutch doctors who are to serve abroad are given a further two year course to fit them for single-handed total responsibility for an area perhaps larger than the Mother Country. This course includes a minimum of Tropical Medicine but a lot of practical training in emergency surgery and a surprisingly high standard of ophthalmology. I learned all my eye surgery from a Dutch CMO in Indonesia whose knowledge of all other aspects of doctoring was contemptible. We have some short 'refresher' courses available for missionary doctors but nothing like this.

[I wonder if a very junior member of the Clergy should dare to suggest that similar considerations could apply to the appointment of Bishops. Almost any ordained priest who has a genuine vocation should be able to fulfil the Sacramental duties of a Bishop once he has been appointed and consecrated with the Gift of the Holy Spirit for that function. This is only a tiny part however of the work of a Bishop today. A Bishop is the administrative head of a large business organization and the qualities required of him are those of a manager in industry. The chief abilities required are business knowledge and efficiency; and the ability to assess, handle and obtain the loyalty of his staff. Skill in handling people is not a God-given gift, it has to be learned, and there are places where it is taught. Just as a young doctor who is to become a surgeon or radiologist requires to return to his studies and obtain other qualifications, it would be an enormous advantage if a young priest who is to become a Bishop were sent to a red-brick university or a management training school to obtain a diploma in industrial management with emphasis on personnel relations.]

In one respect the Second MB course in my day was superior to what it has become. Today a student is only required to dissect one part of the body, and learns the rest of his anatomy from lectures, demonstrations, the textbooks, and prepared specimens. This may or may not be a satisfactory way of amassing the vast amount of information required to pass exams, but it is certainly not adequate as a training for true general practice, and still less as a prelude to specialization. A man going on to a career in surgery has to take for the Primary FRCS a much more intensive course of Anatomy of which he is required to show a hundred per cent knowledge, but there is no requirement, and seldom any opportunity, for him to complete his course of dissection. An Orthopaedic Surgeon, Urologist, or Gynaecologist is thus very likely to spend his whole professional life operating on parts of the body he has never dissected in the cadaver. This cannot possibly be good. When I was working for the Primary, having as an undergraduate dissected the whole body, I was able to get a paid job in the anatomy department at St Mary's preparing teaching specimens, and thus completed the course twice, but very few have this opportunity.

That first term, for until we started clinical work in the hospital itself we kept the University terms with the generous vacations available for study at home, was pretty hectic; and it was probably only the fact that the house at Purley was still not available and that I was living within easy walking distance that enabled me to get so much work done. The Anatomy and Physiology course was a full-time job but there were about ten others who like me had been granted the privilege of starting before we had passed First MB Biology and hence had to do several hours a week cramming under the excellent Biology teacher, Dr Fisk. There seems no doubt that my second failure had been due to sheer bad luck and he refused to take my position seriously; maintaining that I could not possibly fail again. I had all my day's lectures to write up every evening and then spent several hours on Biology, using my own system and writing, for the third time, a complete precis on the subject. In the event, the exam was very easy. The internal results were available to the examiners in Christmas week but Fisk insisted that he was not going to spoil anyone's Christmas by releasing them until afterwards. In my case however as I was getting neurotic from worry, he agreed secretly to let me have mine sooner and a cable reading 'Congratulations on passing' reached me on Christmas Eve. He told me later that he had written and stamped the form days before and simply gave it to his daughter to take to the post office when the results arrived.

With First MB at last safely out of the way I was able to take at least a little interest in the extra-curricular attractions of student life. The Rifle Club had been disbanded during the war but Dickson Wright called a meeting early in 1946 to appoint officers and get it going again. I was still very much a schoolboy at heart and had not really got used to the staff addressing us as 'Gentlemen' and the porters and lab boys as 'Sir', so there was no idea in my mind of applying for office. The old pre-war target rifles had mysteriously disappeared (at least those which were found and said to be them had certainly never seen service this century) but we got a generous grant from Students' Union funds, and were able to start shooting at once on the range of the Marylebone Rifle Club. One learns very early that there are people in this world who will do anything for Medical Students, and others, possibly readers of Dickens, who detest them. The then secretary of this club was one of the former and for a purely nominal fee gave us the complete use of the club premises for one evening a week to use our own rifles, ammunition, and targets. Unfortunately, although we behaved very well and showed our gratitude, this attitude did not last, and about two years later we had to look elsewhere.

None of us were brilliant shots and most like me started off just about keeping in the scoring area of the target but no better. It took me several months to get consistently into the nineties and I have never been of competition standard at .22 shooting. Later in the term however we started fullbore shooting at Bisley, and although still no good I began to realize that this was to be my sport for life.

Shooting at Bisley was like nothing else in the world, except so far as, throughout the Empire at least, local clubs and rifle associations were modelled on it as manifestly the highest expression of the marksman's art. Curiously Bisley shooting was not originally (nor was it then) a sport. The National Rifle Association was formed in 1860 simultaneously with 'The Volunteers' (later to be the Territorial Army) in response to the threat of invasion by Napoleon III. Its purpose was stated in the constitution to be 'To give permanence to the Volunteer Corps, and to encourage rifle shooting throughout the Queen's Dominions' and the whole organization and atmosphere were military. It is obvious from a study of *Punch* in the latter days of the last century, that to attend the Bisley Meeting (The 'Imperial Meeting' as it is still known) was regarded as a highly laudable act of patriotism. Even today, and things have gone down badly in the last twenty years, it is one of the few places where it is respectable and proper for a man to use his military rank even if he was only a temporary officer in the Catering Corps in one of the world wars, and indeed where he is obliged to do so when entering for a competition. If he still has the right he will also not be permitted to collect his prizes at the prize-giving ceremony unless he wears uniform: a source of some profit to Moss Brothers when an important match is won by a man who left the forces half a century ago and who has put on ten stone since then.

In miniature rifle shooting (.22) one shoots in comfort, usually indoors and always under cover, at a small paper target which is never more than a hundred yards away and in nine cases out of ten is at a range of only twenty-five yards; where even on outdoor ranges wind can have no possible effect. The only skill lies in meticulous sighting and holding, and in recent years rifles have grown into such monstrosities that they bear no resemblance to any practical weapon, and serious competitions are decided on an accuracy at this range not of a tenth of an inch but of a few hundredths.

Bisley shooting on the contrary is out of doors in all weathers (and Bisley Common can provide all possible weathers simultaneously), and shooting at a canvas target not less than four feet square and up to six feet by ten, at ranges never less than two hundred yards and up to twelve hundred (which is more than two-thirds of a mile) and in winds such that one may actually be pointing one's rifle at the next target but one.

Even today the greater part of the first week of Bisley is for members or past members of the armed forces using the current service rifle with service ammunition and with the rules designed to mimic active service conditions: although these are more the conditions envisaged in the eighteen-sixties than like anything seen in the Boer War or since. From an early date though provision was made for those who aspired to a higher standard of marksmanship than was possible under these rules. These provisions resulted in two new classes of competition known as 'SR (b)' and 'Match Rifle', the original purely military class being designated 'SR (a)'. To almost all Bisley men of my generation, shooting at Bisley meant SR (b).

These matches were shot with one of the three service rifles officially considered to be still in use, the SMLE (short magazine Lee-Enfield, also known as the 'number one'), the P14 (Enfield rifle pattern 1914), and the new 'No 4' version of the SMLE. The outdated Long Lee-Enfield which had been the mainstay of shooting until the last war was banned. Rifles had to be with barrels 'as issued' but could have target slings fitted and used as a support while shooting. It was also allowed to fit aperture sights with micrometer and vernier adjustment but with no magnifying or telescopic properties. The weapons were thus still essentially service rifles with no additions which were unsuitable for active service conditions. Ammunition had to be the service cartridge issued to us, though traditionally the very best of that year's batch was sent to Bisley for the Imperial Meeting.

The typical SRb shoot was the same as that for the first stage of the King's Prize, two sighting shots and seven to count at each of three ranges, 200, 500, and 600 yards. One was allowed a minute after the target appeared to get each shot off so there was no hurry. One learned to judge the wind in minutes of angle from the angle of the flags on poles up and down the range, and to enter the calculated deflection on the rifle's sight and correct it if necessary between shots. Targets were on counterbalanced iron frames working exactly like an old-fashioned sash window. When one fired, the marker hidden in the trench in front of the target and stop-butt, lowered the target and hence raised a similar frame called 'The Dummy'. This was for signalling only, and was a frame in which a black and white board was put in one of four positions representing a Bull scoring five, an inner four, a magpie three, or an outer two. There was no signal for a miss, and the marker was supposed to give no indication that he knew a shot had been fired but no hit seen. In those days if this happened one had to challenge the marking at a cost of half-a-crown and have the result communicated by telephone. Even if one had made an obvious mistake and was sure one had missed, one was in honour bound to challenge and get a clean target in the interest of one's companion who was shooting next. At that time the rules provided that if when he fired, two hits were found on the target, only the lower value would be signalled but both would be spotted, which would not only cost him a point or more but hopelessly confuse his calculations for the rest of the shoot. I have known a competitor himself to pay for the other man's miss to be sure of having a clean target.

Once the target was lowered, the marker would put on it, a circular disc of contrasting colour secured at its centre by a wire through the bullet hole, put a patch on the previous hole where the spotting disc had come from, and raise the target again to let one see with a telescope exactly where the shot had hit. Every serious competitor had a scorebook open in which he had already recorded the wind, the settings of his sights, and the value of the shot as signalled, and now entered on a printed diagram the exact spot where the bullet had gone. These diagrams were divided by a grid into minutes of angle so that if the shot or a group of shots were not centred in the bull, correction to the sight setting could be made easily.

During the Bisley Meeting, when there would be about sixteen hundred people competing, one was issued with a card for each shoot giving squadding details of time and target number, and if a match were at more than one range the score at previous ranges. When one's detail was called one went onto the firing point just to the left of the peg bearing the target number and put down a groundsheet, rifle, telescope, scorebook and pencil, and a bag containing ammunition and other odds and ends. Groups of three at each target shot in turn, and when all three hundred shooting in the detail were ready a telephone order would be given and the hundred targets would come up out of the marking trench at the same instant. Alongside each group of three on a target would be an army private called the 'Register Keeper' sitting at a blackboard. He would call out as each shot was signalled 'Major Bangstick – a Bull scoring five' or 'Lord Blueblood – an Outer scoring two' and enter the score on the card in pencil and on the blackboard in chalk. One signed the card at the end to show that the score was correct or at least agreed with that on the blackboard – there was no appeal against that after the next shot had been fired.

One could protest if the marking was obviously in error, which in practice only meant if the spotting disc was in a part of the target which could not possibly correspond to the score signalled, but except in extreme cases such a protest was not accepted. Otherwise one's only means of redress was to pay 2/6d. to challenge the marking, which was returned if the challenge was sustained. The fee was not unreasonable as a lot of work was involved and the delay could be serious to one's two companions who might find that the wind had changed by the time they could begin firing again. The register keeper had to call the Range Officer who then telephoned the officer in the butts. The target had to be lowered and personally inspected by the Butt Officer who would then send back a message 'Target twenty a Magpie as signalled' or 'Target twenty, Clear Target' or 'Challenge sustained – the last shot on target twenty is a Bull now being signalled'. Although one had little option, challenging a miss carried a danger of further expense. If one had struck the wrong target, a challenge would infallibly result in the shot being traced back and one was fined a further half-crown. Deliberate shooting at the wrong target, or at anything else on Bisley common except one's own, entailed disqualification for life; but I never heard of it happening.

I was at Bisley practising every Saturday from about March 1946 and bought my first full-bore rifle (an SMLE No 1) a year later. In the 1946 meeting I entered for the King's Prize and for two other individual events. We won the United Hospitals' cup against all the other London Teaching Hospitals. The following year I was elected Honorary Secretary of the St Mary's Rifle Club, a post I held for two years and a Vice President of the University Rifle Club. Considering the vast amount of study I got done in those years it is incredible to me now that I was able to attend to the day to day running of a Rifle Club, arrange weekly postal matches with teams all over the country (few of whom were really interested in competing with us) and compete in almost all their matches; as well as organizing the incredible complexity of getting members down to Bisley every Saturday on privileged train tickets, arranging for targets and markers, feeding them, and getting them all home reasonably sober on Saturday night.

Twice a year we had a match against the Consultant staff for which I had to assemble both teams and arrange the lavish entertainment paid for by our president Mr Dickson Wright. Dickson, Sir Alexander Fleming, and Reginald King were regular members of the staff team, but I had to go round cap in hand to find four others who would compete. I once tried to get Roche Lynch the Home Office Pathologist and expert on the wounds, ballistics, and identification of guns used in murder cases. He told me 'I have never fired anything but a revolver, and whenever I have done that, someone else has always been hanged.' Sir Alexander was the discoverer of penicillin and a keen member of the London Scottish. Sir Almoth Wright our vice president was of the previous generation, the inventor of typhoid inoculation who had thereby at least halved the terrible death rate of the Great War; and the victim of Bernard Shaw's vituperative worthless play *The Doctor's Dilemma*. Anyone who still believes that Shaw was an honest writer or serious thinker should read his preface to that work. He knew what he was doing as he had shared digs with the great man when they were both students.

Another very staunch supporter was Dr Morley of the Inoculation Department (now the Wright Fleming Institute) who had before the war been secretary of the club. Like many of us he was not only totally right-handed but as completely right eye dominant. Target shooting was not his only sport, and when he lost his right eye in a shooting accident he scorned a 'crossover gun' as he scorned a binocular microscope for his work, and killed his first pheasant from the left shoulder shooting with the left eye, two weeks to the day from his discharge from hospital. He was still a far better shot than I shall ever be.

From my point of view though, my most important contact in shooting, or in all the years I spent at St Mary's, was a young man with an artificial leg who appeared for the .22 shooting one evening early in 1947. His name was Michael Porter. He was a superb shot who once made twenty-two consecutive 'Possibles' (Highest possible score) and became our Captain a year later. He is now the father of two of my godsons, and his family together make up almost all my remaining friends in England.

Apart from rifle shooting, I can think of only four times student activities interrupted my studies in the appalling grind between passing in Biology at Christmas 1945 and taking Second MB in March 1947, one of which took only about two hours, another was on a Saturday afternoon, and the others on two evenings a year apart. The tradition of dramatic yet harmless rags still persisted, though there was nothing of the violence and political malice which characterizes student life today. One day in my first few months, the *Daily Express* accidentally transposed the scores in a Rugger match between ourselves and another hospital. I cannot remember which, but it was a quite unimportant match, so it cannot have been Guy's. It was obviously an innocent printers error but an apology had to be obtained. The entire student body took time off to march on Fleet Street and call the editor out to make amends; which he did most handsomely.

Before leaving Bath, or at least before I ceased going there on alternate weekends, I had ordered a sports coat to be made by my tailor, a very old man whose rate of work was quite unpredictable, and who always spoke of the Fuhrer who was at least twenty years younger as 'Old man Hitler'. It was ready for final fitting only after we got back to Purley, which should have meant an expensive railway journey. It happened though that the Rugger Club was playing away at Bath that Saturday, and places for supporters were available in the team coach for two shillings return. I at once became a supporter and went with them.

The journey down was uneventful and spent entirely on singing obscene songs in which a consultant ophthalmologist who was with us joined heartily. I got my coat fitted and was back at the ground before the match started. It was the same field where we held our parades in the days of the JTC at King Edward's. We won, and the journey home was somewhat different. We stopped at every pub en route and the quantity of beer consumed was astounding. Apparently by intuition, Dickson Wright who was president of the Rugger club, as he was for most of the student clubs, found us at one of these stops and stood rounds of something stronger. Nobody however became unpleasantly or dangerously drunk although one or two who had subsided quietly into coma on the floor of the bus could not be woken at journey's end and were dumped in the casualty department for the night. All was very good humoured and almost gentlemanly, and the only potentially dangerous incident was when it got a bit chilly and we closed the sunshine roof; only to find at the next stop that one of our number was on the outside. He clung on without trouble (there were no low bridges) and cheerfully accepted it as a genuine mistake that anybody could have made.

The only other Rugger match I have ever attended except at school was the United Hospitals Cup at Twickenham the following year between St Mary's and Guy's. For some reason lost in the depths of history these two hospitals, and especially their medical schools, have always been arch-rivals in everything and especially in Rugger at which both excel and eclipse all the others. The tradition cannot really be very old as St Mary's is a recent foundation, whereas Guy's was founded by Thomas Guy after he had made a vast fortune by being one of the very few to get out of the South Seas Company just before the bubble burst. However a meeting in this final, which commonly happens as there are few years when the others get a look in, is the occasion for a massive rag which is normally at least as important as the game itself, or as the result.

Guy's always paraded with a mascot, (exactly what escapes me but I think it was a brass helmet) which for some reason St Mary's lacked and always had to make good with a temporary substitute. This year we borrowed (without even having to resort to theft) the Elephant from Chessington Zoo. Early that morning a young woman, one of their female students, incredibly appeared outside our medical school wearing a Guy's scarf. She was immediately attacked in the public street by 'The Admiral', our elderly hall porter, and dragged in as a prisoner;

while the rag committee debated what to do with this unexpected gift from heaven. It was finally decided to parade the elephant round Twickenham stadium with her naked on its back representing Lady Godiva. The project was only abandoned at the last moment when the elephant's keeper refused to co-operate. They had probably let us have the beast with very little protest as an advertisement for the zoo and he must have thought this would be the wrong sort of advertisement. In the end she simply got dressed again and spent the afternoon with us as a pampered guest and then went home with her own people; certainly a much tamer ending than she had anticipated when she wantonly exposed herself to capture.

The rag was not as tame as all that though. Pretending to be put to shame by our effort, the Guy's supporters paraded quietly and soberly round the ground as though following the coffin of a lost friend. When they were lying squarely opposite our stand, every hand went to a coat pocket and the air became mysteriously filled with small white objects travelling in perfect parabolas towards us. A moment later bags of flour were bursting on our heads, and the entire Mary's contingent disappeared under an opaque white cloud. By the time the first of us emerged coughing and spluttering into the open air, Guy's were back in their places looking sedately as though nothing had happened, and play was about to begin.

After such a beginning the match could hardly be expected to make further Rugby history but it did. At one minute to time with the scores equal, St Mary's were awarded an almost impossible penalty kick. Our kicker took a tremendous run up, but then tapped the ball lightly with his foot towards the touchline on his left, whereupon the wing three-quarter ran forward, picked it up, and put it down over the undefended line. We were awarded the match and the cunning of the move was widely applauded in every newspaper in the land. Incredibly it was several days before some busybody looked at the Laws of Rugby Football and found it clearly stated that the ball was not in play until it had travelled forward five yards, which this one certainly had not. A replay was impossible and despite gentlemanly protests from the other side, who like everybody else should have spotted the infringement, we insisted on conceding a draw.

The only other occasions that I remember when student

activities took me away from work (apart from Rifle shooting of course) were the last two 'Hospital Day' collections. They were forbidden once Aneurin Bevan seized the voluntary hospitals as he had no time for charitable contributions (or for charity itself in any sense) and preferred money forced out of the tax payer. He did not mind that these hospitals were built and had always been maintained by gifts from the God-fearing public as he had no objection to robbing the dead. The first of these I took part in was in the autumn of 1946, and I was horrified to discover a week before what was to be the last Hospital Day that in disgusted anticipation of the end, no students outing and collection had been planned. Entirely out of character as it was for me, I then took it upon myself to organize one, which as far as I remember I did single handed.

Apart from making a list of the places we were going to raid, getting collecting boxes from the appeal's department round the corner, and recruiting about sixty fellow students to take part, the only real organizing that was necessary was to call on the local Pickfords Manager to ask for the loan of two lorries, (staffed at their expense) to provide us with transport. Here, although they had always done this, I ran into an unexpected difficulty. Unknown to me there had been some hooliganism the previous year when someone in the other lorry from mine had sprayed the street with a fire extinguisher, and with it by sheer bad luck the chairman of Pickfords Ltd. Neither he nor the manager actually said they would not help us again, but they asked me for an assurance that there would be no further unseemly behaviour. I was only able to promise that I would do my best to prevent it, which they generously accepted, and it is to my lasting regret that although I did so, I was not entirely successful.

Those too young to remember the days before Bevan can have no conception of the goodwill, love, and respect of ordinary people for doctors, and even as a rule for the quite unlovable medical students. All this has been thrown away and the general attitude today, in England at least, is that doctors are overpaid lazy self-important and often murderously incompetent tradesmen. A very large part of the blame for this rests with this uncouth malicious little Welshman and his obsessional class hatred. Certainly nobody in the world, not excluding General Tojo, was less suitable to be placed in charge of what had been the finest medical service in the world, and to be allowed to bully, browbeat, and blackmail members of what had been an honourable and dedicated profession. My own opinion of the man had been formed some years before when a distant young relative from South Africa (where there was no conscription) had left university to come to the Mother Country at his own expense to volunteer to fight for his King. Bevan personally drew his name out of a hat and then as he refused to work as a coal miner under the infamous 'Bevan Boys' scheme, preferring to return to his own country, had him imprisoned for the rest of the war. History may well say that we deserved to lose our Empire.

The evening went well and more quietly than expected. Dressed in long white coats and with stethoscopes sticking out of our pockets we called in succession at all the best hotels, clubs, and restaurants from the Atheneum to Simpsons, from Claridges to the Dorchester. Everywhere we were welcomed and everywhere huge sums were put in our collecting boxes. The only place we met with opposition was the Lyons Corner House at Marble Arch, which perhaps I should not have included on my list as it was not in the same class as the others. We were met by an abusive manager who called us beggars and threatened to call the police if any of us entered his 'Cafe' which he pronounced to rhyme with safe. His language alone was worth fourteen days without the option in any court, and I sometimes wish we had called his bluff. No doubt he had just been transferred from a roadside pull-up for transport drivers (which would be a bad let-down for car men) but his employers deserved the publicity which a prosecution would have involved and not just the loss of custom of ourselves, our friends, and our future patients. Actually I have never believed in cutting off my nose to spite my face, and have on occasion, for reasons which will emerge later, dined there since. The behaviour of the staff was better, but then it could hardly have got worse.

I am unsure whether I am sorry or not that I only discovered after getting back to Paddington that I had been driving round all the best of London in a van with 'To Hell with State Medicine' painted on the front, and 'Bugger Bevan' on the back. People may have thought our manners and morals were little better than those at Lyons.

Music never played much of a part in my life until my very late teens. I never liked Jazz, Boogie Woogie, or any other form of what would be called 'Pop' today, and insofar as I cared about it at all preferred fragments of Italian opera on the wireless and organ music in Church. For some reason at the age of about five I became enamoured of the overture to *Tannhauser* and had a ten-inch record of it for my own small gramophone, but I knew nothing of what that or any other opera was, and even the name of Wagner meant nothing to me. I made up my mind at the age of seven or eight that I wanted to play the organ, and had I been allowed to learn I am sure I would have made as fine an organist as Grandpa, as I would have put more hard work into it than he put into anything. Unfortunately we had a very fine Beckstein piano in the house (a wedding present to my mother from her father) and this was considered good enough for me. It was laid down as an Ex-Cathedra Dogma that you could not learn the organ until you had mastered the piano. I never really believed this, as even then I could see that there was no resemblance between the two instruments or the way they were played, except that the piano had a keyboard resembling one enlarged manual of the organ, but used and responding in a totally different way. It was forty years however before I realized that the complete answer to this absurd contention was that the organ had been in use for two thousand years before the piano was invented. At the age of nearly forty I bought a small Wurlitzer electric organ with but a single octave of pedals, and taught myself to play after a fashion using strips of stamp edging stuck to the keys labelled 'C-D-E' etc. The organ is though an instrument which has to be studied from a very early age and I shall never be able to do much more than play hymns and ballads. To have a son born into a musical family who had the urge to learn as early as that should have been recognized by my father as a gift from heaven, and it is tragic that he did not take advantage of it.

Fairly early in 1946 (I cannot verify the exact date) the house was de-requisitioned and restored. My father and I went down to Purley with a little of the furniture to make preparations for the arrival of the rest with Mummy and Nanor. To cheer things up I switched on the wireless and for the very first time heard the overture to *Die Meistersinger*. I have been an obsessive Wagnerian ever since. I know now that this time was the beginning of the Golden age of Wagnerian opera, and that nothing like it is ever likely to happen again. There will never be another Kirsten Flagstad just as there will never be another Caruso, and this was when she came back to London for a few concerts, to be followed by many years of the finest performances Covent Garden has ever seen.

Until four years before the war, Flagstad, then in her late thirties, had never sung outside Norway: and when she was offered a contract for one year only at the Metropolitan it was to sing only Sieglinde and other second-line roles. She sang Isolde at Covent Garden in 1937 and 1938 when she was regarded as a very satisfactory soprano, but only one of many available at that time. She was not heard again in London until one evening in November 1947 when I, who had never heard of her, decided to spend money I could ill afford at a Wagner concert at the Albert Hall. I was not the only one present, and when after singing '*Dich, teure Halle*' from *Tannhauser*, *Elsa's Dream* from *Lohengrin*, and *Senta's ballad* from *Der Fliegender Hollander* she sang the dawn duet from *Gotterdammerung*, the powers that be decided she must have the status of a permanent guest artist at the Royal Opera House, and keep it. I heard her sing *Brunnhilde* twice in the next few months in isolated performances of *Die Walkure* in English at the second of which the Queen was present, and then next year we began to have proper full performances of *The Ring* with Karl Rankle conducting, interspersed with what must surely have been the greatest renderings of *Tristan and Isolde* ever heard, in spite of what Ernest Newman used to say about them.

Many years later after she had retired and I was a surgeon on leave from Borneo, I was sorting through a box-full of rare records in a collector's shop in Shaftesbury Avenue, when I became aware that the vast mountain of flesh alongside me was Flagstad. I had just turned up a copy of the very rare recording of Frieda Lieda singing the *Lieberstod*, and so I glanced up politely in her direction and said 'This might interest you Madam Flagstad.'

She looked down on it as if it had been a black beatle in the sink and asked 'Have you ever heard ME sing *Isolde*.'

'Yes. Thirty-five times at Covent Garden.'

She stopped looking at the record and looked at me with even more disapproval. 'I have only sung *Isolde* thirty-five times at Covent Garden.'

'Yes. I was there every night.'

'You must be mad. You shall take me to lunch.'

Fortunately I had just come from the bank and had forty pounds in my pocket, which in those days was enough to take the Queen out to lunch. There is of course only one place in London to take a prima donna. I called for a taxi and we drove to the Savoy Grill. As we entered the head waiter took in the situation in an instant and as he showed us to our table Flagstad murmured a few words in a language I did not know (he probably understood a dozen). It was certainly not German but may have been Norwegian. We had an excellent meal with a very acceptable wine, and the bill when it was presented was less than it would have been at the Strand Corner House next door.

☆   ☆   ☆

Once installed in Manor Side and provided with a season ticket from Purley to Victoria, I was given an allowance of a pound a week to cover meals, stationery, and bus fares, as well as everything else. The fare from Victoria to Paddington was three-halfpence but subsequently went up to tuppence-halfpenny, when I used to walk to and from the first stage in Edgeware Road to save the extra penny. Several years ago I got into a bus outside the hospital and found that the fare had gone up to about 7/6d. On my protesting that when I started making the journey it was only three-halfpence, the conductor, without batting an eyelid, replied 'Yes Sir. Those old horse busses were very reasonable.'

Twenty months is not enough for the vast amount the student had to learn of the normal structure and working of the human body, and I am sure that it is much better to do the three year course at an older university, particularly as then, having done as much as any other degree course, one is actually given a degree instead of just a slip of paper entitling one to go on for another three years. With even the minimum of relaxation, the London student has little time for eating and sleeping. I never got to bed before one am and was back (studying of course) on the seven fifty-two train every morning.

The work was interesting but exacting. Anatomy of course was just a steady grind through the dissecting manuals, text-books, lectures, and tutorials; but Physiology involved long hours of fascinating experiments on frogs, cats, and guinea-pigs or more commonly living parts of them. The mythical experiment which Bernard Shaw (in order to disparage doctors in general and Almoth Wright in particular) pretended formed part of every medical course, was not featured.

As on other occasions I was suffering from having nobody with sufficient knowledge to advise me. My father rightly said that medical teaching and the experience available in London was the best in the world, but it did not follow that London University was therefore better. What neither he nor I knew until it was too late, was that all Cambridge students, and most of those from Oxford, went to London Hospitals for their clinical work after passing their tripos; and thus got the best of all possible worlds, getting their pre-clinical studies as part of a proper university education.

At last it was over; the Second MB exam passed in a flash (I did too) and we were free to start the serious business of learning to treat the sick.

There was no vacation for those who passed. Thereafter we would be permitted to take a maximum of two weeks off from a three month 'appointment' with the approval of the chief of the unit. No chief liked it of course, and as future jobs depended on their references there were some from whom it was unwise to ask any time off at all. For the first time the new students were given a three month introductory course in clinical studies before being precipitated into the wards. This proved popular and has been continued ever since. We attended elementary lectures on Pathology, Bacteriology, Medicine and Surgery and most important in the arts of history taking, examination of a patient, and the writing up of clinical records. I find it hard to see how all previous generations of students had managed without this, but they did.

Only on this very elementary course did we have any teaching from Sir Alexander Fleming. Fleming was not a great teacher, indeed he was hardly a teacher at all. Neither was he a great researcher or even I think a great bacteriologist. Nevertheless he was a man with an idea, and an idea so great that it has

95

revolutionized medical science and already saved untold millions of lives and alleviated human suffering and misery more than the work of any other single man, not excluding Pasteur, Lister, or Simpson. Erlich had already experimented with and produced drugs which could be injected and destroy pathogenic organisms without damage to the human body. It was Fleming alone who foresaw that such substances could be the natural products of living organisms. Oddly an unpublished notebook of Lord Lister shows that he was aware that penicillium produces a substance that destroys certain bacteria, and had demonstrated that it was intensely toxic.

The first organism to which Fleming looked to produce such a universal non-toxic antiseptic (for which he coined the name Antibiotic) was man himself. He discovered Lysozyme in his own nasal mucous in 1922. Facilities for mass production of such a substance did not exist at that time and it has never been put to clinical use; though with modern tissue culture and genetic engineering it may some day become worth investigating again. It, or something very similar might even be effective against viruses including Aids.

The important thing is that Sir Alexander's mind was the fertile ground in which the idea of Penicillin was to grow. Professor Charles Pannett who delivered his funeral oration from the pulpit of St Paul's said that for the one and only suitable mutant penicillium spore to fall into Sir Alexander's petri dish was literally a miracle. He described it as 'The Finger of God at work'. No other bacteriologist in the world would have done, and no other spore. All other non-toxic strains are mutants of this mutant. He alone was expecting it and was ready to investigate it, the activity of the new drug and the toxicity (or rather absence of any toxic effect) in experimental animals and man. In spite of all that has been said to the contrary, the credit for the invention of antibiotics is his and his alone. The chemists at Oxford did splendid work, without which nothing but minuscule amounts of the impure drug could have been produced, but they were only technicians. The genius was his.

Sir Alexander was a devout but very Low Church Christian. It horrified him when he visited Spain and the women knelt and crossed themselves as he passed. He gave his discovery freely to the world, and resented it strongly when the Americans took out a patent on the manufacture of Penicillin and even St Mary's had to pay royalties on every vial they made. After the war when it became known that he was a rather poor man, there was a move in Parliament to vote him a million pounds, but predictably it was shouted down by the Labour Party, with Bevan making the most noise.

I have sometimes wondered how much a medical man's inclinations in specialization and his whole future career depend on the accident of his first student appointment. I was allocated for my first three months to Surgery under R M Handfield Jones and Arthur Porrit. Porrit was a New Zealander, a Rhodes Scholar, a leading light in the movement to relate medicine and sport, and a very pleasant and competent teacher. He was so pleasant, sympathetic and charming that his references and testimonials, which he gave freely on demand, were worthless. He was too kind to give to even the most undeserving student anything less than suggested that he was the greatest and most dedicated doctor since Hypocrates, and the fact became known. He subsequently became Sir Arthur, and afterwards as Governor General of New Zealand, Lord Porrit. He was however completely eclipsed by the senior member of his firm (and Senior Surgeon), Mr R M Handfield Jones. 'HJ' (he was the third of that name at St Mary's) was the archetype of the Great Surgeon. He was arrogant, selfish, self important, self righteous, ill mannered, totally intolerant, and the greatest teacher, greatest surgeon, and one of the greatest of men I have ever met. He was also a famous collector of butterflies.

I certainly did not ask to be on HJ's firm. I doubt anyone ever did. I did not even presume to ask to be on any firm, though all the competition was to get on Dickson Wright's. I am very thankful at least I did not know enough to try that. Had I done so I would have obtained at the same time a completely distorted idea of Surgery and a completely distorted idea of Dickson Wright.

Dickson was a combination of a lady bountiful and a Ministering Angel to all the students and student clubs. He was however a devil incarnate to the nurses, his House Surgeons and Registrars, and incredibly to his patients including that vast army of private patients who kept him in Rolls Royces, servants, and funds to support all his benevolent activities within the student body. I have never met a surgeon who could drive a motor car in safety, or one who should ever have been allowed to try. Dickson however was something quite exceptional. In the days before motorways I have more than once known him to overtake at seventy on the near side on an ordinary first class road while leaning out of the window to curse the other driver doing only sixty-five who had not pulled in to let him pass.

Handfield Jones was a tyrant and something of a bully, but a superb teacher who correlated every clinical feature of a case with the surgical pathology involved and could justify on pathological grounds every aspect of treatment. As is probably proper in undergraduate teaching he was dogmatic, but over the years I have found almost all his dogmata to be true. When I joined his firm I certainly had no intention of ever being a surgeon, but since the end of that three months I have never considered anything else. It is interesting to speculate what might have happened had I started my clinical studies on a medical firm.

My second three months was in the Casualty department where we had every opportunity to put into practice the elementary surgical training we had acquired. Each patient was seen initially by the house surgeon who wrote up the treatment required on his record card and then left it to the students to carry out. Most cases were simply for dressings, poultices, or penicillin injections; but a few required minor surgery for the opening of abscesses, reduction of fractures with application of plaster, or excision of warts, moles, or sebaceous cysts; with of course a constant flow of wounds to be cleaned and stitched up. Those that could be done with a local anaesthetic we did virtually unsupervised, but every few hours there would be an operating session on four or five cases at which the HS had to be present. Usually he would just sit in a corner to see that we did not kill anybody, or that if we did he would be able to assure the Coroner that everything had been done correctly; but from time to time he would himself do a difficult reduction while at the same time supervising the student anaesthetist, or give a difficult anaesthetic while supervising the minor operation. I sometimes wonder what things are like now when a patient can take advantage of all the facilities provided at a teaching hospital built and run for

98

this purpose and yet have a legal right to refuse to be seen or touched by a medical student.

It was during this three months that we lost Nanor. She had a heart attack in the garden and lingered on for seven weeks, dying in her eighty-first year. My mother described it as 'a great age' though she herself lived a much more active life to the age of eighty-six. Nanor had lived with us all my life as she was widowed a month before I was born; but until the war spent every winter travelling in the warmer parts of the world. She always took with her a Mrs Lord, a Southport friend from the Women's Lib days who apparently fell in completely with what Nanor wanted to do and in later years was not even consulted about the arrangements which she made for the two of them in London. She would just be told when they were going to start and how much she was going to have to pay. In twelve holidays, during which of course they never used aeroplanes, these two old ladies made two journeys round the world and visited India, China, Japan, Australia, the Americas, the Holy Land, South and East Africa, Rhodesia, and a score of other places in five continents. Only in her last trip to Africa did Nanor go up in an aeroplane to see the Victoria Falls from above. For once Mrs Lord did not join her. It was only several years after her death that I discovered that she was paying all my medical school fees, my father having refused to do so. She had paid many hundreds of pounds into a bank account for me over the years, and had now opened a special account to pay for my further education. She paid into it every penny she had, so that Mummy had to borrow from it to pay for her funeral.

Gynaecology, with which is naturally linked Obstetrics (known for some unexplained reason as 'Midder') was taught by a triumvirate, all of them famous. I say nothing about Alec Bourne whose fame rests largely in the part he played in the legalization of abortion.

Our second Gynaecologist was Douglas Macleod, second or so in line to the Macleod of Macleod and a man with a vast private fortune who had never needed to do a stroke of work in his life if he had not wished to. He was one of the hardest working, dedicated, and kindly men I have ever found in any branch of Surgery. He left himself little time for leisurely pursuits, but when he did indulge in them he did so magnificently. Most top line London Consultants would have a Rolls Royce with a chauffeur, but Dougie had two, the second kept in Edinburgh and said to be driven to Renfrew airport daily in case he should suddenly decide to go to Scotland without having time to call for the car to be ready for him. One would have taken him for an Englishman but he was intensely proud of his family background, and subject to some harmless jesting from Dickson Wright as a consequence. One morning Dickson told him that he had a Macleod among his patients in the Lindo Wing, the most expensive and exclusive private nursing home in London. Dougie put on his best kilt to pay a social call, only to discover a middle-European Jewess who had changed her name from Goldsteiner the previous month.

Leslie Williams, our third Gynaecologist, was a man of quite outstanding ability, character, and bulk. As a devout and practising Roman Catholic he had to be outstanding to have secured a place in that citadel of Freemasonry. His teaching, like that of HJ was precise, reliable, axiomatic and dogmatic and as with HJ wise students would always have a notebook handy to jot down his pithy and immensely practical sayings. With Leslie Bill though there were often less repeatable things to go into the book. He enjoyed life, and regarded all his work as a huge joke which he wanted us all to share in. All his clinical accounts and examples (and clinical teaching consists very largely of narratives of past successes and failures) were punctuated with witty, risque and often downright bawdy remarks, which made everything he said well remembered. (One of his axioms was 'If the Archbishop of Canterbury misses a period for the first time in his life, he is pregnant.') The only thing that ever made him angry was bureaucratic officiousness and inefficiency, and he had plenty of that in the early weeks of the Health Service.

Until Bevan took over, nobody questioned that although the welfare of the patients was paramount, administration was for the convenience of the Honorary Staff and the efficient teaching of the students. A man whose time even then was worth hundreds of guineas an hour, and who is giving it freely to a teaching hospital does not take kindly to having it wasted. It was recognized that if one wanted to have free what would cost a private patient a very large sum, one must sacrifice ones own convenience and wait. The patients for a clinic would all be assembled and documented at least an hour before the great man turned up and if, as sometimes happened, a patient dropped dead just as his turn came, the next must be ready to step into his place without a moment being lost. In spite of the terror he inspired among the clerical staff, the new appointments system would sometimes fail and Leslie Bill would find himself without a patient. He would then open the door into the outpatients hall, where even then there would be two or three hundred people, and before slamming it with a crash which would be heard in Paddington Station, would bawl in the voice of a sergeant major 'God Damn all Planners'.

Only once did I see him disconcerted. A voluptuous blond in the maternity ward was nursing a baby with the most astoundingly red hair, and Leslie Bill asked her 'Has the father got red hair.' As quick as a flash she replied 'I don't know. He didn't take his hat off.' On another occasion a somewhat older patient was sitting in the crowded outpatient hall and looked up at the nurse to ask 'What did the doctor say was wrong with me?' The nurse bent down and whispered in her ear. 'Speak up dearie, I'm very deaf.' The nurse did so. 'Syphilis?' bellowed the old woman, 'Just write it down for me dear. You feel such a fool if people ask and you don't know.'

Some years later when I was working for Shell, one of our senior staff was admitted to the Lindo Wing for surgery. When he was comfortably settled in bed, a quiet knock sounded on the door and a very small and insignificant nurse came in and said 'Sister has told me to get you ready for your operation.' She removed his pyjamas and gave him an enema and a bedpan. She then blanket-bathed him, shaved his abdomen, prepared the skin and covered it with sterile towels, put on his operation socks and short gown, and tucked him up again in bed. She was just going out of the room when the patient asked her 'Tell me nurse – why did you knock?'

Other appointments followed each other at three month intervals including one devoted to pathology. Most of this was taken up with lectures and tutorials, but we had to attend the day's postmortem demonstrations at lunchtime, and personally perform at least four autopsies ourselves, writing them up afterwards in one of a series of big leather-bound books. It was just after the time when the early ball-points were found to have been filled with fugitive ink, and we had to re-learn the now lost art of writing with a fountain pen. It was the custom to have a postmortem on every patient who died in the hospital, and permission was almost invariably obtained by asking the next of kin to 'just sign the authorization for the usual examination of the body'. One has no legal right to perform a postmortem without permission; on the other hand there appears to be no legal redress if one does, as a dead body is not an article of property and therefore cannot be the subject of an action for damages. In any case, if there is difficulty one has only to inform the Coroner that one does not know the certain cause of death (and one never does) and he is obliged to order one. In all the years I was a student I never heard of any trouble, or a case where autopsy was not performed. In addition to hospital cases there was a constant supply of bodies brought in dead (BID), so that there would be two or three demonstrations every day.

The initial examination would normally be carried out by a student under the very careful supervision of the duty consultant pathologist: after which the student would weigh and record every organ, and array everything on a tin tray for the chief to demonstrate and teach on at one thirty pm. At that time a large number of other students would arrive, often with the Physician or Surgeon whose case it had been, and always the house officer in charge who would read the history, narrate the clinical course and try to explain why the Grim Reaper had defeated them all. In loyalty to his chief he would sometimes come early to learn the findings, and might not be above altering his story to make the great man appear to be less liable to error than he really was. No such sympathy was to be expected from the Pathologist, and wordy battles sometimes ensued more suggestive of a collision between two Billingsgate porters than an erudite discussion by two of the leaders of a learned and gentlemanly profession.

In passing it is worth pointing out that Medicine is considered a profession for gentlemen, whereas Surgery most definitely is not. Few medial men do in fact have a doctorate, but they are all given the courtesy title of 'Doctor' to indicate that they are assumed to have received a proper education and to be doctors of a university faculty. In the distant past they would all be Doctors of Medicine or of Divinity, and even today the Archbishop of Canterbury has the right, which is never exercised, to award a degree in medicine to anybody he chooses: which entitles him to be registered and to practice without of necessity having any qualifications at all beyond being a Christian Gentleman. Surgeons however have a different origin and history. They have arisen from and developed pari passu with the barbers, with whom in London they shared the same livery company and the Barber Surgeons Hall. They are not gentlemen but tradesmen. Since late in the last century they have been required to have the same initial training, examinations, and qualifications as a physician but now as a form of inverted snobbery they refuse to be known as 'Doctor' and even the most senior of them who may well have the double higher qualification including a doctorate in medicine (which few Consultant Physicians have) will insist on being known as 'Mister'.

Surgeons in Australia carry a chip like everyone else, and in spite of their own Fellowship being of at least as high a standard as ours, have a sense of inferiority, and are regarded as inferior, unless they have been to London or Edinburgh to take the FRCS there as well. Incredibly, men with only the Australian Fellowship are known in their own country as 'Doctor', and it is only when they have qualified in Britain as well that they assume the more honourable title of 'Mister'.

I have met only one Australian who did not have a chip, and he curiously enough was a Physician. He was a very odd Australian in other respects in that he was a teetotaller. This was not born of any confused ethical or religious beliefs. He just didn't like the taste of the stuff and disliked the effect it had on him and on other people. He came to work with us in the all British medical department of Caltex in Indonesia. For some weeks we handled him with kid gloves to try to avoid offending him, but it seemed to be unnecessary. Indeed far from having an inferiority complex, it almost looked as though he was looking down on us. He was. One evening someone made some remark about England, to which he responded 'England? – Isn't that the place where all those convicts came from?'

Every student is required to spend one month of full-time resident duty on a delivery unit during which time he must

103

personally conduct twenty deliveries, though most manage many more. I did mine at Chiswick hospital overlooking Chiswick Eyot which ever since has provided me with a place to go to watch the boat-race. I kept good records in those days, and a year ago on giving a lift to a young visitor to St Helena, discovered he was a doctor and that the only hospital we had both worked at was Chiswick. He went on to remark that he was born there. We drove to my house, and checking my diary for 1949 I was able to show that I had delivered him. It made me feel rather old.

Some students were put onto 'district' work which meant that they went out with a district midwife to deliver patients in their own homes. One of my colleagues was not renowned for overworking and seldom if ever opened a textbook or attended a lecture. He was quite unconcerned at having to deliver a baby (and the midwife often failed to arrive until the student had finished the job) as he said 'It is a perfectly normal physiological process'. The first time he was called out things went well and he said the same thing. The second time the midwife failed to arrive and he made a panic telephone call for the Obstetrics Registrar. That young man was in on the joke and answered 'Why do you want me? It's a perfectly normal physiological process isn't it?' 'Physiological process be damned,' came the agonized reply. 'This one is coming head first.'

Included in the course, and attended without question or grumbling by all of us including the most lazy, were two or three lectures on Medical Ethics. Few of us came from homes which were not medical or clerical, and we needed this not to tell us what we had to do if we did not want to get struck off the register, but to give us details of the way of life we were all determined to pursue. None of us questioned that, whatever was by tradition permitted to medical students, the moment we became qualified we must adhere to a code of conduct drawn up in the fifth century BC and give up fornicating with the nurses (those few of us who managed to), getting drunk on Saturday nights, and collecting policeman's helmets. Even as students we had some respect for public opinion. Consorting with prostitutes was definitely not done, even for the few who could have afforded it; and the inevitable adolescent boastings of sexual prowess was confined to accounts of wholly imaginary trips to Paris, which we could not afford either. The carrying and exhibiting of a contraceptive in one's wallet was probably only acceptable in clergyman's sons, and in the case of the only one I knew well I noticed a small tear in the wrapping of the one he carried which was still there four years later.

Young people today, even young doctors today, cannot conceive of the change in medical ethics and acceptable standard of behaviour for doctors which has come about since 1948. This is certainly the major factor, the only important factor, which has changed large parts of an honourable profession into an ignominious trade. Abuse, blackmail, and persecution by Bevan explained the changed attitude of the public in the early days of the Health Service; but it is the abandonment by themselves of a code of ethics, not built up over the centuries, but respected, revered, and universally adhered to unchanged for two and a half millennia, which has made the doctors of the New Elizabethan Age what they are.

In the days when I qualified it would have seemed as inconceivable that the setting up of an abortions industry by parliament would induce thousands of British doctors to prostitute their calling by killing unborn children for money, as it would for the clergy to go in for human sacrifice or cannibalism. The fact that an act of parliament makes a thing legal does not of course compel members of the General Medical Council to allow such men to remain doctors, and their status as advisors to the Queen in Council does not absolve them from the sacred duty of maintaining the code of conduct which was expected of them when they were granted the immense privilege of becoming doctors, and which some at least of them were under oath to maintain.

Bevan and the Butler Education Act caused men to be selected for training on totally different criteria to those of the past; and without consideration of vocation, background, or cultural and ethical standards. Nevertheless the men who are truly responsible and on whom the terrible guilt lies are those of my generation and older, who had it in their power to refuse facilities and further training to the corrupted young and to remove their professional status from those who indulged in these wicked practices. We cannot shelter behind the actions of professional politicians who use the democratic electoral process to obtain and retain soft jobs yielding salaries many times what most of them could earn in an honest trade, and who if they lose their jobs are in some cases reduced to living on the dole as they are in fact unemployable. We, the elders of our profession, are the guilty men.

Euthanasia too is not merely murder but what in the past would have been regarded as Petty Treason, the killing of someone towards whom the criminal was in a position of especial responsibility and trust. In South Africa, a country where murder is still punished by hanging, though unhappily there is no worse penalty for matricide, a famous practitioner has boasted in print that he deliberately killed his own mother. In England the family of a very famous Physician have recently claimed that he murdered his king. Perhaps fortunately he is now dead, as that at least still carries the death penalty. I personally am quite certain that the story is untrue, but it is frightening that it could be told and accepted even in this day and age.

I personally have never deliberately terminated a pregnancy, though like Leslie Williams, a devout Roman Catholic, I have once been tricked into removing the gravid uterus of a woman who lied to me with that very object. In Leslie Bill's case the woman even brought him a fake pathological specimen from her non-pregnant sister, but I was less on my guard and simply accepted my patient's lying history. I baptized the miserable victim so that he at least will be saved even if there is little hope for his unworthy mother. That is not to say that there are no circumstances where I would not have been prepared to terminate. I would never deliberately kill one innocent person to save another, though I would have no hesitation in shooting down a criminal who was holding and about to kill an innocent hostage. I have always said that I would be willing to do so if I were satisfied that the mother's life would be saved thereby and that by all human judgement she would not live to deliver a viable child. Only once have I been satisfied that these criteria were met, and I am not certain whether I am happy or not to say that the patient refused operation and did in fact die with her baby unborn. In such cases the baby's life is already forfeit and one is not in any sense depriving it of life. I would be confident that if after prayer I had set out to abort such a case and was mistaken, God would prevent me in some way, even if necessary by letting me see, as

106

did Balaam, an angel with a drawn sword standing in my way.

☆ ☆ ☆

In the summer of 1948 David Griffiths persuaded me to go with him on a fishing holiday to Ireland. It was to be done on a shoe-string as although I could always rely on a reasonable gift of money from my mother on such occasions he was dependent on savings from his job. At that time he was working for a somewhat esoteric quasi-government department called 'The Cocoa, Chocolate, and Confectionery Board' and his duties, which appeared to consist largely of entertaining visiting African Native Chiefs with names like 'The Oggi of Iffi', were not highly paid. We travelled third class via Fishguard on a night when the *Mauritania* was forced to ride out the storm off Cork Harbour, and for the only time in my life I was seasick.

After a few days in Cork we went to stay at a very pleasant fishing hotel in Fermoy on the Blackwater. David professed an interest in fishing but was really only interested in Nature and the Irish, the most astonishing natural phenomena in Ireland. I confined myself to trout fishing and occasional spinning for pike. There was an elderly Irishman who took a continuous interest in me and was constantly urging me to try for salmon. My protest that I had no Salmon Licence was met with what he may well have known to be a classic *Punch* joke 'Is it a Licence you'd be wanting to kill a salmon? Faith, you could kill a man or two round here and nobody would be minding.'

However our object was not only to fish but to see the country, and David's idea of doing this was by hitch hiking. He is now a much more senior and respected member of the clergy than I shall ever be, so I suppose it must be all right, but I confess that I have always regarded it as a form of begging. In Ireland though it certainly worked, provided of course that there were any vehicles on the road to beg from. We got from Fermoy to Dublin and later from Dublin to Limerick with the absolute minimum of trouble. As far as I can remember we got a lift in each case from the first vehicle to appear and it took us from door to door. So confident were we when we wanted to get back from Limerick that we set out at night walking along a deserted road believing that we had only to make a thumbs up gesture to the first car or lorry to approach and we would be spirited to our destination without trouble or expense. It might well have been so, had there been any car or lorry going from Limerick to Cork that night, but there wasn't. About three in the morning we turned round and made our way back to our hotel at Limerick for another day or two, and then completed our journey by more orthodox means.

It was my own custom on these occasions to carry a packet of cigarettes to make some sort of recompense to our benefactor. We neither of us cared much for smoking but if the driver accepted one we would smoke ourselves to keep him company. One time in the front seat of a huge tanker waggon my offer had been most enthusiastically received and we were just lighting up when I saw a notice above the windscreen reading 'No Smoking – highly explosive vapour'. I drew the driver's attention to this and asked whether it was safe for us all to smoke. He replied 'Och yes. It's not petrol we're carrying. It's what they called "High Octane".'

The following summer David wanted to go to Ireland again, but I had set my heart on a holiday in Italy and in spite of his misgivings I managed to persuade him that we could manage a three weeks holiday in Rome, Florence and Paris for forty pounds each including our fares. It sounds unbelievable today as one could not live for a day in any of these places for the money, but things were different then in spite of what people considered the total collapse in the value of the pound since 1939. David told me afterwards that he spent rather less, and I spent only a pound or two more.

We went to Paris and back third class, a journey that took us over eight hours, without too much discomfort, but paid for second class all the rest of the trip. I suppose even then we could have gone by air for much the same but never thought of it. We spent two days in Paris staying with a friend of David's father from the Great War days but saw little of the town. All I remember of the luxury flat were the flirtatious maid and the fact that although our host was a Consultant Chest Physician he refused to speak any language but French. David, trying to make some sort of conversation at the lunch table remarked that I came from '*Une grand belle maison*', upon which the nine year old daughter of the house choked and had to be removed by a nanny. (It has just struck me as odd that I never had one myself. All my friends at prep school had.) The third night we were taken on a tour of Paris, including the outside only of the Moulin Rouge, and then to the Gare de Lyons for the night train for Milan. This was one of my only two visits, and as everything was seen in the dark it has not interfered with my memories of 1937 when I was only ten.

Whether the Rome express is any better I do not know, but that night I swore a dreadful oath never again to go to Italy by rail. The train itself was comfortable and fast as far as the Italian border, though unbelievably cold going through the Swiss Alps; but it then became a local stopping train and at every village the corridors became blocked and even the second class compartments invaded by voluble Italians, nuns, chickens, and goats. We were thankful for a brief stopover at Milan, when we managed to see the outside of La Scala and pay a visit to the Cathedral. We had booked our very comfortable hotel in Florence and only discovered on getting there that there was only one bathroom and that baths could be had by an elaborate arrangement involving the entire staff running round excitedly for an hour or more working equipment apparently dating from the days of the Medici and very possibly designed and built by Leonardo da Vinci. We put the procedure into operation that first night, but when we announced that we wanted a bath the following night as well, were met with stunned incredulity. My Italian was as now rudimentary, and I addressed the astonished multitude in what I fondly believed to be French. '*Touts les Anglais faites du bain toutes les jours.*'

Florence was all we had expected and more. The first evening we wandered into the Piazza della Signoria and as we turned the corner, the Palazza Vecchio suddenly stood before us floodlit like the backcloth of an opera set. I have never seen anything more breath-taking. There are two splendid open-air restaurants in the piazza but we did not use them on this trip. A few days before we left London, a stranger at a bus stop in Paddington had heard us discussing our plans and had told us of a little eating place known as the *Trattoria di Medici* underneath the Ricardi palace where the local cab-drivers went for their dinners. It was exactly that, and even then the most unbelievable value for money. A huge pasta followed by fish or meat, cheese and fruit, with a half carafe of wine cost the equivalent of one and ninepence, and we ate there every night.

It would take a lifetime to see everything worth seeing in Florence, but we managed to see about half of it in a week.

We went on to Rome second class by the ordinary slow train which cannot have been too bad as I remember nothing of the journey; though in those days I knew nothing of the air-conditioned rapido or the excellent air service which went direct from Florence before the airport was built at Pisa. For some reason we had not booked a hotel and fell foul of a tout who promised us a room with bath at a very pleasant new hotel within a hundred yards of the station for a pound a night each, bed, breakfast and dinner. After paying our fares our budget allowed only a pound a day for everything, but we had saved quite a lot in Paris and Florence so we closed with the offer and lived a week in what seemed like luxury. It was probably a very good bargain and established a life-long habit, as although I have never been to the same hotel again, I now always stay somewhere on the Quiranale and know my way about Rome only from that direction. We walked everywhere within the city (I still do) and had money to spare for conducted tours to Tivoli and the Catacomb of St Calixtus.

Arriving back at St Mary's I found myself far from popular. I had not exceeded my leave allowance but the Physician on whose firm I had been placed took a very dim view of my having missed the first week of his teaching. It was not worth much actually. I see from my diary that this was on 6 August 1949 and I was to start sitting my finals only two months later. Although I was of course a degree student, I had elected to take the 'Conjoint' qualification as well. This comprises the diplomas of the two Royal Colleges of Medicine and Surgery, and was devised in the last century to provide a single portal of entry to the profession. Somehow this did not work out and the degrees of the various universities continued to be registrable instead of as had been intended being merely supplementary, and it became just one more way of qualifying. It was not much sought after at that time for a peculiar reason. Almost all students were liable for compulsory military service and once they had qualified were required to obtain a house-job immediately or they would be called up. For me though, being exempt, there was an advantage in qualifying six months early as there was always the danger of failing a single part of the MB and I could then get a job and complete my degree not only at leisure but with the advantage of having some months of practical doctoring behind me and the presence and self assurance that would follow from it.

I sat all the Conjoint final except Medicine that October as well as the MB Pathology and Forensic Medicine, and very nearly failed the latter by knowing too much about shooting. Every medical exam by tradition includes a viva-voce which has to be passed. Candidates are brought up to a table where they sit opposite two examiners each of which is supposed to ask half the questions, though in some cases such as this, one does all the work while the other reads *The Times*. One has to keep talking, unless one has the skill to make the examiner do the talking himself, for a full twenty minutes, when a bell rings and the ordeal is over. The latter technique is dangerous as when an examiner has been tricked into talking on his favourite subject for a quarter of an hour, he may say when you have gone 'He didn't have much to say for himself did he?' On this occasion having talked briefly on hanging, aided by something nasty in a bottle provided as a talking point, Dr Donald Teare suddenly asked me 'Tell me, at what range could you be sure of killing a man with a revolver?'

'Oh, about fifty yards.'

'Good God! Would you be surprised if I told you that you would have the very greatest difficulty in doing it at ten yards?'

'I shouldn't be surprised sir. I should be incredulous.'

'Well I assure you it's true.'

There the matter appeared to rest. It is never wise to argue with an examiner, but I knew that I was right and that I was being marked down.

'Well, I make no claim to be a revolver shot, but I can at least keep them on the target at fifty yards. The Bisley fifty yard target is about the size of a man's chest, and if you hit a man in the chest with a .455 revolver bullet you should expect to kill him.'

This was not well received. Donald Teare was the Home Office Pathologist, and as with Roche-Lynch what he said on revolver shooting usually sent someone to the gallows. On this occasion he just said in a surly fashion 'Oh, of course if you are a Bisley man, there's no point in discussing the matter any further.' He then turned sideways in his chair and looked at the clock. He remained looking at the clock for ten long minutes

111

until the bell rang and then dismissed me with a nod without looking at me. I thought he had failed me, but he hadn't. He had passed me with full marks. He had chosen the question, and the candidate had satisfied him that he knew more about that subject than he did, so he was not prepared to continue with the examination. He simply passed me and waited for the next victim who might know less.

There is a story, almost certainly true, of Sir Gordon Gordon-Taylor who was examining well into his late eighties and who did not like women doctors. One very confident and self assured specimen of the breed sat opposite to him at the Primary FRCS, and the following conversation ensued:

'Tell me the Capacity of the human bladder.'

'Twenty pints sir.'

'Twenty pints?'

'Yes sir.'

'Are you quite sure?'

'Quite sure sir.'

'Then I am afraid Young Lady that you have missed your vocation. – You should paint yourself bright red and get a job as a fire extinguisher.'

The rest of the finals passed without dramatic incident. I took the remaining part of the Conjoint in March and, rather to my surprise, passed. In those days if it was wet or if I felt too tired to walk home from Purley Station I used to telephone from Victoria to ask Mummy to pick me up. This evening, as she picked up the telephone I said 'Dr Crook speaking.'

4

YOUNG DOCTOR

Qualification is always said to be the greatest event in a
medical man's life, turning him suddenly from a despised
snotty-nosed medical student into a respected responsible
member of the most honourable of all professions. Perhaps in
the past this was true, when many young men went straight
from medical school to busy General Practice, perhaps to one
where father was waiting impatiently to hand over to the
youngster the family firm which would be his for the rest of his
working life. Today it carries no right to practice anywhere
outside a hospital for another year, and in all probability life
goes on for the next month or so, exactly as it has been doing.
The new doctor stops wearing a soiled sports coat and puts on
an expensive and respectable three piece suit to attend teaching rounds, and that is all.

In my own case it was a total non-event, and I did not even
remember to say 'doctor' when answering the telephone.
(Before long I was seeing myself as a budding surgeon, so I
never did.) I telephoned Dr Cross who expressed astonishment
that the time had gone so quickly and, remembering the
traditional etiquette of the occasion, went round to pay a
courtesy call on the only local GP I knew, an Irishman. A large
open hand was thrust into my chest, and from the darkened
doorway came the welcoming words 'Go away – the shop's
shut'. He relented later to the point of asking me in, though not
for a drink (the bottle was empty), and advised me to join the
Merchant Navy immediately. Apparently in his youth he
made one voyage on a cargo-passenger ship and still looked
back on it as the high point of his life. The poor man had built
up a fine practice over the years since the Great War and was

much loved by his patients, but the Health Service destroyed him and few weeks later he left for Ireland without even saying goodbye to anyone.

I continued as a student until May, and then heard of a Casualty job going at Putney Hospital. Each Teaching Hospital had a group of small hospitals somewhere in London staffed by its own men and which provided training appointments almost as good as in its own. Putney was unique in that it was shared between St Mary's and Guy's, with top-line Consultants from each, including Dougie Macleod, Grant Massie (senior surgeon at Guy's), and on the Medical side Dr E.C. Warner the dean of Kings. The jobs there were highly sought after and it was an opportunity not to be missed. Unfortunately it was non-resident and travel to and from Purley by train and two changes of bus took nearly two hours each way. I was on duty twelve hours a day except on Tuesdays and Thursdays when it was only nine to one, and alternate weekends, and was paid £350 a year less tax and with no allowance for fares. My allowance of a pound a week dried up of course and I was much worse off than in the days when I had been a student. However it was an intensely rewarding job, and had I played my cards right and wanted it, would certainly have led to a Consultantship in the Health Service in another fifteen years or so. Before long I found ways and means to stay overnight three or four nights a week in a room in the private ward, and life became a little less hectic. The day's work was never finished by nine, and there were often emergency anaesthetics to do at night so I could justify my presence as a non-paying lodger in the eyes of the hospital, though not in those of Bevan and his henchmen if they had ever found out.

There were many odd things at Putney. At that time there were only four men named Crook on the Medical Register, and three of us were on the surgical side of this tiny hospital. I was always called 'Dr Crook' but my namesake who was a general house surgeon was known as 'Mister' as was Mr Eric Crook second surgeon at Guys. Once when in the great man's ward, I overheard one patient explaining to another 'This is the real Dr Crook, the others are really only senior students.' Just before I got there they had an ex-service registrar whom I had known at St Mary's and who shall be nameless, who was more noted for his knowledge and skill than for his diplomacy and tact. On one occasion when a patient was objecting to having his varicose veins done as an outpatient he declared in a voice which was heard throughout the whole department 'My dear sir, I come from St Mary's Hospital where we do forty of these operations on outpatients every Friday; and in the whole of my experience only one patient has ever bled to death in Praed Street.' Every patient waiting in the outpatient hall got up and went out.

These outpatient Trendelenberg operations are done by students, which is why Mary's men tend to regard the surgery of varicose veins with contempt and as soon as they have risen far enough to have any junior leave it to him. This same registrar one afternoon when he had left one to be done by the house surgeon in main theatre, entered after a good lunch halfway through and, swinging by one arm from the door-jamb, gave a Tarzan yell and exclaimed 'Yippee – blood.' It was unfortunate that the case was being done under local anaesthesia.

I finished my six months at Putney in December, and applied for a Casualty job at St Mary's, the post of House Surgeon to Mr Vernon Pennell at Addenbrookes, and, in case both failed, a Junior Registrarship in Casualty at Doncaster Royal Infirmary. To my horror I was appointed to all three posts, and went to ask the advice of Dougie Macleod as to what I should do. Any job at Mary's was worth having but surprisingly, though I know now very wisely, he told me to go to Addenbrookes as I had already had enough casualty experience, I had never yet been a House Surgeon, and Pennell was one of the last of the great General Surgeons. I was left with the problem that I was committed to the other two, and could not be in three places at the same time. Dougie arranged for me to do only three weeks at St Mary's until another man could be appointed, and my conscience made me offer to spend the only ten days I had available at Doncaster. Ten days net pay did not cover my return fare and I tried very hard to get the income tax people to at least let me cut my losses by deducting expenses, which would still have left me out of pocket on ten very heavy days' work. For the first time I fell foul of the class war and learned what petty-minded English civil servants are really like.

Possibly though this ten days was worth the money (and it

did cost me money I could ill afford) as for the only time in my life it brought me into touch with the toughest element of the working class, the Yorkshire coal miner. I cannot be said to have learned to love them but they did get from me a certain grudging respect. Love of money was translated into love of work, and nothing, not physical pain nor mutilation, was to be allowed to delay them one unnecessary day in getting back to their highly paid jobs. In ten days I performed twenty-four finger amputations (all as outpatients and under local anaesthesia), some of which were inevitable but mostly in cases where, with the patient's co-operation and at the cost of several weeks off work, the finger could have been saved by plastic repair and skin grafting. It a man had been so careless as to crush a finger he wanted it off and to get back to work without a day wasted. Other workers outside the coal mines were, as in London, only too glad to go onto unemployment pay, but curiously gave none of the credit for it to Aneurin Bevan or the NHS. The universal expression was 'I want to go on't Lloyd George'. I found it rather pleasing.

These two unwanted short jobs which my conscience had made me do before starting at Addenbrookes left no time for a pause for breath between them. In each case I finished a day's work, leaped on a train, and got late to bed in the new hospital ready to start again in the morning. Returning to London I did at least get dinner on the train (a further expense as the cost of the one at Doncaster had been deducted from my pay) and got to the room at St Mary's in time for a very few hours sleep. The Mary's job was more fun and I wished very much that I had been able to do a whole six months there. There were three of us on the Casualty unit, all contemporaries, and we worked every morning and two afternoons, evenings and nights out of three. It was all good clean fun, but essentially no different to what we had known as students, except that now it was we who wrote the instructions and the students who carried them out: we who sat in a corner during the minor operating lists and the students who did the operations while we provided the tone and the legal cover. The work was hard and we seldom got four hours sleep in a night, and never worked less than a hundred hours in a week, but then that was how doctors were made and how a majority lived their lives throughout history until the New Elizabethan Age.

One evening when I was on duty alone, something quite incredible struck St Mary's. The entire nursing staff was in a panic and the Matron herself, blinking in the unaccustomed light, appeared in Casualty attended by all the senior sisters and sister tutors. Nothing like this reception would have been laid on for the King or the Pope, or even probably for Our Lord on his second coming. The patient was none other than the president of the court of examiners of the Royal College of Nursing. The great dames present would of course all have wished to give me detailed orders as to exactly how I should conduct myself and exactly whom I should call in, but they dared not speak in the sacred presence, and the patient had to do all the talking for herself.

She held out an arm which the most junior student would have recognized from the other side of the street as showing the textbook 'dinner fork deformity' of a Colles Fracture. She surveyed it with equanimity and said 'I don't think it's broken, it's only a sprain isn't it doctor?' I looked at her with undisguised astonishment. She wasn't joking; she really meant it, and really expected me to agree with her. None of the assembled multitude showed any surprise, but then they may have been in a state of trance. I said to her very quietly and politely:-

'Tell me, if a candidate at one of your examinations looked at that and said it was not broken, would she pass?'

She looked at it again with a proper professional assessment and said with a sigh 'No, I suppose she wouldn't.'

She had many years before been operated on by Dickson Wright for some serious abdominal condition, and like all his patients who survived (and there were quite a number of them) worshipped him and the ground he walked on. In the politest possible way she suggested that I might contact Dickson and ask him to admit her to the Lindo Wing and operate on her himself. I was only too delighted to pass the buck, though I had my doubts as to whether ADW would be as pleased as they expected to come out late on a Saturday night to do a trivial procedure on a patient from whom professional ethics prevented him accepting a fee. In a sense I wronged him, for his response was not only logical and in the patient's best interest, but took the form of a loyalty to and support for a junior member of his own profession that Hypocrates could not have

117

bettered. He asked to speak to the patient and told her 'If you wish I will come and reduce it for you, but I haven't done one for thirty years and this young man is doing five or six every day, so he is much more likely to make a good job of it than I am.' The logic was irrefutable so I sent for the duty anaesthetist and reduced it to everybody's satisfaction.

On another occasion I treated a very minor finger injury for Charles Hellis, the gunsmith in Edgeware Road. A few weeks later I called on him to buy a secondhand pair of guns which he fitted to me and installed in an magnificent brass, leather, and oak double guncase all for £120. The dealer who exported them to St Helena for me thirty-eight years later valued them at six thousand pounds the pair. Unhappily Hellis was one of those ruined by the myxomatosis epidemic and had to sell up his stock and premises (the business itself was unsaleable) and emigrate to Canada where I have lost track of him. The absolutely top line firms like Holland, Purdy, and Boss were able to survive, but rabbits were the unacknowledged backbone of the kind of shooting done by the customers for the sort of good value handmade guns made by the second-line gunsmiths of that day. Eton, Harrow and Winchester would survive any collapse in the demand for Public School education, but Lancing and Repton might not.

I finished my three weeks duty at Mary's late one night and was due to meet Pennell in his theatre at Addenbrookes at eight the following morning. I managed a dinner of sorts in the mess and caught the midnight train to Cambridge. Rather to my surprise Robin Tagart, Pennell's Registrar, was waiting to meet me and for about an hour regaled me with stories of his chiefs ill manners, intolerance, evil temper, and sheer impossibility. I was not seriously worried, and would have been even less so now with more experience. I have always found myself able to get on splendidly with the absolute bastards of this world. It is the Jolly Good Chaps I can't cope with. In the event I found Pennell exactly as described, and loved and respected him for it. I was his only house surgeon in history to come back for a second six months, and remained his intimate friend for a quarter of a century.

Until less than a hundred years ago Surgery, being a trade rather than a profession, was taught by the apprentice system; and a lot of the tradition persists. A man's chiefs, and especially his first chief, have a profound effect on every aspect of his career, and I was amazingly fortunate in having Vernon Pennell as mine. He was a little round bald-headed man of sixty who really saw himself as a university don (he was Senior Fellow of Pembroke), a rowing man, and a bon viveur, who lived, when not in college where his rooms were among the most ancient in the city, in an old rambling house in the Huntington Road. His wife had left him as happens with so many great surgeons. A surgeon who is any good has to be a perfectionist, and perfectionists are by their very nature quite impossible people to live with. Wives don't like this. His housekeeper acted as hostess whenever he had guests to dinner at home or in his rooms, and he married her when they were both in their seventies as soon as his wife died. Her name was Margaret Nesbit. She found Vernon an interesting change after Rupert Brooke.

Vernon was an outstanding perfectionist even for a surgeon, and rightly could not tolerate his good work being spoiled in any way by the imperfections of his juniors or nursing staff. This made him cross: and as our work was always at least slightly less than perfect, he was always at least slightly cross. When anything was very wrong he was very cross. There was one thing about him though which Robin Tagart told me on that first evening which I firmly believe to have been true, though fortunately I never had to put it to the test. He said 'Pennell may say very unkind things to you about yourself and the way you do your work, but remember that if you are ever in trouble and have done your best, he will stand up for you against the whole world.' I regard this as the finest thing that can be said of any chief and resolved that it should always be said of me.

There were other charming points in his character and the way he looked after his houseman. In the past a house-surgeon was paid an honorarium of forty-five pounds for his six months' work. Under the NHS he was paid £175 less tax on £225 (because he now had to pay for his filthy food and for living in squalor on twenty-four-hour call) which for most of us amounted to about twice as much net. For a few with private incomes it came to much less. Pennell could not resist making at least one remark every day about the huge salaries young doctors were getting, so different from when he was young.

Almost every other house officer in the land was in fact worse off as he had lost the right to numerous perks, particularly to a share of his chief's fee when he assisted in the care of a private patient. This Pennell refused to recognize, paying me these fees just as he would have done in the past; and when I thanked him, as I always did knowing that I was probably the very last houseman in the land to be so privileged, he would say, 'You don't have to thank me, its your right.'

His previous house surgeon had relieved his feelings on departure by writing a story about him in the *Lancet*. He did not mention Pennell by name but everyone knew who it must be. A few weeks earlier he had got irritated with a perfectly harmless old man, who like him suffered from an enlarged prostate. Among the usual routine questions, Pennell asked how long it took him to empty his bladder and the poor man did not know.

'You must know. How long does it take you to empty your bladder?'

'I'm very sorry Mr Pennell, but I just don't know.'

'Nonsense. Every man knows how long it takes him to empty his bladder.'

'Well if it comes to that, how long does it take you?'

'Two minutes, dead.'

On one terrible occasion I was assisting him on a case when things were just not going well. He made five or six attempts to pick up a small bleeding point deep in the wound, getting more and more irritated with each failure. The theatre was hot and I was tired and shifting from one foot to the other to stay awake. By sheer ill-luck, just as Pennell finally caught the thing, my foot touched the 'down' pedal and the table went down a foot so he lost it again. His breath stopped; he turned purple and for a moment was quite incapable of speech. In that moment I managed to say 'I am terribly sorry sir, I can't think how it happened.' He swallowed three or four times and then grunted 'It's perfectly obvious how it happened. You put your foot on the pedal.' There the matter rested.

This of course is the secret of dealing with people like that, including myself when I grew up to be like Pennell. Never argue. When he is wrong just keep quiet. When you are wrong apologize profusely before he has a chance to go off. It always works. On one occasion he became outrageously abusive while he was assisting me to do a rather difficult appendix he had trusted me with. He went so far as to say 'You'll never make a surgeon. You'll never pass the Fellowship in a thousand years.' I kept quiet and he spent the rest of the case brooding on what he had said. Once the last stitch was in he started pouring out absurd compliments like a court jester. 'You have done him proud. I hope you are on the staff here when I need an operation etc., etc.' He finished up by asking me to dinner that night in his rooms to a small party consisting of Masters of his own and other colleges, to their obvious astonishment. He was a good host but always picked and matched his guests with great care. This was definitely not one to which he had planned to invite me. He was not to know that it was my twenty-fourth birthday.

Such cases were not common. He was too conscientious to be happy trusting the house surgeon with the knife. If the patient was his, his was the entire responsibility. I have had the same trouble myself and have never learned to delegate. I must be about the only surgeon of consultant rank in the world who has personally done a morning and night round seven days a week throughout his life. It is not good for the houseman. Even so Pennell did not do it and the time I spent working for him was the most valuable training I have ever had.

Ethical problems are with a surgeon constantly, or should be. Vernon Pennell once said to me that it is much more important to be operated on by a gentleman than by a good technician. Faced with a decision in the middle of an operation, the latter will only be concerned with whether a curative procedure is technically possible. A gentleman will however put himself in the place of the patient and ask 'If I was this patient and know what I do, what would I want to be done?' which frequently results in a quite different decision. It is remarkable how few surgeons will themselves agree to a total gastrectomy, although they readily inflict it on their patients. It is of course much more difficult to do this when the patient is of a different culture and lives with a set of values quite foreign to the surgeon himself. Operating on an English woman known to have three children, one would not hesitate to improve her chances of survival by a procedure which rendered her sterile, but in a Muslim woman one would be submitting her to a fate which she might well consider worse than death. Her children

121

will be well cared for in any case, but if one sterilizes her she will be relegated to the place of second, third or fourth wife and treated worse than a slave. There are many such situations where a proper decision can only be made after a close study of the patient's environment and way of life.

My most agonizing ethical dilemma has resulted from a rare disease called Thalassaemia, and I am still very doubtful that the course I have been following over these cases is morally justified: but having once committed myself I have been unable to change my policy and refuse treatment. Thalassaemia ('Watery blood') is a familial condition in which a child is born with abnormal haemoglobin (haemoglobin F). There were two large family groups in Sabah, in one of which all the children were sufferers and in the other rather more than half. The child is born apparently normal and remains so until the age of about five, though the family themselves recognize that he is doomed rather earlier due to the ever deepening purple colour of the skin. He then begins to suffer from anaemia which responds well at first to iron therapy and later to blood transfusion. These transfusions though have to be repeated at ever shorter intervals starting at about every six months but near the end a pint of blood is needed every week or less. At the same time the spleen gets bigger and bigger until from weighing a few ounces as it should do at that age, it is about a third the weight and bulk of the whole child.

I knew nothing of the condition; but when the first case was referred to me reasoned, rightly, that removing the spleen would not only make the child more comfortable but stop the transfused blood being rapidly destroyed, as the spleen is normally the only organ which destroys red cells: although if it is removed the liver and bone marrow will take over the function in time. The result was an immense success, and I did not realize that I was committing myself to a hideous situation over the next dozen years and more.

Both these families are devoutly Roman Catholic, and produced babies like rabbits. As soon as the condition was recognized it would be explained to the child, who was brought up in the full knowledge that he was never going to grow up to adulthood, that in time he was going to have to start going into hospital for regular blood transfusions like his brothers and sisters, becoming more and more ill, and that when he was almost at death's door Mr Crook would take his spleen out and give him almost exactly two years of healthy life again, after which he would suddenly go downhill and die. They were the happiest and most friendly children I have ever known, always with a Rosary beside the bed or between the fingers. I have never known one to cry and seldom saw one not smiling, even with a transfusion being put up or lying on the operating table waiting for the pentothal to be run into the drip. Before I left I had splenectomized more than twenty of them. There was no way out. I could never refuse to do what had come to be expected of me. The parents were perfectly happy that they were producing a constant succession of immortal souls destined for certain salvation. The children were happy with the exactly circumscribed lives they were leading before going on to heaven. The only person who was bloody miserable over it was me.

When my time was up, Pennell begged me to stay for another six months, a thing he had never done with any other HS several of whom had been thrown out within six days. I wanted though to do the Primary Fellowship course at the Royal College of Surgeons but came back to him for a further six months in 1953. These three jobs at Addenbrookes and Putney were the only complete training posts I held. The rest of the time until I got my higher qualification and went abroad was spent in study, and what were supposed to be short term locum appointments at Registrar level at Putney, St Mary's, and Hillingdon Hospital, though some of them lasted much longer than planned. I also spent one term as an anatomy demonstrator at St Mary's, teaching students and prosecting a body for teaching purposes. I spent so long on this corpse that I became quite fond of him and wished I had known him sooner. He was probably a nice chap.

During the Primary course I used to wander round London attending lectures here and there, and one afternoon just as it ended, quite by chance walked into the Medical School and saw a notice asking for a locum for a few days in the Shell London Office. The pay offered was princely (five guineas a day plus lunch in the senior mess) so I rang up and offered my services. Little did I know that the whole direction of my life was being changed. It is not profitable to speculate what might have happened on such occasions if things had turned out differently, as I am quite sure these things are not due to chance. Had I not gone into St Mary's, had a friend accosted me and taken me across the road for a drink or even distracted my attention for a moment so that I did not see the notice, I should have remained on the course that was leading me to a minor consultantship in the Health Service, and almost certainly death before I was fifty from chronic bronchitis, though by then I should probably have had a wife and four children. These things cannot possibly be due to chance. God does not make each one of us different from anybody else, tailored for one particular place in his plan for the world (as I am sure he does) and then leave it to chance whether we see a notice or not.

I knew nothing of Shell or the Shell Empire which employs more people than the total population of Switzerland, and if asked would have said that it was a company running a lot of little garages who sold petrol. I was surprised to hear over the telephone that they had nothing much to do with Shell-Mex house on the embankment, and that the medical department was on the seventh floor of St Helens Court, a mews off Bishopsgate built around the ancient St Helens Church. I presented myself there the next morning to find that I was working as one of five medical officers (I cannot remember who was off sick or on leave at that time to make a place for me) whose duties consisted of supervising the organization of a vast world-wide medical department of thirty-five doctors and many hundreds of nurses, physiotherapists, pharmacists, x-ray and laboratory technicians, and other ancillary staff. Our principle everyday duties however, and the only one with which I was trusted for a long time, were the medical examination of all Shell staff and their families on their way to or from overseas areas, and all those applying for work in the huge organization of offices and installations in Britain. The Shell pension scheme, and the provision for staff who died or became disabled as well as for their dependants, was the finest and most generous in the world, and for this reason the checking for medical fitness on entry as well as supervision throughout their dependence on Shell was meticulous. It was the result of my stupidity and became my misfortune, that I deduced that such concern for the welfare of staff when they became sick would imply an equal concern for them when they became redundant.

Four of these doctors were permanently attached to the London office. They are all dead now. The departmental head was Rupert Scott, a charming country GP who had the good fortune to have treated the Chairman and been a member of his lodge in the immediate post-war days when it was decided to set up a co-ordinated medical service for the group. His number two, Dennis Cousins, was an Irishman, one of the very few Roman Catholics among the senior staff (for the same reason that Leslie Bill was the only one at St Mary's) and one of the instigators of the movement to co-ordinate medicine and sport. He was thus an intimate friend of Sir Arthur Porritt, and as all four of them were Mary's men, the whole Shell Medical Department tended to become a preserve of the one Medical School; hence the notice which had brought me in.

Dennis wrote, or rather drafted, a large number of papers on sport, in the most astonishing disjointed prep school English and then passed them to me to be 'Ghost written' for him to present to the society as I had, to use his own words, 'The gift of the Blarney'. I was very happy to do so, although it often took me several evenings a month which should have been devoted to my studies, and I am quite sure he would never have denied my authorship if asked. A few years after he died however I noticed in a bookstall (in Columbo of all places) a book devoted to the subject: and picking it up saw to my astonishment that I had written it. There was no acknowledgement and no mention of my name at all. Several of the chapters purported to be written by other very senior members of the profession and of the association, so it would appear that unknown to myself I had been ghost writing for them too.

The remaining two permanent staff were Lindsey Webster, an elderly surgeon from Borneo, and John Laurie, the youngest. Lindsey was the oldest serving Shell Medical Officer and had worked in Sarawak as their only Surgeon for twenty-five years before the Japanese arrived. Miri was described as the best hospital in South East Asia, and I was a little surprised when I got there to find it a series of open wooden huts connected by covered ways. I know now that this description was true in respect of the work done and its reputation depended entirely on the twenty-five years of dedicated service by Lindsey Webster. He was operating the morning that the Japs arrived, and had the good fortune to be called between cases (while the next was being anaesthetized) to go to the ward to see an emergency. He arrived there to find all the patients and ward staff murdered, and on returning to the theatre found everyone there bayonetted to death including the patient on the table. Hirohito's Sons of Heaven had moved on, and somehow he survived, to spend the rest of the war in Changi gaol.

He was not well treated by the Japs, and on his release was immediately posted to a trouble spot in South America without his family, unable to speak a word of the language, and under the orders of men who were unashamedly pro-Nazi and did not even recognize him as a qualified doctor. On his return to London he worked in an isolated office by himself and it was only some weeks later he discovered that the Medical Department was being run by Rupert Scott. In due course he moved to St Helens Court as a junior Medical officer under Scott, and remained there doing routine medical examinations on healthy staff and recruits until he reached retiring age. I last ran into him shortly after in a pub at Hampton Court a few weeks before his premature death which was certainly brought about by his privations during the war. He was a little bitter that he had not been allowed a visit to Miri before being paid off, as was common practice in such cases, and that when he proposed to go at his own expense to the place where he is still spoken of today as though he were a god, he was advised that this would be regarded as very improper in a Shell pensioner when the Company had not seen fit to send him. He repeatedly warned me against attaching myself to the company.

Shell always believed in buying the best, at least where the Medical Department was concerned, so there was one other memorable character among us who was not in fact Shell staff. Efficient routine medical examination even then demanded chest x-rays. Today almost any doctor can read a chest x-ray with reasonable reliability, but it was not always so: and when chest radiography began to become routine towards the end of the war, especially mass miniature radiography, it was said that there were fewer than six men in the country who could

126

read a film with sufficient reliability to make it worthwhile. Shell was not interested in saving a few shillings per case by using miniature films, but they were prepared to pay for the very best opinion on their full-size films as well on x-rays of all sorts sent from overseas for advice. The best meant Peter Kerley; who came in twice a week to read our films from all over the world.

Peter's opinion was universally acknowledged as the best in the world. He was the only man who had the certain knowledge and the courage to say that his King had cancer and had to have his lung removed. Incredibly he too was a chain smoker and died ultimately of lung cancer. He was a completely outgoing sporting type who travelled almost weekly up to Scotland for salmon fishing or deer stalking, but unhappily not a Christian. Only once have I seen him discomposed, but on that day he was a very badly shaken man. He arrived one afternoon with two x-rays taken by himself, and a pathology report signed by the Senior Pathologist of the Westminster Hospital.

These x-rays were of the pelvis of a young woman. She was no ordinary young woman. She was a young woman so rich that she could afford to have her x-rays taken not by a technician in hospital but by Peter Kerley himself in the immensely expensively equipped set of rooms he kept for his private patients in Harley Street. But money gives no protection from cancer, and the first of these films, labelled and dated by PK only three months before, showed her right pelvis completely destroyed by what could only be one of the most deadly forms of this disease. With it was a pathology report from one of England's foremost pathologists on a biopsy of the tumour. Bone tumours are always pretty deadly, and this was the worst of them. The patient was a devout Roman Catholic, and her doctors very properly told her that nothing could be done for her, that she was going to die in a very few weeks, and that she would do well to make her preparations.

She didn't. Instead she went to Lourdes. The second x-ray was taken by PK that day, and that is what had made him shake. A student could have said that it was without any possible doubt of the same patient. There are ways of telling with absolute certainty. The deadly tumour was gone; and in it's place was a normal healthy pelvis. Now a lobster can grow

127

a new leg when an old one is lost but this patient wasn't a lobster; she was a young woman who had faith in God.

On this first occasion I only worked for a few days, but over the next few years I was there at intervals for periods as long as three or four weeks. The pay was very welcome while I was studying and the hours did not interfere with much of what I wanted to do. Otherwise until I joined the Shell staff in May 1957 I was doing a series of surgical locums as house officer or registrar, making little money but getting a vast range of experience, at a number of hospitals including Addenbrookes, Putney, St Mary's, and Hillingdon the hospital serving London airport and the cinema studios. Not many doctors have had to examine dozens of men dressed as Roman Legionaires and Centurions writhing about on the hospital lawn with food poisoning.

Considering the amount of study and practical work I had to get through in six years between qualifying as a doctor and becoming an FRCS, it is incredible I found any time for sport at all. I gave up regular shooting at Bisley, but took part in the July meeting every year until I went overseas and about two years out of three thereafter until the mid-seventies.

Serious service rifle shooting was of course impossible without regular practice, but in the last few years before I qualified I became very keen on Match Rifle. This is a very specialized sport indulged in by only about seventy or eighty people, all either very young or very old. It involves shooting at ranges from 900 to 1,200 yards with special rifles which are permitted to have telescopic sights and with precision ammunition. The rules still say that the cartridge must be suitable for military purposes, but little attempt has ever been made to enforce such a rule over the rifles, all of which are custom built, and no two of which are alike.

A small number of competitors use traditional looking rifles with reasonably conventional telescopes mounted on them. The classic match rifle however (which is much cheaper to make and more fun to use) looks like nothing else on this earth, and is fired lying on one's back with the barrel between the legs. The standard long heavy barrel (which everybody has to use) is mounted on any solid action which is strong enough to withstand the very high breach pressure of the match rifle cartridge. No modern service action will do, and most of those used have not seen service since the Boer War, or even the Crimea. The sights are telescopic but there is no telescope, the convex front element being mounted at the muzzle where a conventional foresight would be, and the concave rear element on a long folding bracket coming up from the heel of the butt. One thus gets a sight radius of nearly four feet, perhaps twice that of the service rifle. Firing in the back position gives steadiness equal to that of a machine rest, there is a spirit level under the foresight to avoid cant, vernier adjustment of the sights, and a cartridge which will hold better than a minute of elevation. Even at 1,200 yards the bull is equal to two minutes of angle, so that with holding and sighting errors eliminated were there no wind any competent shot could put every one in.

There always is wind however, sometimes changing from shot to shot from fifteen to twenty-five minutes. With only four minutes separating a dead-centre bull from a miss, this frequently means that the rifle is pointing at the next target but one. Everything depends on wind judging which is only learned over a period of many years. The attraction of this sport to me was that an experienced man who has not fired a shot perhaps for a year or two can always outshoot the youngsters who have been practising every week since Christmas. There always are plenty of youngsters. This is a university sport and the match between Oxford and Cambridge is one of the chief events of the meeting. These university men (and today even young women) make up a third of all the match rifle fraternity in any one year. Very few stay on after they leave university, possibly because they cannot afford their own rifles, but those who do or come back make up the other group whose average age is probably nearer seventy than sixty.

For some reason the Cottesle match is the most sought after of the individual Match Rifle events. It ought to be fairly easy to win as it consists only of a single shoot of twenty rounds (plus sighters) at 1,100 yards, which I have always found to be an easy range, and as far as I know nobody has ever achieved a possible. In 1953 I tied for first place with a ninety-seven but went down badly in the tie shoot. The very elderly late Lord Cottesloe was present on the firing point to congratulate the winner of his trophy, and as I finished considerably earlier than the others, we both thought I had won it outright. I therefore for the first time swam above his mental horizon and he noticed

129

me.

He said 'Of course conditions are very easy tonight.'

Much as we all revered the old man I wasn't going to stand for that when I thought I had won and replied 'Well not so very easy. The sun is setting right at the end of the butt.'

'OH yes; but you remember at Wimbledon it used to set in the very middle of the butt.'

Now the NRA has not shot at Wimbledon since 1889. I looked at him and realized that he was speaking in absolute seriousness and regarding me as a contemporary.

'I am afraid Wimbledon was a little before my time, My Lord.' I managed to say without smiling.

He looked at me sadly and said 'Yes I suppose it was.'

I have never wanted to shoot with any other sort of match rifle but the classic back-rest type. Those who use more conventional weapons with simple snipers or sporting-type telescopic sights, we call 'Belly gunners'. What they say of the position we use cannot be quoted in a book for publication in a Christian country.

Shooting for me always meant rifle shooting (with an occasional few minutes relaxation on the revolver range) until after I qualified, when I suddenly felt the urge to try the shotgun. I bought a very nice pair from Hellis and went down to the Arundell Arms Hotel at Lifton in Devon. There has been an inn on that site at least since the nineth century and it has now become probably the most comfortable sporting hotel in England. In those days it was run by a retired Army Officer named Major Morris who owned the local canned milk factory and ran the hotel largely as a hobby and for the entertainment of his Army friends. It had, as it has now, many miles of fine trout and salmon fishing on the Tamar and its tributaries, but also had about a dozen shooting beats where one could get rabbits, pheasant, partridge, and especially snipe. the hotel was not advertised then or for twenty and more years afterwards, and until then one only heard of it by word of mouth. Nine out of ten of the guests were army men and their wives, and like Bisley it was one of the few places where it was normal for men to be known by their military rank. An outstanding feature has always been the food, and even in 1950 the chef was earning twenty guineas a week.

A month or so before I first went there, somebody had

suggested to the Major that there were in fact gentleman to be found in other professions and for three weeks only an advertisement appeared in the *British Medical Journal*. For the next quarter century the hotel was the preserve of army men and doctors, and they probably still make up the majority of the clientele. It has become, next to Cambridge, my spiritual home in England, and the place which I use as my base whenever I visit the country. It has also played a major part in my carrying out my duties to my godchildren. For many years the hotel has had as professional fishing coach Roy Buckingham, a former national casting champion. Each boy for whom I have accepted the duty of Godfather has been brought up in the faith and brought before the Bishop in due course. I have always considered it my duty also to teach them or have them taught to fear God, Honour the Queen, and cast a dry fly for trout. Roy has been a invaluable help.

I passed the Primary Fellowship in due course, more by skilled examination technique than by knowledge of anatomy. Everything depends on the vivas, and in particular on the anatomy viva. In undergraduate exams, provided one does not make a mistake which would kill a patient, the examiners are out to discover how much the candidate knows with a view to passing him. In each part of the Fellowship however, they have to fail at least eighty-three per cent of the candidates, all of whom know enough to pass, and they are out to find as quickly as possible any small gap in a man's knowledge which will justify failing him. The secret of success is to try to steer the conversation onto something one really knows well and then keep talking until the bell rings. One is always warned never to use an eponymous name for a structure unless one knows all about the man whose name it bears. This can however be turned to one's advantage. The examiner gave me an occipital bone with an unfused rear portion said to be common in Inca skulls and which is known as the '*Os Incae*'. He was obviously hoping I would say this so that he could floor me with his knowledge of American pre-history. I had accidentally discovered that it was first described by Goethe, an amateur naturalist of some distinction, so I called it the '*Os Goetheri*'. I had not really expected it to work, but he may have been tired and off his guard for a moment. Anyway he rose almost with an audible plop like a trout taking a mayfly, asked 'Who was

131

Goethe?' and I was away. I had worked my way through Goethe's Faust to Marlow's Dr Faustus, the superiority of Marlow's work to any other Elizabethan drama with the possible exceptions of Romeo and Juliet and Hamlet, and was already deeply into Philip Massinger before he was able to call the meeting to order. I passed.

☆   ☆   ☆

Bachelors like many other pathological entities come in two sorts, the true and the false. The true bachelor has deliberately adopted the state as a way of life that suits him. The false knows very well that it doesn't, and spends the greater part of his life in hope though gradually diminishing anticipation. Bachelor surgeons are almost all of the latter kind, and curiously they are bachelors because they are surgeons and surgeons because they are bachelors. Many a young man with good prospects has married young and found he cannot afford to continue his long and arduous training it he is to support and do his duty by his wife and family, but there is another factor. As I have said before, every good surgeon is a perfectionist and he will not consider as a wife anyone who does not strike him as perfect. Few young women are. There was a story I heard many years ago of a very old man who was asked why he had never married. He explained 'Life is very like walking through a wood looking for a walking stick. Every time you find one you think that if you go on a little further you will find a better, and before you know it you have walked right through the wood.'

I had never considered for a moment remaining a bachelor, and I started looking for a wife in my twenties while still a house surgeon at Addenbrookes. Indeed it is only in the last five years that I have recognized that the situation is hopeless, and that I am now in a third category, The Resigned. Four times, after long consideration and planning have I asked a girl to marry me, and in each case only after a reasonable time to think it out has she said no. I am still astonished that each one turned out, long after I had made up my mind, to be from Cheltenham Ladies College. I don't know why this should be. I cannot in retrospect see that they had anything in common except that I liked them and they did not like me and, leading the sort of life I have done, only a tiny proportion of the girls I

132

have met can have come from that school. There must be some hidden characteristic that made me pounce whenever I saw one. Obviously too there is some far from hidden feature in my character which makes Cheltenham girls shy away.

Perhaps unknown to myself I was not really looking for a wife but for a suitable mother for my children. I have managed to survive without the consolation and companionship of matrimony, but I should never have done so had it not been for the numerous children for whom I have so often been able to play at being father. In some ways this has given me the best of both worlds. I am amazed at the readiness with which people have lent me their offspring to take on long holidays all over the world, and at times have actually thrust them upon me when I was known to be so willing to take them off their hands for a few months. I have three pairs whom I call my godchildren, though in two cases only one brother is genuinely so and the other calls me 'Godfather' but is only an honorary godson. There is also a solitary goddaughter by whom I certainly have not done my duty as it is just not feasible for a bachelor to disappear into the blue with someone else's little girl. But however much fun this has been in the past it is little consolation when faced with a bleak and unloved old age. I certainly could not have qualified as a surgeon had I married in 1953 (and surgery has been everything in my life) but if I had my time again and had to choose between a wife and the Fellowship, I should be a fool not to choose the wife.

I developed a splendid technique for proposing marriage. The vitally important thing is that the girl shall hear you out and not walk out on you before you have properly stated your case. One place where you can be sure of this is when you are driving at seventy miles per hour on the motorway. I discovered this even in the days before motorways, and used the long straight road across Salisbury Plain where one could get up to eighty for about twenty minutes before getting to Stonehenge, a delightfully romantic setting for further cold-blooded discussion of the details. Only once has this method misfired and the consequences then have in fact turned out splendidly. I was always entirely honest in what I was proposing and put all my goods, good and bad, clearly in the window. This was the last time, and I had to tell her as a possible adverse factor that I already had six godchildren whose

133

parents I had promised that if they were orphaned I would adopt them and bring them up as my own. She had to accept therefore that there was always the remote possibility of sudden unexpected additions to the family. I had been stalking the unfortunate girl for four years since she was eighteen, and I thought this revelation made a favourable impression on her. It did: but not in the way I intended. She had got tired of waiting for me to come to the point and when I finally did she realized she did not want me and at once married another surgeon. Four years later I got a letter asking me to stand godfather to her offspring 'As it will be such a comfort to me and Brian to know that if anything happens to us you will look after him.' There was another brother already which made eight. The girl's name was Valerie.

I have always considered my own family resembled nothing so much as the cast of a mid-Victorian melodrama (people say much the same of me), but Valerie's father outshone them all. He was a High Court Judge and four years before when I called to take her out for only the second time he invited me into his study, placed an open outstretched hand flat on his desk and asked me sternly 'Young man, what exactly are your prospects?' Valerie was furious when I told her many years later, but I loved him for it.

I see that I have said nothing about food and drink, which have played a significant part in my life; and neither have I on the subject of smoking. Smoking is a vice as of course are gluttony and drunkenness but unlike these it cannot be said to be merely a vicious overindulgence in something that is otherwise harmless and acceptable. We smoke, if we do so at all, simply to give ourselves pleasure. I have obtained great pleasure in pipe and cigar smoking in my time, thought I think I can say that I have never got any real enjoyment from cigarettes, and I have some doubts that anyone ever does. Most boys start smoking cigarettes simply because it is the thing to do, and possibly because they think it makes them look manly. To do it for this reason is of course a confession of a sense of inferiority and awareness of a lack of any true manliness; as a boy who is advancing at even a normal rate for his age has no need to do so.

I at least had a little excuse for starting to smoke. I was two years too young to be employed in the Civil Defence, and I reasoned, very possibly rightly, that if I smoked vast numbers of cigarettes while on duty it might give the impression that I was older. I never enjoyed it, but curiously enough it never made me sick; and the habit (and it is only a habit – not an addiction) remained with me for a dozen years. With an income which in real terms has never been generous, I could not afford to smoke more than a very occasional one in England; but overseas there were no such problems. On two occasions in my early years of overseas service I have stepped ashore at Liverpool on a regular 120 a day and, after finishing the tin, given it up completely for the duration of my four months' leave. This alone gives the lie direct to the story that it is an addiction drug which produces withdrawal symptoms and that only the most courageous can give up. Hashish is an addiction drug and I am in complete sympathy with hanging those engaged in the trade; but tobacco is not.

Pipe smoking though is enjoyable, and I think in most people an excusable self indulgence, provided it is confined to consenting adults in private. There is no excuse for blowing smoke over anyone else or smelling out a public room or someone else's house. There certainly is a slight risk to one's health and even to one's life, but is there anything which gives pleasure which does not carry some risk? There is always at least a chance of getting a salmon fly in the eye, a golf ball in the neck, or a writ for maintenance on the breakfast table. For some people however the risk may become unacceptable and therefore morally unjustifiable; since our lives are not our own, and St Peter may not accept the same definition of suicide as a charitable coroner. In the middle seventies I began to get pre-cancerous changes in my mouth, so advanced that I had to undergo several biopsies to be sure that they were only pre-cancerous. With regret but no difficulty, I gave it up. I still have an occasional Havana cigar: also more than an occasional pinch of snuff. Nobody has yet produced any evidence of danger from snuff taking (as they certainly will), probably because it is comparatively rare. Also the changes in my mouth were very obvious, while nobody can see what is going on in my nose.

Alcohol is another matter. Fermentation is a natural process and God gave us wine 'To make glad the heart of Man'. I am not prepared to listen to Christian teetotallers who say that St

Luke of all people thought '*Oenos*' meant unfermented grape juice. Our Lord drank wine (and incidentally made it the basis of the most Holy rite of his Church). Those who say wine drinking is wrong are claiming a moral superiority over their God. They will probably be eaten by worms like King Herod, and a good thing too.

My mother's family were 'Temperance Workers' and her mother President of the Southport Womens Temperance Association for twenty years. Probably up to the great war alcoholism was a serious problem among what were called 'the lower orders' and efforts to discourage the drinking of spirits (which were often crude and poisonous) and beer (which in those days was alcoholic) were laudable; but even then this had nothing to do with the drinking of wine. In spite of the high incidence in France today of cirrhosis and alcoholism, this is due to brandy, and I very much doubt that even in the days of the four bottle men anyone has ever come to harm from drinking unfortified wines. They would have done better in any case to have chosen another name for their organization. Total abstinence is as intemperate as drunkenness.

Not all abstainers were as bigoted as my family. Even my mother's father, accepting that by preaching only total abstinence they were fighting a losing battle, became a founder shareholder in Trust Houses Ltd. This admirable institution was not intended to make a profit (although of course none of its shareholders, especially Grandpa, were averse to doing so) but was founded for the express purpose of providing restaurants and hotels which would give good value for money and serve good wines without there being any financial inducement for the staff to encourage people to drink. Wine was to be sold at cost, with only the minimum of markup for the labour involved in serving. Most of my life they have clearly been adhering to the Trust and remained loyal to those who provided their capital at uneconomic rates for the furtherance of what they saw as good Christian principles. The company appears now to have passed out of Christian control and I have had a few unpleasant surprises in recent years. Not only have I encountered what appear to be full-time wine waiters who are only too anxious to urge on me something more expensive than the excellent house wine, but I have been charged at least three times the wholesale price of such wines and the wine waiter has been very ready to accept a gratuity for his services. I trust these are only isolated incidents.

As a consequence of this family obsession I had not tasted a drop of alcoholic liquor until I was fourteen. (I know this is not grossly abnormal. Bernard Shaw once said he had not smoked until he was twenty, not drunk alcohol until he was thirty, and had no sexual experience until he was twelve.) I was however somewhat incensed when a doctor said I was to have a glass of red wine every day and a small glass of brandy at bedtime, to hear my mother protest that I was very much opposed to it. I had in fact no views on the subject whatever. I had though the good sense to protest at every glass how horrible it tasted, and that I could only sip it if I was not going to be sick; and to remark each morning how much better and stronger I was feeling. As anticipated my mother decided that any medicine so unpleasant must be very good for me, and the dose was doubled. It was many months before she began to have her suspicions, and decided that I did not need to be as well and strong as all that. Even so, it was only after Nanor died in 1947 that I admitted at home that I was really very fond of wine with my dinner.

As a student with practically no money, my gastronomic indulgences were confined to an occasional lunch at the ABC near Edgeware Road station where one could get an individual steak and kidney pudding for ninepence. The rest of the meal cost no more than in the students' canteen so I used to be able to afford it about once a week. I was then getting an allowance of a pound a week to include my bus fares and everything else as well, including ammunition for .22 shooting. Of course as always Mummy helped me out from time to time with a gift of ten shillings or a pound. It was only when I qualified that I was able to go out for an occasional luxurious dinner costing never more than thirty shillings, and usually little more than that for two. When in London, Michael Porter was my usual companion on those occasions as we had almost identical tastes and an equal degree of poverty. Last year he gave me dinner at a roadhouse outside Birmingham which was no better than those we used to have at the Corner Houses and with a wine not so good. I think his bill was forty-five pounds for the two.

These dinners at Lyons were quite astonishing. There were then Corner Houses at Marble Arch, Coventry Street, and

Charing Cross, as well as one at Tottenham Court Road which I doubt I have ever been in. The wine list was superb and included a Chablis and a vintage Chateau Talbert each at 6/6d. a bottle. Few of the table wines cost more and if one had enough people to drink it (and we never had) there was incredibly a 1904 Cockburn at thirty shillings. It is still drinkable (indeed I think at its best) but the last I was offered was priced at a hundred and fifty pounds. Half bottles were available at half price and we usually shared a bottle of claret and a half of Chablis with the fish. We seldom 'went dutch' but alternated as to who played host, the other taking the wine bill which was under ten shillings as against about a pound for the food.

The food though had to be seen to be believed. The Corner Houses were ridiculed by *Punch* as providing for the lower middle classes the sort of food they wanted, in a pseudo-opulant setting that they would consider the height of luxury. The ridicule was grossly unfair because that was just what they were setting out to do and they did it superbly well. To add to the effect there were always in addition to such things as fish and chips and chicken in white sauce, a few really excellent dishes at what must have been well under cost. In September and October the Marble Arch branch would always offer oysters, correctly served at five for 1/9d., and roast grouse, with everything that went with it for four shillings. The peculiar choice in the number of oysters may have been a pathetic attempt to conceal the difference in price from their Cumberland Hotel next door; and the grouse, which was always perfect, was probably what had been rejected by the Cumberland as too ripe for their own clientele, which were still very much Lyons' customers. One great joy in eating food like this at completely uneconomic prices was that one was entirely surrounded by people eating fish and chips at 3/6d., and in knowing that they were paying for your dinner.

We always went for a banquet and had one. I have always believed that a meal should have a proper structure (which is why I love sea travel and detest the present British Airways first class) and if Michael did not quite agree with me, he always fell in with my ways. We would have seven courses: Hors d'oeuvres, Soup, Fish, an Entre, Meat, Pudding and Savory. Soup never cost much more than a shilling, Herring with Mustard

138

Sauce was 9d., and there was always a choice of two or three savouries. Pudding would usually be a Rum Pancake but at all these establishments there was from Christmas to Easter a superb rich Christmas Pudding served with a real vanilla ice cream. I had not then acquired my obsession with Stilton, but I can well believe it was available. As I have said the bill was never over thirty shillings for the two of us and it provided a whole evening's entertainment. In later years when we had more money we occasionally went to a rather more expensive restaurant called 'Chez August' at 7 Carnaby Street. It has long since gone to make room for the psychedelic splendours of the new Elizabethan age, but at that time for a few pounds one could get the best Provencal cooking I have ever tasted. We used to be the first in when it opened for the evening, and the last out. Douglas Macleod once told me that between the wars one could entertain a girl at the 1/9d. table d'hote with wine at Pinnoli's going on to a couple of stalls at Covent Garden and still show change out of a pound. He was probably speaking of a gold sovereign, but even so it would not be easy to do the equivalent today for the sixty pounds or so that a sovereign is worth. What fascinated me was why he ever bothered to do so and remembered what it cost. The Savoy would surely have been more convenient.

Once at Addenbrookes I was of course exposed to the gastronomic delights of all that is most cultured in English life. From the beginning I used to get occasional invitations to the High Table at Christ's (where David Coombe was already a Fellow) and at Pembrook (on the invitation of Vernon Pennell). These were however few and far between and I made a point of going out at least once a fortnight for a really good dinner by myself. This was not difficult as there are a number of very good and inexpensive restaurants in Cambridge including the Blue Boar (which used to serve the finest Jugged Hare I know and has recently substituted a Jugged Venison which while not a classic dish is every bit as good), the Bath Hotel, and at that time the Garden House Hotel. I once spent a very pleasant study leave there, but it has since been the site of undergraduate rioting, when a friend of mine had his table overturned and his wine thrown over him and shortly after it was burned to the ground. There is now an 'International' type hotel on the same site, said to be owned by a group of Arabs.

Best of all however was Miller's Restaurant which was owned by Finlaters and not run for profit but to enable undergraduates to acquire a taste for good food and wine at prices they could afford. It provided a four course table d'hote menu every night at which classic dishes and Game featured regularly. If one had a guest, a special dinner could be ordered the same morning and the price would be the same as if it had been the menu of the day. The wine list was superb. In the fifties I was drinking the 1933 and 1934 Chateau Calon Segur at nineteen shillings a bottle, and when supplies began to run short they made me a private bin 'Special reserve Mr Crook' which lasted me until 1963. The last bottles were drunk when I was driving my father to Southport after selling Manor Side in September of that year. He had seldom had a dinner so good and the icing on the cake was provided when the wine waiter asked 'Your own wine sir?'

I have never been a rich man, and never shall be now, and am very careful on how I spend what little I have; but there are certain things on which I never economize. These include first class travel by train, ship, and aeroplane, The Opera, and especially good food and wine. My principle in all things is always to buy the best (which is never the most expensive) or the cheapest (which is never the worst). The road to ruin and dissatisfaction is to go through life buying the equivalent of the second cheapest claret on the wine list; always a tenth rate wine kept for stockbrokers entertaining their typists. I take no pride in motor cars or pleasure in driving so I always have the smallest and cheapest second hand car which will do the job. Two old Volkswagons (the second for when one of them is off the road) are a lot more use than one new Rolls Royce, and cost a thirtieth as much. I buy my shoes at Woolworths and throw them away when they become shabby. Nobody suspects this as I have my suits made by Ah Chum, the finest tailor in the East. George Maddocks (Judge Maddocks, father of Valerie and grandfather of my two godsons David and Henry) once glanced down from my new Ah Chum suit to the shoes I had bought the previous week at Woolworths in the Strand and remarked 'You obviously don't have your shoes made in the East.' I replied, 'Oh no, of course these are made in London.' He sighed complacently and looked down at his own hundred guinea pair. 'It's always best to have shoes made in

London.'

In the case of wine however the best, except in my own home, has passed beyond the price I can afford. In England and Europe I now always order the house wine and only once have I been dissatisfied. No restauranteur can afford to have a poor house wine, and sometimes when one has ordered an exceptionally good meal and demonstrated that one knows the good from the bad (or rather the excellent from the good) it is obvious that an even better wine has been put in the decanter. The only time this system has let me down was at an airport many years ago when I was entertaining the Porter family prior to taking the children away to Italy. It was obviously assumed (quite rightly in our case) that no customer would ever come back, and the fluid in the decanter was certainly not wine at all. It suggested dilute commercial alcohol coloured with red ink. Even the children wouldn't drink it. In Italy itself (in spite of some study of books on the subject) I have seldom found a named wine that was pleasing; but the house wines are, to my taste, always excellent. Of course if one likes the harsh Tuscan wines that come in wicker covered flasks (not the Chianti Classico which matures like a claret) then they are always available. Italian ships always have a huge wine list and on a long voyage I always try half a dozen wines the Wine Steward recommends, then ask for what the Captain is drinking, and finally finish up by drinking for the rest of the trip one of the few poor French wines they carry at twice the price of their own.

[I think at least a partial explanation is that unlike the wines of France, a very large proportion of Italian wines are made to be drunk very young, sometimes with a couple of years or less. Some of these have had extra must added and undergone two or even three fermentations. One needs to know exactly the class of a wine one is being offered as the others take almost as long to mature as a claret and apart from those in flasks there is nothing on the bottle or in the name to tell you which is which. The date which appears on the neck of the bottle may be to enable you to select a well matured good vintage, but just as likely may be the equivalent of the labelling of food and drugs with an expiry date. Another factor, at least if it is true of any wine, may be that many good Italian wines do not travel.]

Food without wine (or meat without mustard) is like a kiss

without a moustache. If one enjoys the pleasures of the table, wine is worth a great deal of study; not to learn what the experts say you should like, but to learn what you do like; and then it is worth spending money on. If one is one of those unfortunate (or just possibly fortunate) individuals to whom food means nothing, then one should simply buy fuel for the body as cheaply as possible. But never, never say 'I don't make a god of my stomach'. this is the remark of a boor, or still worse of a typical bloody Englishman.

Bisley 1954 was not a good one, at least for the Match Rifle fraternity. It had cost me a lot to get there. As usual nearly penniless I had got myself an indefinite locum job with Shell. Five guineas a day plus lunches (but from which I had to find my own first class fare from Purley – no Shell doctor could of course travel third) hardly sounds generous, but it was princely compared with anything I could earn in the health service and I wanted time to study. The only snag was that it did not entitle me to any leave and that I could only take unpaid leave if I found my own locum, and one that would be acceptable to the company. Fortunately Michael Porter was even more hard up than I was and willing, indeed eager, to sacrifice his two weeks holiday from the hospital in order to earn money at such a rate. He was able to continue to live at St Mary's and they continued to pay his National Insurance contributions; where-as Shell always maintained that temporary medical staff though not of course typists and clerks were 'Self Employed' and their insurance was their own affair.

It was with the consciousness that I had put just about everything I had in the world into it that I settled down on the 900 yard firing point for the first match of the meeting. What I did not know, and what nobody knew, was that ICI had made one of their rare blunders over the ammunition. A quantity of low-powered pistol propellant had found its way into some of the precision hand-loaded cartridges, and no one could tell which. About half of the boxes were as well made and as reliable as ever, but the others contained cartridges with so little power that they would barely blow the bullet out of the rifle. My first sighting shot was a miss as was my second. Arthur

Hales who was shooting with me volunteered to watch for the splash of my third shot. I checked my sights, my elevation, the wind, whether I had got the wind on the right way, the target number, even the fact that we were at 900 yards. 'Ready?' he asked. 'On aim' I grunted through the knot in the handkerchief clenched between my teeth. The aiming mark came into my foresight and I gave the trigger a firm squeeze.

'My God' said Arthur.

'Where did it go?' I asked.

'You are bouncing them off the 800 yard firing point' he said.

There was only one thing to do. I scrawled 'Retired' across my score card, picked up my tackle, and with bitterness in my heart trudged back to Fulton's the gunsmith. I had hardly left the firing point before I was joined by Admiral Hutton, as morose as I. Together we plodded back, cursing the armourer who had rebedded our rifles. Together we handed our rifles to Robbin Fulton for another rebedding, and together we ambled back to Stickledown to see how the match was progressing in our absence.

Over the Stickledown firing point there hovered a visible purple haze of obscenity. The eighty best shots in the Empire were lying there. Almost everyone had now had a series of misses (in many cases the first in half a century) and everyone had something to say about it. It is a characteristic of the educated Englishman that when driven to extremes he never swears in his own language – possibly because English is so totally inadequate for the purpose. The men who had made the Empire and defended it through three major wars and a hundred minor skirmishes from the frontier to Dakar, were expressing their feelings in twenty or more languages, the most recognizable of which were Urdu and Cape Dutch. My own humble exclamation of astonishment 'Gott in bloody Himmel' was hopelessly outclassed and very properly ignored.

The Match Rifle community is very much a law unto itself. Virtually the whole Council of the NRA with the Chairman is present on the firing point, and decisions to alter the rules or suspend the regulations can be taken in a few minutes. The match was abandoned, much to the disgust of Arthur who appeared to have been the only competitor to have opened three boxes of good ammunition and who had scored a seventy-three, and a meeting arranged for after dinner at the English eight club.

The situation was peculiar. ICI had admittedly made a terrible blunder at our expense. But then ICI had for half a century and more been donating this immensely costly ammunition to be issued free for all the Match Rifle events, without which generosity few if any of us would have been able to compete. If they simply said 'Sorry chaps', as they did, there was nothing for us to do but accept the situation with a good grace and hope it wouldn't happen again.

Actually what they proposed at the evening meeting was that we should shoot the following day's matches with the service cartridge, and in the meantime they would get supplies of ammunition from previous years. There would not be enough of any one year for us all to have the same, but it was hoped to arrange for each competitor to be given enough for his own needs from a single batch.

Unfortunately there is a technical difficulty here. Every cartridge burns the 'Lead' of a rifle barrel; and the exact place where it burns it is dependent on the muzzle velocity. Actually these special match barrels will shoot quite well with the service cartridge if they have been used for nothing else, but after a few hundred rounds of 'Streamline' through them the accuracy with the service cartridge is very poor, and what is more serious, even a few service rounds will ruin a Match Rifle barrel for the precision cartridge. A new barrel even in those days cost thirty pounds, a small fortune to many of us, and certainly a lot more than we could afford for one day's obviously highly unsatisfactory shooting. I was not the only one to decide to cut out Tuesday's matches and wait for the arrival of the new ammunition.

There was however one small hope. It was always possible that Michael was not getting on at Shell and would be pleased for me to abandon my highly expensive and now unwanted holiday and relieve him. I telephoned him as soon as the evening meeting was over. As expected, relieving was the last thing he wanted. 'But there is nothing for you to worry about,' he said. 'They want you to go to Nigeria.'

☆   ☆   ☆

I must be one of the very few men who have actually failed

School Certificate Geography, due largely to my confusing the Panama Canal with the Suez Canal and filling almost half my paper in answer to a question on the construction of the latter with an essay on the hazards of yellow fever and the difficulty of raising ocean-going ships eighty feet by means of locks. Later in my life I had similar trouble distinguishing Montreal from Vancouver, and the Canary Islands from the Philippines.

It happened that I did however know something of Nigeria, thanks to the headmaster of my pre-preparatory school who beat me for repeatedly calling the black citizens of the United States 'Niggers'. Not having read Mark Twain as I had, and being too stupid or ignorant to realize that the vast majority of these people originate in Nigeria, he attempted by the ancient and classical educational method to teach me that the term 'Nigger' was correctly applied to the Nigerians and to no-one else. He really was an extraordinarily stupid man even for the proprietor of a tiny school for tiny boys. I only just escaped similar treatment for enquiring, with more perspicacity than he could comprehend, whether the story of Noah's Ark was not 'just a parable'. I think that what may have saved me then was the conviction that he was dealing with Satan himself and was out of his class.

Nigeria at that time was not an oil-producing nation and indeed outside the oil companies few people were even aware of the possibility that there might be oil to be found. Apart from the first dry hole at Enugu, the wildcat wells then being drilled were the first in the country, and so far not one drop of oil had been seen.

The reason I was suddenly wanted was peculiar, but quite characteristic of the way an oil company works. The most important oil-producing country in the Shell Empire, and also the most politically sensitive, was Venezuela; and when the Venezuelan government decided to sponsor an international conference lasting six weeks on malaria control (a subject on which South American doctors knew less than nothing), it was at once decided to send a doctor from our worst malarious area to show our admiration for everything that Venezuelans did. It mattered nothing that the doctor concerned knew not a word of Spanish (the language of the conference), off he was packed. His replacement was to have been John Laurie from the London Office who was then on his honeymoon. John responded by developing 'Honeymoon Appendicitis' a few hours before he was due to depart, leaving the entire expatriate community in Eastern Nigeria without a doctor.

I rushed to St Helens Court, was vaccinated and inoculated, and on 21 July was on a plane bound for Brussels, Rome, Cairo, Kano and Port Harcourt. The first of the overseas jobs which were to be my life's work had begun.

5

BLOOD AND OIL, BAD MIX

['I have taken the title of this chapter from a huge
road-safety advertisement outside Singapore Airport
"Beer and Petrol – Bad Mix".']

For many years I was convinced that Sabena was the worst
airline in the world, and for all I know it may be true as I have
never flown with them since this first overseas journey in 1954.
Nevertheless I now think that airlines change completely over
the years and Quantas of which I formed a similar impression a
year later, had by the seventies become one of the very best.
After all there was a time when people of discernment used to
fly British.

In view of the shortness of my proposed tour, Shell only gave
me a tropical kit allowance of twenty pounds, even though the
outfitters to whom I was sent rightly pointed out that one
needed every bit as much kit for six weeks as for six months.
Twenty pounds though went a lot further then than now, and
although I was sadly out of pocket (and my salary was to be
only £120 a month) I had to buy two suitcases to contain it. I
checked with BOAC as I was travelling on their ticket and the
flights were said to be in tandem, and was assured that the
smaller was acceptable as a cabin bag. On arriving at London
Airport I was rudely told that it wasn't, but on my appealing to
a hostess of the British airline was let through, only to have the
scene repeated with even worse manners in Brussels. We flew
there in a dirty Dakota which had probably last been cleaned
in the thirties and used by the German transport command
ever since.

The new and splendid Super Constellations were then

147

flying, but Sabena flew us to Kano in an elderly, and then almost obsolete Douglas aircraft, I think called a DC4 or DC6. All planes in those days were liable to interminable delays for servicing and it was annoying rather than a matter of much surprise that we had several hours to wait before take-off. I have always considered that really good and well-served meals in the air are the chief justification of the enormous supplementary cost of first class travel, which is why my travel agents now have my file labelled 'Never flies British' and it is always a disappointment to have to take dinner on the ground. Most airlines do however try to make such a meal acceptable, especially a national airline in its own nation's capital: but the food in Brussels was as bad as school dinners in wartime, and as sparse. No wine was served and when I asked for it, pointing out that it was an all first class flight, I was told that I could have one glass only. A tenth-rate white vin ordinaire was brought in a thick tumbler and incredibly when I asked for a second it was refused.

We boarded the plane ultimately to find the accommodation no better than in the Dakota, and the seats so close that one could with difficulty, get in at all. The seating plan which we had been given at the time of booking was duplicated in the pocket of the seats ahead of us, and when my neighbour complained that it bore no resemblance to actuality was told by a smirking and unwashed steward that this plan referred to the 'Royal Sabena' flights of which there was only one per week (at the same fare) and that they had to put twice as many people in the ordinary first class.

Dawn broke over the Sahara of which I got my first and as it has turned out my only view. We were flying of course in this aircraft at a very low altitude. Kano airstrip was simply a bit of desert bounded on each side by an interminable row of oil drums on each of which was perched one vulture. The birds craned their long necks to watch us come in and then slowly followed us with their eyes as we landed and taxied to a stop, exactly like the two following the fall of the witch in *Snow White*.

The airline had not got their last laugh out of me though. Following a breakfast which was very good as it was the work not of the airline but of a negro contractor, I was called to the desk (I was the only passenger there at the time but they would not of course come to me) to be told that my baggage was overweight and that I would have to pay out of my meagre cash if I did not want it sent back to London. They admitted that the weight was recorded on my ticket but claimed that their scales were 'Better than the British use' and the decision was final. I have seldom yielded to demands for bribes and still less to demands with menaces, but I had to this time. I had great difficulty in getting a receipt, and in any case never got my money back. I had been given a letter from Shell undertaking to pay any excess, but Sabena had taken it off me at London. I never checked to see how much the Company was charged.

I remember nothing of the flight to Port Harcourt nor of the ninety mile drive to Owerri, but I arrived tired and happy about teatime and went exhausted to an early bed.

Next morning I called to see the manager. George Evangouloff was one of the most dominating and flamboyant characters I have ever met, and yet a charming and very competent administrator. He and all his staff were fully aware that he knew more about any man's job and could do it better than the man himself, with but one exception. It is rare to find such a man who will acknowledge any exceptions: yet George made no pretence of being in any position to criticize or question the opinions and decisions of even the most junior of medical officers. Industry in general and oil companies in particular would do much better and waste fewer lives if there were more like him. Like all exiled Russians he was said to be a Prince, which in his case may just possibly have been true, and his sense of humour was both Russian and princely. His invariable reaction to an embarrassing or amusing situation was to call for champagne. Once while taking my coat when I was his guest, he dropped and broke a pocket hypodermic syringe and said 'Oh dear will that cost you much money?' On my replying 'No but it will cost Shell much money', the immediate response was 'Ah Doctor, I think that calls for Champagne!' One night at a bachelor party we got him playing 'Are you there Moriarty?' He enjoyed it immensely but on leaving felt bound to remark 'Are you there Moriarty is a very good game, but in Russia we should play it with sabres.'

Owerri camp was a group of about sixty fairly solid bungalows, without of course air-conditioning which I had never seen

149

in those days, and with atap windows and mosquito screens. There was no effective mosquito control as the jungle, which came to a hundred yards of the camp boundary, was impenetrable to spraying, although it was done from the helicopters as much as possible. There was a tiny hospital situated in a bungalow just across the road from mine and like it in every respect except that it had been enlarged slightly and some of the interior walls removed. The manager lived in a slightly larger one about a hundred yards away, and there were office blocks, a mess and a commisary. I know now that this was an absolutely typical small oil camp and have seen dozens exactly similar in other parts of the world. I am told that some American oil companies make their camps exact duplicates in every area so that a newcomer can find his way about, drunk or sober, from the moment he arrives.

There was a fairly well run Government hospital across the road from the camp, and Owerri town was about two miles away. It is not easy to get people to believe just how barbarous the area was at that time. The white man's law and civilization extended for ten yards on either side of the main road, and beyond that was timeless Africa. The law said that all meat exhibited for sale must have the hide on. The operative word was 'Exhibited'. All the meat exhibited was goat or the almost unchewable Indian beef, but under the counter was said to be always human flesh available at a higher price.

One of my own staff, an African dresser, had a father die at the Government hospital and went there to collect the body and take it home for burial, draped conveniently over the cross-bar of his bicycle. On the way he was overcome by a call of nature, and being a modest chap propped the bicycle with father against a tree and retired behind a bush. When he returned, the valuable bicycle was still there but the body was not. Only on two or three occasions did I go into an African's house for food and I always had uncomfortable doubts about the palm oil chop. Naturally they would only give me the very best, and it was always delicious.

I was of course very young and inexperienced, and totally lacking in any real knowledge of medical or tropical diseases. Even so in retrospect I am not proud of the standard I was practising. I had one very experienced expatriate sister to help and advise me, and I fear I accepted without question her

150

account of what was normal and acceptable. Undoubtedly malaria was omnipresent, and I think it was true that whenever a native developed a fever from any cause, latent malaria at once became clinical. The result of treating each and every fever with Mepacrine showed this to be the case and 'therapeutic test' is a perfectly valid and respectable means of diagnosis when no other methods are available. Unfortunately though, other methods were available, or were claimed to be. Every patient with fever (which meant at least sixty per cent of every clinic) was sent for a blood smear, and all the time I was there I did not have a single positive result. I was told, and in my ignorance readily accepted, that this was perfectly normal and that the organism would not be found in the majority of cases where the clinical diagnosis was undoubtedly malaria and where the patient would respond at once to anti-malarial treatment.

I know now that this was absolute nonsense. Since that time I must have seen and treated many hundreds of cases of malaria in my surgical patients, and not once has the laboratory failed to find the organism. I knew no more about laboratory technique than what every medical student is required to do in his practical exam: but then any student who was given a blood film to stain and failed to discover malaria if it were present would certainly be ploughed. I am sure that all these patients had the disease and that had I carried out the test myself, I would seldom if ever have failed to find it. I am surprised that even if the African technician did not know how to do it, he did not automatically report them all as positive. He was a Christian and may have had a religious objection to telling lies, but then he had many children and several wives to support, and could not risk his job by being discovered to be incompetent; as he certainly would have been had I stayed much longer. I suspect my predecessor had caught him out reporting a slide as positive when there was nothing to be seen, and that for the time being at least he had decided it was safer to see nothing.

I do not really think that there was any serious concern for truth on his part. Shortly after I left there was a scandal over a domestic servant whom I had examined and passed as fit who died of both pulmonary and renal tuberculosis in spite of the normal urine report, and my own negative report on the chest x-ray only three weeks before. It transpired that every candidate who wanted to be accepted was paying four weeks' wages to be shared among my staff. If he did, the urine report was negative, and I would be shown a chest film which I had already reported as normal. Otherwise the white of an egg would be stirred up into his urine and I would be given a chest x-ray showing unmistakable tuberculosis. Heaven help me, I used to wax eloquent at the company having to supply cash to its patients in the Government Hospital so that they could bribe the nurses to bring a bedpan, and never noticed the beam in the eye of my own department.

My duties were essentially to provide clinic services for the company staff of all races, with occasional house visits to expatriate wives and children. In addition at least once every week I had to make an inspection of the clinic and hygienic conditions of one or more of the field camps where about twenty men would be living for a stint of three weeks or so without their families. These were usually deep in impenetrable bush accessible only by helicopter. They were of two kinds, seismic parties and 'wildcat' drilling rigs, parties who were drilling a hole, not where oil was known to be because there is no way of telling whether there is any oil, but in a place where the seismic survey shows that the oil would have accumulated if there was any. The whole operation was managed, under George Evangouloff, by a charming Dutchman named 'Dry Hole' from his distinction of having drilled twenty-two dry holes in succession. As making hole cost even at that time up to five thousand pounds a day, and each hole could take several months before being abandoned, he had not up to then proved a very profitable investment to the group. During my brief stay however the first useful show was obtained, and he remained to see the Nigerian Oilfields emerge as among the most productive in the world. There was also a company office and bungalow ninety miles south at Port Harcourt, presumably to manage the import of equipment and materials and some excellent flats for expatriate families at Onitsha on the Niger river.

All but one of the seismic parties were operating on dry land from tiny and primitive camps which had to be moved every few months as the survey of the surrounding area of jungle was completed; although sometimes when it became clear that a wildcat well would need to be drilled in the vicinity they would be turned into semi-permanent hutted camps to be taken over later by a drilling crew. I visited all but one of these land-based seismic parties, and watched them at work as well as carrying out my medical inspection. Seismic surveying consists essentially of making a loud bang and then listening to the echoes from the different layers of rock below. When this is done at intervals across country in a straight line, a diagram can be prepared showing how each layer curves upwards or downwards. Except in South America, oil is always found in limestone layers though there is still some dispute whether it has formed there. When an oil-bearing limestone layer is topped by an impervious stratum, it is necessary to find a dome-shaped point where it will accumulate (limestone is always wet and oil floats on water) for the other people to drill into.

The bang is made by a small charge of dynamite lowered into a shallow hole drilled by a tiny portable rig on the back of a lorry. Some distance away are a series of sensors or microphones which record what they hear on a strip of paper like that of a seismograph. Indeed the thing is a seismograph recording small man-made earthquakes. The natives do not take kindly to this being done to their land and large sums have to be paid out to get permission to do so. In one case no amount of dash (i.e. cash) would be accepted as the witch doctor at the village five miles away whose chief owned the field said that the water god (Ju Ju) lived there and that if he was angered they would have no water. The village had an unusually fine spring in the main street and permission was at last obtained by bringing in an English lawyer who drew up a contract that if the spring failed any time in the next twenty years the company would lay on piped water for them from a very distant source. The deed was signed and the seismic party moved in. The very first shot produced a fountain of water from an unsuspected underground stream, and the spring in the village dried up instantly. Shell engineers were unable to repair the damage, and the piped water supply was said to have cost them over a million. I believe they are still having to maintain and service it thirty-five years later.

I always made a whole day's work of these visits and had lunch with the crew in their mess which would usually only be

153

a smallish tent. Almost all the field parties were staffed by English personnel, but two were all Dutch. The English would be eating essentially school food, but the Dutch would explain that 'A Dutch lunch is just Breakfast over again', which is splendid if you like Dutch breakfasts. Each man would cut himself an inch-thick trencher of bread about six inches square from a specially baked loaf and butter it thickly. On this would be placed in order, served by a succession of stewards like a rijstafel, a layer of thinly cut cheese, fried fish, and fried meat. One or two would top this off with a layer of English marmalade supplied by the Shell caterer (probably in error) reminiscent of the way an American will put strawberry jam on his bacon and eggs. It is less surprising in an American as all their cooking is sweet and sticky like their love-life, but these Dutch oilmen are tough and should know good food when they are at home in Holland. Perhaps the explanation is that these do not. The English have always sent their very best people overseas, while the Dutch and the Americans in general send their worst: which explains the present state of Puerto Rico, Hawaii, and South Africa.

My helicopter pilot was not present on these occasions. The service was provided by Pest Control Ltd., a crop-spraying firm which does not normally carry passengers. They had only two machines, two-seater 'Bell' models which even then cost thirty-five pounds a flying hour (about £700 now) to fly and maintain. The Sikorsky helicopters which I used the following year in the Gulf cost just twice as much but then would carry freight plus nine passengers as against one in the Bell. Few of the field parties were more than an hour away and the pilot would usually put me down and call for me again in the evening. I can only remember one occasion when he stayed and I was grateful, not for his presence but for the loan of his equipment. In a very isolated camp the message came that the headman at a village about a quarter of a mile away was sick and wanted the doctor to come to him. My dresser said it was absolutely safe but he had proved unsatisfactory and unreliable in other ways, so I asked the advice of the party leader. He said that nothing on earth would make him go but that perhaps a doctor would feel duty bound to risk it when a man was in need of him. He said that they seldom ate a white man, but added thoughtfully that they might think a doctor would be very

154

strong medicine and worth having even though unpalatable. He also said that it was a pity I hadn't got a revolver. I borrowed a Very Light pistol from the aircraft, reasoning that if the worst came to the worst a Very Light discharged into a crowd of hungry Nigerians would probably inhibit them a lot more than just shooting six of them; and might give me time for a getaway. In the event everything went amiably and quietly. The chief's sickness was merely the common one of having taken one more wife than he could cope with at his age and he wanted an injection 'for strength'. I gave him a shot of multivitamins which would certainly do him good and might even help with his problem, and was obliged to join him in a delicious palm oil chop. I didn't ask any questions about it.

On the whole the drilling parties were more fun as there was more to see. When one has seen one seismic shot one has seen the lot, at least as regards those on dry land, but the drilling rigs and the men who run them are a study for years. A wildcat drilling requires at least as much in the way of staff and equipment as any new well in a producing field, and frequently very much more. One outfit which was looking for oil only very near the surface was using a portable 'Failings' rig mounted on the back of a lorry, but all the others were using huge structures like smaller versions of the Eiffel Tower, known as 'Ideal 50' or 'Ideal 100' rigs. These were driven by a big diesel engine with another smaller one alongside it to work the derrick. The drilling floor is elevated on a scaffold some twenty feet above the ground and on it is the turntable driven by the main diesel and through which the drill pipe passes. Below this are two powerful valves, the blow-out preventers, which are closed if the pressure in the hole suddenly rises to prevent the drilling mud and drill string being blown into the air on a column of high pressure oil or still worse by gas. The public is under the impression that a 'Gusher', which is the lay name for a blow-out, marks the triumph of a drilling operation, but it is in fact almost the greatest disaster which can happen. Very rarely the opposite phenomenon occurs, but it had done so sufficiently recently for it to be fresh in the minds of everyone. A large drilling rig had tapped a fairly superficial gas pocket which was holding up a flimsy shell of hard rock. When the gas blew, the thin dome collapsed and the whole installation, platform, rig, engines, office, and drilling crew, disappeared underground to be immediately covered by the cave-in without a trace of where they had been.

Most of a driller's time is spent in the monotonous task of standing watching the turntable and drill pipe turning and the gauge which marks the bottom hole pressure. If he is wise he also keeps an eye on the colour of the drilling mud and whether it has oil in it, and also that his native crew are awake. If a blow-out starts there may only be seconds available to avert disaster. One of the blow-out preventer valves is supposed to close automatically, but the crew has to be ready to close the other by sheer physical strength with a big wheel like an enormous version of the valves on a water main. Also the diesels, lights, and all other sources of ignition have to be shut down in moments. Even so, when disaster strikes the gush of oil and gas almost always catches fire within seconds. Costs are such that the rig has to be run continuously day and night. The most unwanted duty is 'The Graveyard shift' in the small hours of the morning which falls to the most junior of the drillers or to someone who has put up a black and whom the company is hoping will resign.

At irregular intervals it is necessary to change the drilling bit, a mammoth task when it may be on the end of seven or eight thousand feet of drill pipe. Such a 'round trip' can take days and costs tens of thousands of pounds in lost drilling time. The 'drilling string' is pulled up one section at a time, each length being somewhat shorter than the height of the derrick. As soon as the screw joint between two sections appears, the pipe below is locked from falling (a vitally important step) with wedges placed in the turntable, and unscrewed. This unscrewing is as simple as unscrewing the parts of chimney-sweep's mop, but being on a larger scale cannot be done by hand. It is done by two big spanners each about ten feet long and worked by steel ropes attached to their handles and pulled by a windlass on the shaft of the smaller diesel; the one which works the block and tackle of the derrick. Once the joint has been unscrewed part of a turn, the drilling turntable is run for a few seconds in reverse, and when the upper section is free it is winched up and put vertically in a stack to wait until it has to be screwed on again and replaced. Once the bit is exposed, it is quickly changed and the procedure reversed until the new bit reaches the bottom of the hole and drilling can be started again.

Sometimes the wedges are not properly placed and the old bit, with anything up to three miles of pipe, drops down to the bottom of the hole. When this happens the first thing to be done is the dismissal of the driller and his chief (the 'tool pusher') who may well have been asleep in his cabin at the time but is still responsible, and very probably everybody else on the rig including the small boy who brings the milk. Next the whole mess has to be got out of the hole. A very few drillers are good at this operation which is called 'a fishing job', but there are specialists who have an uncanny knack of feeling what is going on at the end of a drilling string, just as a trout fisherman can feel what is happening to his fly, and they are often summoned from the other side of the earth for a difficult case. The fishing problem, is not always a lost string of drill pipe. Total obstruction to further making a hole can be caused by a dropped spanner, a broken bit, or even the tool-pushers cork leg. These are all well known complications of an oilman's life, and provide a good income to anyone who can make his name as an expert in dealing with them.

There are other reasons for stopping the progress of the drill. The whole object of the exercise is after all to find oil, and there may be several strata where oil might be found. In the Persian Gulf there may be five or more. When the drilling bit reaches one of these layers it is pulled up and an instrument called a 'Johnson Tester' substituted. This just takes a sample of the fluid at this level without any attempt to find out how much there is. Usually this is all that is required, and after the test the tester is replaced by the drilling bit and the making of hole proceeds as before. If oil is found though there are a series of other tests to be performed, culminating in a 'Production Test' where the well is pumped for several days to assess whether it is capable of sustained production. In completely new areas where the geological structure is unknown, everything may be stopped in order to let down a special bit with diamond teeth to cut a core of rock for microscopical examination.

Probably my finest memories of this assignment are of the water-born seismic party at Warri. Today this is the centre of one of the world's largest oilfields, but when I knew it, it was a tiny camp in the midst of a swampy river delta which was not only almost uninhabited but not even explored and mapped.

Maps certainly existed but the helicopter pilots quickly discovered that they bore no resemblance to reality, and they were frequently in serious trouble looking for hills, valleys, and landmarks which if they existed at all were several hundred miles from where they were shown to be. My total incompetence in matters geographical once more led to near disaster. Indeed it apparently did lead to disaster to a company vehicle and a possibly very deserving one of God's creatures with several wives and uncountable children. It was just possible to get to Warri by road in a period of nearly three days, but there was a better method. It was within about thirty miles of Abba (or just possibly Agbor) where we had a seismic party and a helicopter landing pad. Anyway I confused the two names and sent my car and a driver to Agbor (or just possibly Abba) with instructions to wait there until I descended from the clouds, and then drive me to Warri. The mistake was discovered a few minutes after he had left and a second car dispatched to Abba (or was it Agbor?) and the mission accomplished without further difficulty. The interesting thing is that the first car and driver never returned; and up to the time I left nearly a month later, no trace of them had been discovered. Admittedly the people in the area were reported to be 'Primitive and untrustworthy' but surely they would hardly have eaten the car.

The base camp at Warri consisted of three strangely luxurious bungalows separated by about twenty yards of well-cut lawn from the Warri river. One of these was reserved for the manager and his wife, who had a delightful miniature Dachshund. In the river immediately opposite and about five yards from the bank was an unsightly tree stump which for some reason annoyed them. Two men with a chain saw and a rowing boat could have removed it in ten minutes, but it was decided to use dynamite. The company was only licensed to use dynamite for seismic shooting so a government dynamiter had to be called in. He arrived just before I did but like a plumber without his tools. He was given an exploder, some cable, a box of detonators, and a twenty-two pound case of explosive. It was not a sensible thing to do as one stick would have been far too much and unsafe a mere twenty-five yards from the house; and dynamite is not nice stuff to try to cut into small pieces, particularly in a hot climate where it tends to get rather sensitive.

I was just congratulating my hostess on having such a beautiful house, when all of a sudden she hadn't. We were standing on either side of the front door, fortunately a modest four feet apart or one at least of us would certainly have been killed. The door was wrenched from its frame and dashed to splinters on the opposite wall. All the windows and their frames were torn out, and the ceiling split from one corner to the other. My chief concern was for the dog, far too well-bred to be exposed to such goings on, which was convinced that the world had come to an end and was protesting loudly that it hadn't expected the day of judgement to be as bad as this. Suddenly a large black face appeared where the window had been, grinning happily from ear to ear.

'Big Bang Master.'

'Yes. Bloody big bang. How much Dynamite?'

'Whole case. Twenty-two pounds.'

I went to spend the night in the houseboat of the seismic party itself. There were four boats in the little convoy which was slowly surveying a large area of Nigeria from the convenience of the river. The houseboat provided accommodation for the expatriate team as well as offices and the cabin where the radio equipment and seismometer were kept. There was a similar one for the African staff, a sizable floating dynamite store with no engines which had to be towed, and a little fast motorboat, the 'Shooting Launch' which laid and fired the charges. I was given a good dinner and put to bed in a comfortable cabin but for the first and last time in my life under a mosquito net.

I was woken quite early by an apologetic seismologist who wanted to remove a small box from under my pillow. They had been using the radio for some time when somebody remembered that I was sleeping on a box of detonators and it is not unknown for one to be fired by the power from the transmitter. I dressed and went on deck to see what was going on.

The seismic sensors or microphones in these waterborne outfits are mounted on floats at intervals on a cable of about a hundred yards length, towed behind the boat carrying the seismometer recording machine. The mother vessel sails very slowly along the river, a navigator checking and recording its position continuously from landmarks on the bank. The shooting launch sails round her firing first a shot about two hundred

159

yards astern, and then another the same distance ahead. Two pounds of dynamite with a detonator in a polythene bag is let out on a safe length of cable suspended under a big red balloon floating on the water. The firing signal is given from the mother vessel as soon as the position is established and the seismometer running, and there is a fountain of water and spray as though a depth charge had been exploded. The little shooting launch then speeds astern and does it all again. It is a wonderful spectacle for a man making his first cine film as I was of my whole trip. I had bought an 8mm camera with a hundred feet of film for twenty pounds the night before I left London, and ultimately used a further two hundred feet bought in Port Harcourt. I have never been interested in photography except for records of overseas travel and for teaching surgery, but this was the first of some thousands of feet of my travels round the world. I became very keen without bothering to think why I was doing it. It was only when my father died a dozen years later than I realized I was doing it for him. I still have a Bolex and a Leica but have hardly used them since.

John Laurie took a long time to recover from his appendicectomy, but arrived in about two months with his new wife and an evening temperature. I took a few days showing him around while I made arrangements for my return trip and then flew to Lagos to board a ship for Liverpool. My locum contract expired with the job although this carried a paid leave entitlement of one week for every month worked, which just about covered the extra time for the journey by sea. I had as yet no intention of joining Shell or any ambition beyond a consultantship in the Health Service, and reasoned that this might well be the only chance I should ever have of a sea voyage. As things have turned out I have made twenty-eight voyages (excluding those to and from St Helena) and this was to be not only the first but the shortest of them. I think I have spent a total of nearly two years of my life on board ship and I have loved every moment of it.

The journey to Lagos was in an incompletely converted Bristol Freighter in which we could still see the gap between the loading doors at the front. These aircraft (there may only have been one) were all that Nigerian Airways were running, though they had to buy something else a few weeks later when one of the wings fell off. We stopped at Benin City for refuelling. The landing was all right but the stop outside the terminal (an atap hut with a bar) was sudden. On getting out we found that the front wheels had sunk a foot or more into the melting tarmac. The captain looked at it long and sadly, and then went inside for a beer. Ten minutes later he came out again clutching his second foaming pint, and looked at it even more sadly. He then went back and called for volunteers to push his aircraft out of the hole. All the passengers and airport staff came as well as any locals who were passing including a small group of school children, and by pushing on the under-carriage and tailplane managed to manhandle it back onto the runway. I was the only one who did not help. I had a film to make and this was too good to miss.

The very few children who go to school walk many miles there and back, each with a pen, a ruler, and an ink bottle neatly arranged and balanced on the top of the head. Those who can however will buy a satchel, even if this means going without other less essential things. The film shows one boy of about thirteen pushing manfully while wearing a magnificent new leather satchel, but no other clothing whatever. The star rating however goes to the future prime minister (he may even then have been elected) in spite of the heat immaculately dressed as for the city, pushing with one hand and holding in the other at shoulder height a birdcage containing a canary.

My host at Lagos was a charming man with an even more charming wife. He had been happily married many years and told me 'I first saw my wife when she was playing roulette at Monte Carlo and said to myself "That's the girl I am going to marry".' His only other interest in life was polo and he took me to the polo club that evening to watch him play. This was the first time I had seen or even heard of an air-conditioner. I was astounded at walking into a dry cool climate after the hot sweaty conditions I had got acclimatized to in the previous two months. An elderly friend who served abroad before the war once said to me 'Life in the tropics has been revolutionized by three things, air-conditioning, sterilized milk, and long playing gramophone records.' I agree with him: but I am astonished how many people, and even great hotels like the Raffles, will buy expensive tea and coffee but will not pay for the milk, and put up with milk powder or the even more repulsive sweetened condensed.

Apapa sailed for Liverpool the following day and although I had no previous standards with which to compare her I think she was a very good ship. The first thing I did after unpacking was to go down with my card to the Surgeon's cabin and offer my help should it ever be needed. This has become a lifelong habit and on this occasion as on so many others made me a friend. Reggie Armitage was a Lancastrian, though nobody would have suspected it. He had elected to take his medical at Dublin University and had returned home with an Irish degree, an Irish wife, an Irish religion, and an Irish accent you could cut with a knife. Like most converts he was more Catholic than the Catholics, and at once went out to the medical mission at Emakuku to convert the heathen and had thence gravitated to the shipping line. He was a wonderful companion and at once invited me to his table where in the course of the one voyage we drank the ship dry of every claret on the wine list.

Before leaving the Emerald Isle he had somehow acquired a Mastership in Surgery at the University of Cork, of which he spoke most disparagingly, almost certainly neither in justice to them nor to himself. He was thus more highly qualified in surgery than I was. When therefore the prospect arose of having to cut a passenger for appendicitis, I suggested that he should operate and I should give the anaesthetic. He refused absolutely, saying 'I am under contract to treat any first class passenger for two guineas a day. If I operate I shall get my two guineas and you can charge perhaps five as anaesthetist. But if you operate and I give the anaesthetic, I shall still get my two guineas, and you can charge fifty.'

The week after we landed he had been asked to be best man at the wedding of a friend at Brompton Oratory, and invited me to be present. There had been a monumental stag party, but all would have been well if at the very last moment it had not been discovered that the groom had not been to confession for a year. We all waited somewhat embarrassed while he went off sheepishly with the priest to one of the confessional boxes. The embarrassment was worse when the priest returned alone and to say that he was terribly sorry but that he could not give the man absolution until he was sober. Ignoring the tearful protest from the bride that she certainly wouldn't marry her if

162

he was sober, we took him across the road to the Kardoma Cafe for an hour and poured black coffee into him. We got him just sober enough to be absolved but not enough to refuse to be married. I decided to cut the reception and go home.

Perhaps the rest of the company were not quite up to what one would meet on the Union Castle boats or the P & O. The first morning of deck sports I dutifully entered for the shuffle-board. I had no sooner appeared than the wife of a Resident bore down upon me and asked whether I was good at it. I explained that I didn't know as I had never played before. After all the only place one can learn is on board ship and it was my first voyage. 'If you haven't played before, you had better go away' she said. 'You will only make a fool of yourself and annoy people who want to play properly.' I went away and have never entered for deck sports since. There was also an African magistrate on board who had recently achieved notoriety by passing a flogging sentence on an English expatriate for keeping a fox terrier which had nipped a Hausa trader. He was inclined to give himself airs at first, but there were a few settlers on board of the old school who let him know that if he returned to his own country he was likely to lose more than the skin of his back. I have heard that he has since done very well in the grocery trade in Balham.

We arrived in Liverpool on a bright October morning and to my surprise my mother was on board to meet me and go home with me on the boat train as though I had been away for years.

I maintained my contact with Shell and worked a few weeks in the London Office but for the most part concentrated on study and locum work for practical training. The technique of operating is not hard to learn, at least for those who are reasonably good with their hands at things like making model aeroplanes. Some very able surgeons never do learn clean and careful dissecting technique, while others whose meticulous dissections are a joy to watch are so incompetent at diagnosis, assessment of what needs to be done, preparation of the patient, and post operative care that their results are terrible and they are not surgeons at all.

163

I had not yet seriously considered a career abroad, so it was the English Fellowship I was working for. In England this is essential for any worthwhile job but overseas, especially in the East where almost every worker in the past has been a Scot, the Edinburgh College which is much the senior is far more highly regarded. I sat the English Fellowship in May and failed. I met Eric Farquharson of Edinburgh at the college bar afterwards and he told me that I ought to have passed (he was examining and it was Ian Aird, a rejected Edinburgh man who had failed me) and urged me to come up to Edinburgh next time. I might possibly have done so had not fate whisked me away to Singapore, and by the time I got back I was committed to life in the East so I should have done so anyway. I had already decided that private study was not sufficient and that if humanly possible I must get onto the very restricted course at the English College. These courses were limited to about twenty places of which only two were available to UK residents. I thought it possible that once abroad again I might be able by using a Singapore address to trick them into giving me one of the places reserved for colonials, and so it proved.

This time I had to miss Bisley as an emergency situation had arisen. The Shell installation on Pulau Bukom, an island five miles outside Singapore harbour, had grown very rapidly and at least one full-time medical officer was essential. They had made the mistake of appointing a first class Singaporean of Indian race at a time when ideas of racial equality were most definitely not accepted among oilmen even if in theory they were by the Company, and he was treated like dirt. He was paid a salary less than that of the most junior expatriate and although a house had been assigned to him he never got it. An even more race conscious Eurasian in the engineering department had said 'If that man gets a house I resign.' As the office Manager said 'What could we do? the man had twenty years service and the doctor was newly recruited.' When I said that the engineer should not have been given a chance to resign but dismissed without a reference, I was told that I understood nothing of management: which I am proud to say was true.

Unknown to the company this doctor was gambling on the rubber exchange and when the rubber boom came made himself a millionaire. There was a story told me by a director of a crucible company which had a reputation for working its staff hard on not overgenerous pay. One of their travellers was lost somewhere in the Outer Hebrides trying to sell crucibles to the crofters, when it became known that he had won the first dividend on Littlewoods. There was some speculation at head office as to what his reaction would be to sudden wealth. He was a Scot and did not waste words, particularly on telegrams, but in due course one arrived for the managing director. When decoded it read 'Bugger you stop rude letter follows'. I gather the reaction of our millionaire doctor was much the same. He was replaced by a newly recruited Englishman but they had got into the habit of treating doctors badly and although he got his house, he was refused a motor car. Riding a bicycle in Singapore temperatures around a tiny island with three hills is not good for a man who has spent all his life in a cool climate, and he was ill within days. He was good at spot diagnosis and just before he died after less than three weeks of it he was heard to say 'If this is Polio, I am killing myself.' It was.

Bad news travels quickly, and before I left I knew something of what had happened. I was in a strong position to dictate terms and as I was only going for a few months I did not need a house, but I stipulated that I must have transport. I was given a Willis Jeep and later a Land Rover, so I at least survived. Actually after a week or so I decided I wanted a house and got one. I started for Singapore by air on 5 June and left for home by sea two days before Christmas. The invitation was strangely welcome to me (did I half suspect where it was leading?) and I remember walking round the garden a few minutes after the telephone call from Shell singing 'The Road to Mandalay'. There was only a token kit allowance as I had already had one of twenty pounds, but I managed to get the essentials using about fifty out of my own pocket and within a few days I was sitting in the Kensington air terminal with my parents who had come to see me off listening to the announcement of my flight to Rome, Cairo, Karachi, Singapore, Darwin, and Sydney. Daddy said 'This is the modern magic carpet.'

I see that I have been boring in my very Bowdlerized account of travel at that time by Sabena, and have indicated that I was not all that impressed by Quantas. To be fair, Quantas Empire Airways did very well by me, and I was well looked after in real comfort, well fed and supplied with good wines, as in those days the Australians made no effort to palm

165

off their own on passengers who had paid for first class. Even if they had done badly by me I hope I would have forgiven them as we were told we must 'Those who trespass against us'. It is an interesting theological point however how far we have the duty to forgive those who trespass against others. What turned me against this airline (and I have already said it has since become the best in the world) was the way they treated a young boy sitting next to me. He could not have been more than seventeen and looked a couple of years younger.

I don't think I have ever seen anybody more airsick or seasick than this poor child. In two and a half days he had to refuse every meal, drink, and snack that was offered. He was obviously on his way out to his first job and half an hour before we landed he made a desperate attempt to get himself into shape to meet his new employers and so asked for a small glass of brandy, probably the first he had ever tasted. As it was not a mealtime they made him pay for it.

Progress with the Super Constellations was leisurely, although it was the best and most comfortable means of air travel I have ever known except for the brief period when the upstairs lounge of the 747s was used for its proper purpose. Flights for the East left at one minute to midnight on Sundays (which was a great boon to people like me as I got a whole day's pay for that minute) and arrived in Singapore at five o'clock on Tuesday evening. There was still a night stop for those going on to Australia, and the airline provided a tour of Singapore on Wednesday for transit passengers before starting off again in the early afternoon. These were the last long distance flights to have a separate aircraft for first class passengers, and the food and service were markedly better than in the rear cabin of the two-class flights. (The young may not know that in a piston-engined aircraft it is the rear which is most free from noise and vibration, and in two-class flights that was where the first class cabin was always placed.)

The impact of Singapore on a young man who has never strayed outside Europe is staggering. It is said that a man who tastes the fleshpots of the East before he is thirty never comes home and I have never known it to prove untrue. Certainly in my case I had never considered living or even travelling east of Suez, but by Christmas I knew I should be happy nowhere else. Today it does not need to involve a radical change in lifestyle as it did to the characters Somerset Maugham wrote about, but it must mean a completely changed outlook on the world and one's fellow men as well as intimate contact with, though never assimilation into, a civilization which is much older than our own and in many ways far superior. The Chinese have been living in an elegant cultured civilization since a thousand years before we stopped going about dressed in blue paint. He never forgets it, but has far too much natural good manners ever to let it show. Other races when they come into contact with the white man's technology find it necessary to assert their own native history and culture (often as in the case of Africans and Malays almost entirely mythical). The Chinese has no such need. He recognizes that the European is good at physics, biology, and chemistry as well as at making motor cars and aeroplanes, just as a silkworm is good at making silk, and he makes use of those things with gratitude. He has no desire though to emulate us or to pretend to be our equals in such things which although very useful are essentially beneath him.

The result is that he will cheerfully accept what we would consider menial work and supervision by a person culturally far beneath him, without any suggestion of servility. In Sabah I later met three brothers, meeting together on terms of perfect amity equality and mutual respect. One was the most highly qualified and gifted physician in South East Asia, a man who had he remained in London, as he was urged to, would have risen to be PRCP. The second was the Prime Minister. The third brother was a lorry driver. All met together on terms of equality, and certainly none would have considered another his social better or inferior. Just possibly, although they were all devout Roman Catholics, they would have looked up to a fourth brother (had there been one) who had become a Buddhist monk or a renowned philosopher, but certainly not to one who had been made Pope. All these things were of the West, useful and perhaps lucrative, but of no essential importance in their eyes.

When I arrived on Pulau Bukom a few days later I found that since the death of my predecessor all the work had been done by a Chinese dresser of great ability and experience (he was trained before the war by Lindsey Webster) who was so well loved and trusted that the expatriates always spoke of him behind my back as 'Dr Leong'. An English male nurse who had reached such a position would have got above himself and become insubordinate (as all European male nurses do sooner or later anyway), but Leong at once reverted to his proper status and position. We have remained friends for life and his manner towards me is always superficially that of a respectful subordinate: but if I was so unwise as to ask to marry his daughter I should very soon be told which was the superior race and who was the presumptuous barbarian. The girl too, if she was foolish enough to marry me in defiance of her father (mother would not be asked) would be cut off from her own people and be regarded as something worse than a fallen woman. Prostitutes are necessary even in a Chinese society, and even a young woman who becomes the mistress of a European (known as a 'sleeping dictionary' as this is the only way of learning Chinese which ever works) is not beyond the pale. This is a matter of business. But a girl who marries outside her race betrays everything Chinese culture stands for, and she and her children are social outcasts.

The airline took us with the Australian transit passengers to the Raffles Hotel, then still the undisputed finest hotel in the country and recognized as one of the seven 'Great' hotels of the world. (The others were Shepherds, the Imperial at Tokyo, the Peninsula, the Taj Mahal, the Waldorf Astoria, and curiously the Savoy.) Since then many modern 'International' hotels have sprung up, all exactly the same with swimming pools, gymnasia, coffee shops, and computer controlled drink dispensers in every chromium plated room. The Raffles has made concessions recently in the shape of a refrigerator and small bar in every suite, a television set (which is immediately removed on request) and, horror of horrors, a swimming pool in the palm court, but otherwise it remains the same as ever. I always stay there.

Bukom was one of those mysterious industrial complexes which an outsider finds it impossible to understand what it is for. An island little more than a mile long and half a mile wide, it was covered almost entirely with oil tanks. There were however two villages (grown up before Shell arrived) a clubhouse, a bachelor mess, a block of four small comfortable flats, and about fifteen houses scattered about on almost every bit of land that was unsuitable for an oil tank. Some of the villagers had nothing at all to do with the company except to get free medical attention and transport to and from Singapore, but most tended to be employed in some way in the Company's business. Along one side of the island was a series of eight wharves, each solid with pipes for pumping oil in and out of the tankers, and the adjoining strip of land was protected by a high metal fence as 'The Installation' within which were offices, laboratories and workshops. The great mystery was what actually got done there. Admittedly on very rare occasions a ship would come alongside for bunkering, but otherwise the whole enormous installation (and in terms of throughput it was the biggest petroleum installation in the world) did nothing but pump oil out of tankers into its tanks, and oil out of its tanks back into tankers.

As I understand it, and even after working there for nearly six months I am not quite sure I do understand it, Bukom was a 'Blending and storage installation', but with the enormous flow of oil in and out twenty-four hours a day, seven days a week, even the huge tank farms could only hold enough for a few days had the supply ceased: and for the most part tankers were taking out exactly the same blends as other tankers were bringing in. I knew this because as a senior officer in an oil installation I got a detailed account on my desk every morning of everything that was going on; what ships were discharging what cargo and what others were loading: just as in other areas I should have had the day's drilling report and the progress of each of the seismic parties. A tanker always has several tanks each capable of being loaded with a different product, and frequently finds all of them filled with what its customers wanted to sell but which nobody on its scheduled voyage wants to buy. It then unloads into the tanks of a place like Bukom, and immediately reloads from adjacent tanks with what is wanted at its next port of call. In between it probably has to wash out its tanks with sea water and blow them out with steam. One would have thought that careful planning of tanker voyages could have worked out an easier and cheaper solution, but apparently not.

Blending was apparently the lesser of the two operations carried out, but it is at times necessary. Every oil marketing company has its own particular blends, almost certainly not better than anyone else's but of course always claimed to be, and these do differ. Blending is done at every level and on every scale from one of the mammoth tanks in a tank farm, to the tanker lorry on its way to the local petrol station, and perhaps sometimes in an oil drum behind the manager's office. At Bukom it usually took place in the tanker itself. The calculated quantity of each of the constituents would be pumped into the same tank one after another and left to mix as they slopped about in the rolling ship. There is a freemasonry among oil companies as between oil men, and if a company finds itself short of one of its own products, it regularly asks a rival company to make it some. What is sold as the most wonderful petrol in the world from a petrol pump bearing the name of one company is most unlikely to have come from that company's own oilfield, been transported in the company's own tankers, and spent all its existence in the one company's hands. It may be so, but if so it is just a coincidence.

Until the war Pulau Bukom was, by modern standards at least, very small, more than half of the island still being covered with virgin jungle. It fell undamaged into the hands of the Japs, and after they had taken a suitable number of the staff to the end of one of the wharves and cut their heads off, they enlarged it to serve the whole of their 'Co-prosperity sphere'. It remained in perfect working order until after the Japanese surrendered and then the American air force attacked it as they did Sandakan and destroyed both. After it had burned for a week, the Bukom installation was rebuilt and restarted, but Sandakan was a washout and the capital of North Borneo had to be removed to Jesselton where it remains.

I arrived to find a small but attractive little hospital with two long wards but no patients in them, no operating theatre, and no x-ray facilities. Except in an emergency there would be no need for inpatient facilities, Singapore being only twenty minutes launch ride away,and the only useful part of the building was the doctor's office and a small laboratory. The building was already condemned; and under construction on an area of recently reclaimed land was a new clinic whose design my predecessor had not exactly approved but was reputed to have seen and not objected to. I never believed the story and consider it a gross slander on the dead. The new building was one of three, long and thin, two of which were together to make up a new school, and the third appeared to have been designed as a milking shed but was to be called a hospital. The concrete slab for the floor had been poured the day I arrived, so nothing could be done about its shape, but I was able to tear out the whole interior plan and design what must be the longest and thinnest hospital in the world. Management suddenly insisted that it must be called a clinic on the grounds that it was not intended to have beds in it and that a hospital always had beds whereas a clinic did not. (Oil company managers are not taught Greek and have no idea of the meaning of Klinos.) Actually my new design provided for inpatients but I kept quiet over the Greek as I wanted it called a cottage hospital. It was not all that important and I thought I had lost the battle, but it appears I had not and 'Pulau Bukom Cottage Hospital' it remains to this day.

I had to get down to work within minutes of arriving, but next day attended to the routine of putting on a suit and calling to see the Manager. 'Tommy Thompson' was filling in the last few months before his retirement, and although he and his wife (with two children) had been working there when the Japs came, they had worked in almost every Shell area as well. He was a very good sort but very much a company man. I remember him saying 'You may become a very great man but you must always remember that Shell is greater.' I am not quite sure that the few doctors who made the company their careers would not have said the same (and two of them were great doctors) but to me then as now it was sheer heresy as well as being nonsense. He was by way of being if not great, at least a very good and honest man in his job (the combination of goodness at the job and honesty is not easy in oil company management) and one well worth having as a friend, but he was completely overshadowed by his flamboyant wife Hilda.

Hilda was perhaps the most splendid and, if her own stories are to be believed, the most amoral character I have known. She was very far from being immoral, and although perhaps she did not go to Church as often as one might wish, her kindness, sympathy, and generosity made her loved by all who knew her. She had the presence of a dowager duchess, and when she chose could speak and behave like one. At other times her language was calculated to bring a blush to the cheek of an East Coast Road whore, and on at least one occasion did so. Another time on a lavishly provided picnic on an island outside

171

Singapore harbour, a remarkably unattractive Malay oozed up to her and was sent away with a quietly passed ten dollar bill. She leaned over to me and whispered 'That's my little bit of blackmail.' The story she told me was unprintable but a few minutes later her husband also whispered to me 'Hilda doesn't think I know about that man but I do. I am paying him too.' Frankly I did not believe a word of it.

Almost all the disreputable stories about Hilda rest on her own word, but one is very widely believed and appears to be true. She was in a prison camp in Sumatra in 1945, and she claims that on the day after Japan surrendered the camp commandant called a meeting of all the inmates to make friends with them. All previous general assemblies such as this had been for the prisoners to witness one or more of their number being bayonetted to death for some minor misdemeanour, but this time all was sweetness. The Nip announced that the war was over, that all their differences must be forgiven and forgotten, and that they were all friends again.

When he had gone Hilda asked the others what they intended to do to the man. Everybody was frightfully British and forgiving. The poor chap must be terribly depressed at his country being defeated, and it would be grossly unsporting to rub it in. In short they were not going to do anything except be nice to him so that he would not feel it too badly. Hilda said 'Well I am' and went up the steps to his office, the guards bowing politely as she passed. She went in and cut his throat; and the guards bowed again as she came out. It was all very bad form of course: almost 'Non U'.

Some years later returning from the Royal Opera House with Hilda resplendent in a model evening frock, furs and diamonds and looking every inch the dowager duchess, I was seeing her onto the sleeper coach at Euston and asked the ticket inspector where I could get a platform ticket (for Hilda's benefit I called it a 'titform placket') and what it cost. He showed me the machine and telling me that it was still only one penny added that it was the only thing that had not gone up. Hilda looked him straight in the eye and in the accents of Lady Bracknell remarked 'Not the only thing.' The poor man nearly fell through the ground.

The work on Bukom was much the same as at Owerri except that there was little malaria. There were five thousand people on the island, mainly in the two villages, but also a floating population which I estimated at several thousand from the tankers. This figure represented not only those loading or discharging at the wharves or waiting their turn in the anchorage, but also those on their way to us who had sick men aboard waiting to be seen by a doctor as soon as they arrived. We had to have plans for a major disaster such a tanker fire, and of course some major injuries would not live to get to Singapore without emergency treatment on the island. I persuaded the company therefore to let me plan the new hospital with a reasonably well equipped operating theatre, I think three small wards, a small x-ray department and a bloodbank. I collected two bottles of blood every fortnight from the General Hospital in a refrigerated bag, and returned the previous two for their immediate use. The life of one expatriate with a bleeding duodenal ulcer was certainly saved by this before I left.

Changing the blood provided me with an excuse for a day in Singapore every two weeks, and I always managed to find some reason for a visit every other week as well. 'Dr Leong' covered in my absence as ably as before. Indeed as regards treatment of the sick I cannot honestly say that they benefited at all in having me there. I was thus able to visit each of the main hospitals in the colony and meet all the prominent local medical men including Professor Shears who subsequently became the Dominion's first president. Hilda accompanied me on several of these occasions and sometimes took me for lunch to the Tanglin Club. If I was alone I usually had a superb lunch at the Raffles. Shell was incredibly generous about this sort of thing and bills for taxis and meals were paid without question. Indeed they were so in all matters financial, and perhaps it was lack of suitable information that made their medical salaries, while adequate, far from generous. Hospital doctors overseas in those days were paid little more than at home, and I suspect that those who determined company salaries were quite unaware of how much private practice added to every doctor's income. However we were always given first class passages by air or sea, full overseas salary while travelling, living costs in the very best hotels, and generous allowances for expenses on board ship and at purely imaginary stopovers when going by air. They may at times have driven me to the verge of gibbering imbecility or even of murder, but on the whole they dealt very generously with me and as I shall say later I have no regrets that I served with them.

There were some things in Singapore at that time, and for all I know are still there, which are so unbelievable that few writers dare to mention them even when they have seen them with their own eyes. Chief among these are the streets of the dying and the child slave market. There are two small streets in the town which are reserved for healthy people who are going to die within a day or two. The house I visited, which I think was typical, was clean, comfortable, and beautifully furnished. There was one downstairs room containing a coffin, chairs for visitors, and a small dining table. Upstairs was a comfortable bedroom. The elderly lady who had moved in that morning, and was the mother of one of my staff, appeared to be in perfect health, was smiling and cheerful, and acted just as though she was entertaining us in her own home. She, like all the others in the adjoining houses, had decided that it was time to die and had come there to do so. She proudly showed us her coffin, the traditional cabinet-sized portrait that would be put on the front of her hearse, and I think the scrolls which her children would be putting up in her memory in their family shrines. It is said that nobody having come there lives more than four days. There can be no question of poison, otherwise the custom would certainly have been stamped out. These people simply decide to die and do so.

I did not see the so-called 'slave market' (the locals do not call it that but the expatriates did) but I have met many people who have and have no doubt it existed at that time and for twenty or more years after. The buying and selling of children and babies was universal throughout the East, though in Malaysia at least it has now been illegal for about a dozen years and has to be kept reasonably secret. Until then, whenever it was known that a girl was going to give birth to an unwanted baby, there would be queues of people in the hospital bidding against each other. The price was of course higher for a boy than a girl and would represent several month's pay for the buyer. I personally thought and still think it a very good thing. The baby was going from somewhere (perhaps not even a proper home) where it was unwanted, to one where it was wanted very badly and would be loved and well cared for.

When one has paid that sort of money for a thing one treasures it. Once the bargain is struck, proper adoption procedures are followed and the baby becomes the legal child of the purchaser. The buying and selling of older children is perhaps less common but still widespread.

The Chinese are intensely practical people, and it was obviously to everyone's benefit that this trade should be properly organized; so that buyers could make a proper selection of what was offered for sale, and sellers be sure of a fair price. These markets were held about once a month. Singapore was then a Crown Colony and there were two or more British magistrates always present to see fair play and complete the adoption papers, and police to preserve order.

While I was on Bukom one of the Chinese staff died in the Company's service, too soon or too junior to qualify for a widow's pension, but the company offered his widow, who was far from young, a lump sum in consolation. We were at the time demolishing a number of 'Bungsaws' near the installation (small warehouses on stilts over the sea) and she asked instead for one of these to turn into a Chinese Restaurant. It was given to her and after deducting its scrap value, the rest was given her in cash. With this she went over to Singapore and bought six small boys, bringing them back to the island as her legally adopted sons and thus entitled the live there and go to the Company school. She fed and clothed them well, and outside school hours they acted as staff for her restaurant. She did so well that all of them in due course were sent as paying pupils to the Harbour-board school, recognized as the best in South East Asia. If she is still alive, which I would doubt, she will be living with the eldest 'Son' as the loved and honoured matriarch of a huge family. Otherwise there is a scroll to her in each of the six family shrines. We must not judge Chinese customs by the standards of our own much newer and in many ways much cruder civilization.

Although these things still go on they have now, in Malaysia at least, been forced underground, as usual as a result of abuse of an otherwise excellent system by the Americans. Nobody objected to childless American couples coming over to buy a child and take it home as an American citizen. The trouble started when dealers started buying them in quantity for resale at a profit in the United States, and the world press got hold of the story.

☆　　☆　　☆

After nearly six months a new MO was recruited, and very
shortly afterwards reported that the work was too heavy for
one man and was supplied with a junior. He was British but
only half English and the other half French. He had a
charming French wife and two small children. I did not leave
immediately but the night before I sailed home (after they had
both had some time to meet and assess everybody) as I was
getting out of their car at my flat Mrs deRenzy Martin put
both elbows on the seat in front of me, looked me straight in the
eye, and asked 'Tell me Michael, do you think anyone on
Pulau Bukom is quite sane?' It was a good question and one I
had not considered before. I am afraid I floundered. 'Yes of
course, there's old . . . , well perhaps not him but what about
. . . No not him of course but surely . . .'. etc. I still am not quite
sure what I should have answered to such a penetrating and
un-English question.

The deRenzy Martins did not know that they were moving
into a haunted house. Senior bachelors are not easy people to
accommodate. I don't think the company ever really grudged
me a house, but married men are inclined to think that having
a wife and family is something virtuous and presumably
beneficial to the company and entitles them to special privileges at the expense of those whose very bachelor status enables
them to get much more useful work done in the week. I have
always therefore been palmed off with a house nobody else
wanted, which in the East always means one believed to be
haunted.

It does not worry me as any supernatural or spiritual forces I
have encountered have always been harmless or even benevolent. My house, which this young family moved into, was
probably the most attractive on the island, but even so I am
surprised that they took the risk of giving it to a young family
man whom they badly needed to retain. The managers were all
Freemasons and possibly assumed that as the doctor and his
wife were devout Roman Catholics they would not believe in
ghosts: being quite unaware that they would, and would
believe (or according to the teachings of their Church should

176

have believed) that all such phenomena are satanic.

The house was built on a hilltop which, like every hilltop on a small island close to a big town like Singapore, had been used as a Chinese Cemetery. The graves had simply been covered over; but in laying the foundations for the pillars which raised it ten feet from the ground, four coffins had been removed and buried beneath the centre of the building. I had great difficulty in finding servants at all and none would consider staying there after nightfall.

It was my custom every evening to settle in the sitting room with a pot of coffee and a brandy and cigar to listen to one act of a Wagnerian Opera. From where I always sat I could see through the dining room into an archway which opened into the kitchen. In this archway at some time every evening would be an elderly bearded Chinese. He never spoke or moved into the rest of the house, and showed no response if I spoke to him. I doubt even if he was aware of my presence. He was obviously quite harmless and I said nothing to the deRenzy Martins about him, nor to anyone else. There was always the chance that neither of them would be able to see him, as proved to be the case.

I paid them a visit about two years later and very discreetly managed to enquire if they had experienced anything abnormal. I found a situation horribly like that in James' 'The turn of the screw', subsequently made into a nightmare play called *The Innocents*. The interior of the house had been stripped out and rebuilt, so that the haunted archway was now just an alcove in the children's bedroom. Nothing had frightened them and they considered as a great friend the old man who came to see them every night, but asked their parents repeatedly why he never spoke to them. The doctor and his wife were unusually sensible people and, although by then they were, I think, fully aware of the situation, had like me decided that whatever was there was completely harmless. They took great care not to frighten the children, and did nothing about it. It was after all a very nice house and the children were very happy.

I am sure this was the right approach. There are people who are probably completely insensitive to these things as well as others (the spiritualists call them 'mediums') who are hypersensitive and who even attract such phenomena. I think most normal people are essentially neutral but fully aware of spiritual forces, even if from religious motives or because of materialist convictions they close their minds to them. All spiritual entities I have encountered have been as harmless as rabbits, although I believe some exist which are diabolical and as dangerous as tigers. If there were such a one in my house, or a tiger in my garden (as has happened to me in Sumatra) I should take the strongest measures, but I have no objection to rabbits hopping about the lawn and just leave them alone.

I sailed for home two days before Christmas on *MS Wilhelm Ruys*. At that time there were very few Dutch in the Far East although they returned briefly a few years later. The passengers were therefore all British (except for Prince Chula of Siam) but the ship very Dutch and the officers and crew very very Dutch. She had a sistership the *Orange* (nothing to do with the Union Castle/Safmarine vessel later of that name which at that time was *Pretoria Castle*). Actually although they were always called 'Sister ships' they were not identical and in theory were owned by different companies, though I was told that like Evenrude and Johnston motors, the difference was more apparent than real.

Dutch officers do not demean themselves by sitting at tables with the passengers and neither does the Captain. They all sit together at the Captain's table, and nobody in the whole dining saloon is served until they have all taken their seats. On special nights the doors are closed so that nobody can get back to the bar, and the Captain makes a speech in two languages (so that his officers know what he is saying) lasting about half an hour, during which time nobody is served with food or drink. I have travelled on a number of Dutch ships and have learned to bring several bottles down with me so that my table at least can hold a 'Symposium' (drinking together) and if things get too bad, as they did on one occasion, a glee session.

The following year both the *Ruys* and *Orange* were holding a mid-voyage party of this sort, with the Captains each making a long speech with all the officers present and each ship in the charge of a deck apprentice, when they ran into each other (quite literally) off Aden. *Wilhelm Ruys* was able to complete her journey, but *Orange* was very nearly sunk and only just managed to make that rather unattractive port where she stayed for several months for repairs. There were of course some staff changes as a consequence, and my mother sailed about ten years later on a barely seaworthy tramp steamer under the command of one of these former captains.

The Dutch do one proud in a number of ways, and there was a band to see us off from the quay. As this floating chunk of the Nederlands' Indies set sail, the band played *Scotland the Brave*. I had however been brought up, as a result of Nanor's travels every winter, to believe that Christmas at sea was a wonderful experience. On the *Ruys* there was one small Christmas tree in the bar . . . and nothing else. There were no services, no party, and no other decorations. Those who protested were told that the Dutch celebrate St Nicholas day on 6 December instead. Perhaps not all of them subsequently met people who had been on the previous voyage who were told that as all the passengers were English, they now celebrated Christmas. It must have saved the company a lot of money, though there was a lot of expensive noise from the Officers quarters on New Year's Eve (Sylvester Abend). In fairness this ship had a splendid reputation among the travelling English who do know what they should be getting for their money. Apart from the total non-event of Christmas I had no complaints (though others had) and I thoroughly enjoyed the voyage. It appears that, on this voyage only, the crew were on the verge of mutiny (possibly for financial reasons) and that as a consequence the officers were sulking. People who travelled on her a few months later said she was as good as ever.

I have made at least twenty-eight sea voyages not counting the short trips to and from St Helena. Most have been between UK and Hong Kong, Singapore, Bombay, Perth, or Sydney. Several times with the canal closed, I have come home round the Cape, and once only in 1975 through the Panama Canal. I have always maintained that Sea Travel is much cheaper than going by air, and certainly if one is going to have to pay hotel bills at the other end, even today the three, four, five, or six weeks one spends in a first class single cabin with bath and duty-free wines will undercut the cost of the first class air fare and the same period in a good hotel, paying for one's food, wine and entertainment. In the past it was less than the hotel, food and wine alone, and one got the travel and entertainment completely free.

Five times I have been on a ship going through the Suez Canal, and twice I have left the ship to spend the day on the overland trip to Cairo. It is fun riding round the pyramids on a camel, and both these trips were made before the Tutankamun exhibition in London. To anyone who did not see that, a visit to the Cairo Museum is imperative if one is to claim any proper understanding of the history of the western world. On the first occasion I was on *Wilhelm Ruys*, and on completing the day in Cairo we learned that the ship had run out of the channel in the Great Bitter Lake, and we had an extra day in Port Said as well. Similar unexpected delays have marooned me in San Francisco and Marseilles, in each case in the notorious water-front areas; but I found all three a great deal less immoral and offensive than the London of today. Also one has to lunch on the Marseilles waterfront if one is to have a standard of what *Bouillabaisse* should be. Even half a mile inland it is inferior. The same probably applies to *Moules Mariniere*, but I formed my ideas of what it should be like in the days of the dinners at 7 Carnaby Street and find the authentic one insipid.

San Francisco is worthy of special mention. I arrived there in mid-winter and had no intention of going ashore, but shortly after docking I walked past the Pursar's office and saw an advertisement for San Francisco's first Antique dealer's fair. I took a taxi and found it to be about three times the size of the one at Grosvenor House. In San Francisco 'Antique' means anything made before four o'clock the previous afternoon. The rooms were filled with the most amazing junk, from pre-war Box-Brownies to genuine George VIth pepper pots, from souvenirs of the 1948 Olympic Games to spares for the Model T Ford. Bang in the middle was a Hester Bateman cream jug. Somehow it looked familiar. There are always at such shows a few bookshops which sell not only antique books but also books about antiques, so I went to one and looked at the Hester Bateman book. As expected that very jug was illustrated on the dust cover and the frontispiece. Examination of the text showed that she had only made two of that design and that they were of different sizes. I went back to the stall and measured it, finding that it was the very one pictured. It was thus a known piece, and was priced at $500. I had exactly this

180

sum on me in traveller's cheques, and knowing that I could easily sell it the next week in London for £1,500 bought it. It was the only thing in the whole exhibition that I would have considered even worth sending to a Church Bazaar.

I have always joined in things like frog racing and Bingo (at least until I took orders) but the ordinary ship's sports and competitions do not interest me. The only exception is the General Knowledge quizzes. These are very easy to win if one takes the trouble to pick or organize a table properly. One needs to have a Lawyer, a Doctor, a middle-aged lady, a young thing of either sex, and either a ship's officer or someone else who knows something about seamanship. Picking a table like this I have over the years been able to win four times out of five. I can only remember one occasion when a table such as this composed entirely of returning expatriates, was defeated by every television-watching Englishman on the round trip. The question was 'Why do elephants never eat penguins', and the totally incomprehensible answer given 'Because they can't undo the silver paper'.

The only out-door sport I ever indulge in on a ship is clay pigeon shooting, which today is not often available. On one trip from Sydney to Venice on *Marconi*, the ship's newspaper announced one morning 'four pm Clay bird shooting on the first class sport's deck'. I turned up on time to find one steward with a pair of guns and a box of clays, and a rather bored trapman with his trap. I waited half an hour for someone to come and shoot with me, and at four thirty they packed up and went away. The same performance was repeated three times a week for the whole voyage. Two days before arrival at Venice, the paper announced 'Final of the clay bird shooting championship'. I went to the Pursar's office to protest that they could hardly have a final of a championship when only one competitor had ever turned up, and not a shot had been fired. I was told that there had been over fifty entries in the tourist class, and that as a result of stiff competition they had now got it down to the last four. The ship is so large that one could not hear gunfire at the stern, and I should have remembered that all the best and richest Australian farmers, who live with a gun under the arm, travel tourist as they will not dress for dinner or mix with the stuffed shirts who do.

I remarked that it was a bit hard, as had I known I would

certainly have gone down to the tourist class to join them. I was thereupon offered a bye to the final; and although I knew and said that I was not remotely of their competition standard, accepted it just for fun. They put me on first and threw me ten birds of which I killed nine. None of the others got more than eight, so I picked up their silver cup they had been shooting for the whole voyage, and carried it back to the first class. I genuinely expected to be shot in the back, and still don't know why I wasn't. I knew exactly what they were saying.

Although I must have spent a total of nearly two years on board ship, there is little else worth telling about it. The whole beauty of sea travel is that nothing ever happens. Only once have I crossed the Pacific from Australia to Panama, and the incredible experience of crossing the international date line appeared to impress nobody but me. It is incredible all the same. Even at school I had been told about the mythical extra day; and it is mythical: it has no real existence. Day and night are made by God, but this one, insofar as it is there at all, is made by the engines of the ship, and is confined to the ship and those on her. The people behind you in Fiji don't get it. The people ahead in Hawaii don't get it. It has no existence even for the fish in the sea alongside. Yet it looks just like a real day. One get's up, has one's usual three meals, watches the sun set, and even fills in a space one makes for it in one's diary, and yet it has no existence whatever. It is all very odd.

Arriving back in mid-January, I flew off again in May on yet another short-term locum assignment, the last as it happened, to Doha in the Persian Gulf. The three months in between I filled with intensive study and hospital visits for teaching rounds and demonstrations, but managed to maintain my contact with Shell so that I was the first man they thought of when they realized they had a man due for leave and no replacement planned.

Qatar is a little peninsula sticking out from Saudi Arabia, so unimportant that even its border with that country was undefined rather than disputed, and no two maps showed it remotely in the same place. There was only one town worthy of the name, Doha the capital, and another Wakra about thirty miles south which comprised only a brothel and a group of mud huts around it. Until a very few years earlier there had not even been that and the only industry was pearl fishing.

What the bedouin really lived on at that time I have never been able to discover as the tiny Persian Gulf pearls could have had very little sale value and there was not enough fresh water to make much of an industry taking in one another's washing. However by the time I arrived there was an oilfield on the opposite side of the peninsula and the Ruler had an income of about twenty million. This was distributed to the few inhabitants by the simple expedient of giving it away, largely to the bedouin sheiks who passed it on to their own people. Generosity of this sort, and not only to their fellow Muslims, is a characteristic of the Gulf Arab and it is not impossible that in the past the country was getting money from Saudi Arabia. The Ruler would sit at a table outside the palace every afternoon to meet anybody who wanted to speak to him, and if a man wanted money for any good purpose (especially to marry and thereby 'complete his religion') he was given it, usually much more than he had asked for. The result was of course that no Qatarie would accept a job (except oddly as a driver, which like riding a camel was considered a gentlemanly occupation) and even completely unskilled labour had to be imported. Personal domestic service for the Royal Family and the minor sheiks was of course provided by negro slaves, as it is today in Arabia, but even they had to be fed.

It is almost impossible to drill a hole anywhere in the Gulf area without finding oil but until about two years before nobody had bothered to look for it under the sea. Then with almost every square foot of dry land acquired by some oil company, Shell bought a concession on the sea bed and started geophysical and seismic surveying from a ship, the *Shellquest*. The doctor I was replacing had begun as a Ship's Surgeon, and followed them ashore when the seaborne operation came to an end and a permanent camp was established on the outskirts of Doha for drilling crew and their families. The camp was just like an oil camp anywhere else in the world except that every house and every other building was air-conditioned as a unit with a big machine outside in the desert; for apart from the white mud-brick town everything else as far as the eye could see, and for that matter all the rest of Qatar, was white desert. There was the usual clubhouse and the usual tiny hospital, differing only from others in that having been designed one afternoon by Dennis Cousins (who was no surgeon) the very well equipped and furnished operating theatre had been combined with the outpatients consulting room. This would have made sterility a bit of a problem had we ever had any surgery to do, but we never had.

In addition to the usual ritual of calling to see the manager, here I had on my first day to make an official visit to meet the Ruler. As I entered the throne-room he and whole court rose and he held out his hand limply, deftly slipping it out of mine so that I could not grasp it. I drank the necessary three cups of clear brown coffee and then withdrew. The expatriate Government Medical Officer who was with me genuflected as though in the presence of God.

All the government doctors were an odd lot, the oddest of all being the State Medical Officer, the dourest of dour lowlanders into whose head no operation known to surgery could have inserted a joke. With an ambient temperature of 120 to 140 every afternoon he went about invariably in a European-weight three piece suit. He once told me that he was prepared to admit that drinking to excess could be harmful, but drinking in moderation was essential to health in a warm climate. He had drunk his two bottles of whisky a day for forty years and he said he could never have survived without it. I found later that two bottles was only his basic ration, taken strictly for reasons of health, and that he was not averse to unlimited social drinking as well. I called on him once on business at nine in the morning, which is nearing the end of the working day there, when to my personal knowledge he had been up all night at a Shell party. It was Ramadan so he locked the door and opened a drawer of his filing cabinet marked 'State Medical Officer only: Strictly confidential'. It was full of bottles. He put his hand in at random and pulled out what mercifully proved to be only a half bottle, tore off the cap and threw it into the waste paper basket. There were two tumblers on the desk. He poured half into each, threw away the bottle, and pushed one over to me. We started our discussion.

He was an unusual man in other ways. He had spent eight years in the Sudan, where although a bachelor he had a large house with two bathrooms, as I always had. His hobby was anatomy and the second bath was filled with embalming fluid in which he always kept a corpse so that whenever he had a few minutes to spare he could do a bit of dissection. Nobody had

184

ever seen him drunk and indeed he was always stone cold sober.

Work at Doha was essentially the same as at Owerri. There were the expatriate staff and families to visit, and local staff to treat strictly on an outpatient basis. There was only one field party to visit: but as it involved more than an hour's helicopter flying time each way, it too took a whole day once a week. The whole enormous land based operation was maintaining a single drilling rig sixty miles out in the Gulf. Movable floating platforms are a commonplace now but this was the first in the world. It had so far drilled one dry hole and was now at its second location.

This platform did not actually float by itself as some do today (and have therefore to be registered at Lloyds as ships) but was a three storey metal structure supported by huge telescopic legs which could be retracted to allow it to sink down on supporting barges which were floated under it whenever it had to be moved. This design led to disaster the very next time a move was attempted and the whole rig I knew was lost in a storm when the barges went out of control and smashed the legs; but subsequent models were self buoyant. The structure contained a small air-conditioned hotel as well as a helicopter landing platform and on the same level the drilling floor of an Ideal 100 rig. The diesels were there too but the fuel store, mud tank into which mud was constantly gushing out of the hole and from which it was pumped down the drill-pipe, as well as the blow-out preventers were below. Lowest of all, usually only a few feet above water level, was a small jetty to which supply boats could tie up and from which the sporting would fish for shark and parrot fish. I say 'usually' a few feet above water level because the swell in the Persian Gulf can suddenly rise to forty feet, which was what wrecked the whole outfit some months later on her next move.

Probably this job would have been boring if it had not been for the opportunity of seeing Arab life at its most typical before the serious impact of Western culture. I had already seen all the interesting technology of the oil industry (except for the refinement of drilling through the sea) had enjoyed all I wanted of oil-camp life, and got used to travelling by helicopter; although here I did at least have the chance to fly one. Also as a budding surgeon I had already had my fill of general practice and never again wanted to be called to see a neurotic underworked housewife or a snivelling unspanked brat with a cold: but in the few months I was in Doha, the astonishing impact of Arab life made up for it all.

The Ruler gave a dinner party the night before I left for the whole senior staff. There were no tables and we sat cross-legged along one side of a rich carpet about two yards wide and fifty long. The court sat on one side, with any odd sheiks who had dropped in, and we sat on the other. Along the carpet were huge dishes up to four feet long containing whole roast sheep and goats and as the dish of honour a young camel, as well as plates of rice and some weird side dishes. There was no conversation but occasionally our host would throw an eye or other tasty morsel to an honoured guest. We all ate with our hands of course, tearing the flesh from the dishes near to us and passing bits round to others. The heads of the sheep and goats lay scattered round about, and at one point a barefoot negro slave brandishing an axe ran from one end of the 'table' to the other chasing a chicken. Nobody deigned to notice either of them of course.

Less than a week later I was lunching at the Royal College of Surgeons and overheard an Egyptian post-graduate student saying to an Indian 'Yes, camel is said to be a great delicacy but I have never had any.' I was able to lean across the table and say 'I had some last Friday. It was delicious.'

A very aged member of the Royal Family, then in his nineties, had given a smaller party for the Shell bachelors some weeks before to celebrate his recent marriage. He took it upon himself to give them some very well-meant fatherly advice. Speaking through an interpreter he said 'You are each very young now, but some day I hope you will be an old man like me and will take a new young wife. If you are wise you will not sleep with her every night. If you do you will exhaust yourself and make your other wives jealous. You should take them strictly in rotation. In that way you will preserve tranquillity among your other wives, and will look forward all the more to your new wife when her turn comes round.'

The Suez crisis began to loom while I was there and the Ruler was away in Switzerland when Nassar called a general strike against the British throughout the Arab world. Very wisely the Ruler decided to fly home, which gave Shell the wonderful opportunity to avoid the strike by giving everybody the day off, declaring it to be a public holiday to celebrate the return of the Ruler. It was a masterstroke and all would have been well if the Ruler's plane had not broken down at Bahrain. The whole road from the airport to the palace was lined with people waving Qatari flags and Union Jacks, when agitators began to spread the rumour that the Ruler could not come as the accursed British had arrested him in Bahrain. The situation was very ugly and a murderous crowd descended on the British Advisorate in the main square opposite the palace.

They had reckoned though without the very aged father to the Ruler who was Regent and who had run the country long before the British came. He appeared outside the palace gate at the head of his body-guard of twelve slaves, and wielding a double-handed sword with which he went through the crowd like a knife through butter. We had all been told that there was a British Cruiser hull-down on the horizon which would rescue us in an emergency. As loyal subjects of the Crown we accepted the story as duty bound, but I think most of us were amazed when she actually appeared and a landing party of marines marched into the main square in the best tradition of gunboat politics. Of course if it had not been for the old man with his sword, it would have been too late (as it was with General Gordon) but it was a great comfort to see that Britannia still ruled the waves and that these things did really happen, even if sometimes too late.

I was already entered for the very exclusive Royal College course before I started off for Qatar, and had arranged to meet my mother at Rome for a few weeks holiday on the way back: but Shell muffed the dates, and as there was finally less than a week to spare before the course started this was cancelled and I spent just three days at Beirut and another three in Rome by myself. Beirut was then a beautiful city and I have spent several very happy holidays there on my way to and from the East. Central to the European holiday area was the comfortable St George's Hotel within a few yards of the St George's Club and English Church. There were several reasonably safe Arab restaurants nearby where if one took no notice of what was going on upstairs (every third building in the town was a brothel) one could get excellent Arab food and a bottle of arak, the native spirit not unlike absinthe but which is drunk much more diluted and is probably reasonably harmless.

I took a conducted coach tour to Byblos and Baalbek. The coach was full of well behaved Americans but the pleasure of the trip was considerably mared by an ill-mannered Australian woman in the seat ahead with a voice like a hacksaw who asked me to put out my pipe as the smell was making her sick. A few minutes later she and her husband lit up revolting Turkish cigarettes. I leaned over and very politely asked her if she had any objection to my smoking again as she was doing so herself, only to be told that she had no objection to smoking but could not put up with what she elegantly described as 'The stink of that pipe'. To get away from them at Byblos I went into an Arab Cafe and ordered coffee and a Hookah. The wretched woman walked through, saw me sitting cross-legged puffing away, looked at the Hookah, and said 'That's much better' which of course gave her game, set, and match.

The Fellowship course was based on St George's Hospital but included lectures, demonstrations, and clinics all over London. I was not only just the only Englishman present, but virtually the only European. Considering that by then the cost of all medical and surgical education in Britain was borne by the taxpayer (the state having seized, confiscated, or unashamedly stolen the funds with which to provide it), and that falsified but universally accepted government figures showed that Britain had a gross excess of doctors and surgeons, this was not unreasonable. But it was a bit hard on those dedicated young men who had a genuine desire to serve the people of the Empire (which they equated with that of George VI and of the King Emperor of their childhood) and who had no intention whatever of joining the rat race of socialist medicine in the Mother Country. The course was orientated towards the English Fellowship exam, and I think one, and only one, of the others passed. I unashamedly went up to Edinburgh, and passed too.

6

BORNEO SURGEON

Becoming an FRCS marks the watershed in any Surgeons' career. Before that he is just another young doctor. With a Fellowship he has not just got his foot on the bottom rung of a ladder, he is of a different order of creation. A bank clerk who is destined to become the Manager of Securities and Investments in his banking group will experience the same thing when he first becomes a securities' clerk. He may well continue for years in the same branch under the same manager, but he is no longer just another clerk with a chance some day of rising to management. He has ceased to be a banker and become a financier.

The beginning of this chapter thus marks a quantum break in my life. True I did three further relatively short jobs in oil companies and from force of circumstances did a certain amount of general medical work, but I was no longer a General Duties Medical Officer, I was a Surgeon and any other duties were merely to fill in time when there was no surgery for me to do. Furthermore although everything had been arranged (without my knowledge) for me to go to Borneo once more as a locum, I insisted that I be recruited as Shell permanent staff, which means I must have decided by then to make a career overseas rather than in the Health Service. Even so the Borneo appointment was said to be only temporary, as it in fact proved. I managed to shoot the Bisley meeting and flew off at the end of September.

The Shell operations in Borneo started three years before the Great War at Miri in Sarawak, where I spent most of this tour, but I went first to Seria in the tiny independent Sheikdom of Brunei. The much bigger Seria oilfield there was only discovered in 1929, allegedly as the result of the Miri Manager riding his horse along the beach there on a Sunday morning and seeing an oil seepage. There was now a huge Shell area extending for over eight miles along the coast from the little town of Kuala Belait at the mouth of the Belait river to the Oilfield itself. There were then two or three oil platforms a few hundred yards offshore (so close that they were served by cable cars instead of helicopters) but most of the wells and drilling rigs were on dry land. A producing well does not require a permanent derrick over it and can receive occasional maintenance from a travelling portable rig, though some had a structure smaller than most drilling rigs mounted permanently.

There was a small clinic in the working area and another for women and children about two miles nearer the town. The hospital, which had five doctors and specialists on its staff, was in the town of Kuala Belait, as was my house, and in between were the Company offices, expatriate houses, and a lavishly fitted Club and Hotel. The club swimming pool was perhaps the best in South East Asia. I still had some general duties in the clinics, but there was almost a fulltime Surgical practice, and I was very happy there. Wards and theatre were well equipped and there was always a qualified specialist anaesthetist (with the FFA diploma).

There was one rather sad case that deserves mention. A young Dyak made the six week journey down river to apply for a job with Shell and was directed to the recruiting office. When he was almost there, walking along the sea wall where a lighter was being loaded, a load of oil drums being swung out by a crane broke his leg and lobbed him out into the South China Sea. A small boat was launched, and he was fished out and brought to the hospital where a nail was put into his femur. While he was recovering a member of Staff Department visited him in the ward, put him on the company payrole, and started his sick pay. As soon as he was fit to work he was sent back to the recruiting office to sign the necessary papers. Lest he be knocked down by another load of oil drums it was thought safer to send him in the back of a Land Rover. It wasn't. The poor man had never travelled in anything faster than a canoe and knew nothing of inertia and relative velocities. Seeing a friend at the roadside, he stepped out at sixty to have a word with him and was back within half an hour to have a nail put in his other femur.

Staff department sent another recruiting officer to get him to sign the papers in his bed, so that when recovered he could be put straight onto a safe job close to the hospital in case he should need it again. In due course he was sent to do his first morning's work sweeping out a storm drain. It should have been a very safe place, being an underground pipe six feet in diameter. There was nothing to knock him down, nowhere for him to fall, and nothing to fall on him. It was the dry season and only a trickle of water at the bottom of the pipe. Every drain in a refinery area or an oilfield though is liable to have traces of oil in it and petrol vapour around it. It was a long walk, and just before the end he stopped to light a cigarette. For all practical purposes he was standing in the barrel of a seventy-two inch gun. This time he was blown a full quarter of a mile out to sea, and they had to launch a somewhat larger boat to bring him back. As they hoisted him aboard he announced that he had had enough and was resigning. After a week or two recovering from flash burn he returned up river having been on the payrole for over five months without having done a stroke of useful work.

There is an apocryphal story of another Shellman who was on the payrole for a quarter of a century without working. He was said to have been an expatriate recruited in 1941 who arrived in Seria just in time to be caught by the Japanese. His salary was of course paid monthly until his release at the end of the war when, unlike Lindsey Webster, he was sent home on leave until there was a job ready for him. He was noticed again when he reached sixty-five, when despite his protests he was retired on pension.

In spite of all Lindsey Webster had told me about Miri, I was sorry when the time came for me to leave Kuala Belait hospital to go there.

My Amah and I travelled to Miri by road with all our luggage and household equipment in the back of a Pickup and my little dog on my knees. As we passed the customs post on the Brunei/Sarawak border, we waved to the revenue officers and they waved back. I found I had been given a beautiful elevated timber bungalow, not even haunted, in a nicely planned camp on the peninsula at the mouth of the Miri river. There was nothing else on this peninsula except the Hospital and Golf

191

club (and of course the usual Shell hotel for visitors) and the town was on the mainland approached by a chain ferry).

My first sight of Miri hospital was a bit of a shock, Lindsey Webster having described it as the finest in SE Asia. I soon realized he was referring to the standard rather than to the quality of the buildings. There was a solid concrete-built central unit of offices, laboratory, consulting rooms, and operating theatre, from which five long wards (open plan with covered ways and in fact merely long wooden sheds) radiated out like the fingers of a hand. The work load was tremendous, serving as it did not only all the Shell staff of Miri and the Lutong Refinery about five miles away, but the entire population of the fourth and fifth divisions of Sarawak. The medical staff comprised two only but they were almost always specialists (a Surgeon and a Physician) and they worked entirely as consultants. The general duties were performed by superbly trained 'medical assistants', who as I have said in an earlier chapter are usually better at such work than a newly qualified doctor. My outpatient dresser subsequently became prime minister. He was better at that too than any we had in England then or for many years to come.

It was at Miri that I first learned to be a surgeon as distinct from learning surgery. The hanging judge knows that he can always be overruled, the hangman only obeys orders. In spite of what he is told at his ordination, a priest has little doubt that if he wrongly refuses absolution the matter will be corrected by higher authority; but the Surgeon is on his own. If he kills he kills.

The true General Surgeon, like the true General Practitioner is extinct in Britain and in most developed countries, but like him survives in developing countries and in small hospitals run by missions and oil companies. He has nothing in common with the so-called general surgeon elsewhere who merely treats, and in many countries is only permitted to treat, those few conditions that the surgical specialities do not want. In most countries this means hernias, varicose veins, the spleen (which is the only abdominal organ which does not interest the Gastro-enterologist the urologist or the Gynaecologist) and quite wrongly the thyroid gland. Even haemorrhoids are now considered to belong to the Proctologist, and the Thymus to the Thoracic Surgeon. Most surgical skin conditions are considered to belong to the Plastic Surgeon, and even the tonsils to the Ear Nose and Throat specialist. In many countries these absurd restrictions have the force of law, and a surgeon who operates outside his field may be prosecuted and/or struck off the register. The ultimate absurdity is the inclusion in 'General Surgery' of the thyroid, an organ which should never be approached by anyone who has not made a profound study of it. I would be very willing to let a competent true General Surgeon operate on my stomach, prostate, or even gall-bladder, but there are certainly not three men in the world today whom I would willingly allow to explore my thyroid.

The true General Surgeon is a specialist in his own right, and it is the most demanding of all specialities. He needs to have an answer ready for every possible surgical problem, and the skill lies in having only one answer and being an expert in that one operation. In my last hospital I probably did twenty Gastrectomies every year. Almost every Gastro-enterologist has designed a new gastrectomy of his own, but he also keeps at his fingertips eight or more other essentially different operations from which he chooses the best for each particular case. One hopes he does each equally well, and as he is a specialist in a very limited field, he can be expected to do them all very well. If a General Surgeon such as myself tried to select from twenty different operations for each of the twenty cases he does in a year, he would do them all equally badly. Over the years I developed and standardized an operation (not exactly that described in any textbook) which I was able to do well and which if not always the ideal choice, was a very satisfactory procedure for every patient needing to have his stomach out.

It was the geography of Sarawak which made the surgery at Miri so wonderful. Patients from the upper reaches of the Baram River and the Kalabit Plateau had to undertake a six weeks' journey to get there, and tended to wait until they had something really worth treating. I had some of the most enormous goitres and spleens to remove that I have ever seen. One girl of twenty had certainly the largest thyroid I have treated, and would willingly have kept it had she not wanted to get married and her intended told her to get it removed. It proved an error. With the huge swelling gone she became a very pretty girl, and when I said goodbye to her and wished her every happiness in her coming marriage, she paused thoughtfully and then said that she wasn't going to get married just yet as she felt she was worth much more now and was going to look for a much better young man.

Disasters of this sort were not confined to native bachelors. A Shell man who wanted to marry a girl from home had to pay her fare out but it was refunded by the company as soon as she qualified as his wife. One unfortunate of my acquaintance paid for his girl to come by sea and had the wedding arranged for the day of her arrival. Instead she married one of the officers on the ship, leaving my friend nearly three hundred pounds out of pocket.

Another young woman arrived from the Kalabit Plateau with a harelip baby. She held a handkerchief to her mouth all the time and when I asked her why, removed it to reveal that she had a complete harelip herself. I suggested that I should do both on the same day but surprisingly she demured. After gazing long and fondly at her offspring she evidently decided that if the worst came to the worst she could easily get a replacement where that one came from, and said that she would wait and see how I got on with the baby first. Actually for the reasons given I was much more experienced and successful with adult cases, but I got an excellent result with the baby and mother then agreed to the operation on herself. She too got a perfect result, but left on her six week journey home with the handkerchief still clutched to her mouth. She had known nothing else all her life and would have felt naked without it.

I was having a very heavy clinic one morning when the telephone rang and a caricature of the voice of the music-hall Scotch comedian said 'Ma name's John Hector MacSporran.' I was not in the mood and before banging the thing down shouted 'And mine's John **** Bull and I'm in the middle of examining a patient.' A few minutes later it rang again and an apologetic voice but with a nasty hard edge to it said 'Arm vera vera sorry, but ma name really is John Hector MacSporran, and arm Her Majesty's Resident at Marundi.' Incredibly he was not even the only one. There were two of them in the same Colony.

Most of the time at Miri my opposite number was a recently recruited physician named Peter Abbott, as keen as I was, and we sometimes forgot that we were really working for Shell and not just for humanity in general; once with disastrous consequences. We had a few days' notice of the visit of an immensely senior member of management, and rejoiced in the discovery that we were completely full up with really worthwhile cases. We proudly took him round, showing him all the wonderful work which was being done, confident that he would be impressed by the value the company was getting for its money. Not being commercially minded however there was one vital point we had overlooked. At the end of his tour the great man said 'Yes, very good. But tell me, how many of these patients are Shell?' Our two jaws dropped simultaneously: we had never given the matter a thought. Investigation revealed that although the hospital was full to capacity and working flat out, there was not a single company patient in it. As a result we were ordered to reduce the number of our beds, and hence the amount of expensive work we could do, and arrangements were put in hand to give the hospital to the Government in return for services rendered to the company and paid for on an item by item basis. Thus ended 'The finest Hospital in South East Asia'.

I think I was happier at Miri than in any other place I have lived and worked. I was young and at last, having found the tropics suited me, fit. I was working perhaps an average of eighty hours a week but found time to enjoy life as well and to make occasional shooting trips into the jungle where there was pig, Chinese pheasant, pigeon, and the occasional clouded leopard. I carried a birdshot cartridge in the left barrel of my gun and one loaded with nine 'SG' slugs in the right for dangerous game (and a surgeon who treats the local sportsmen knows that pig is dangerous game). The clouded leopard was not really dangerous and asked only to be left alone. I once met one face to face while walking up a pig in a deep track in thick jungle grass. We could both see that a pig had passed that way, but his nose told him which way it had been going, and I must have been walking in the wrong direction. It was an embarrassing situation for both of us. I didn't particularly want a clouded leopard skin and it is not healthy to molest leopard with only one lethal shot available. He only wanted to get on after his pig. (They don't eat people.) After a long pause he obviously decided that one pig was very like another, turned round and ambled off. I let him go.

Of course as the only surgeon I could not be out of touch with the hospital on these occasions but I was able to borrow a Jeep with a radio telephone installed. The Jeep would be parked at the point where I entered the jungle, with a small boy on board with a blank-cartridge pistol who would fire two shots if a call came for me. I was sometimes accompanied by the future prime minister who was a superb shot and owned a fine English sidelock. Unfortunately he saw himself rather as the head keeper helping a shortsighted elderly duke, and would never fire until I had missed with both barrels; when he would apologetically pick off the bird for me at about fifty yards.

Another attraction of Miri was that it was not all Shell. There was a *Punch* story of a Yorkshireman returned from his first trip to London saying to his wife '*Eee London's a woonderful* place. Believe me Martha, there's folk in *Loondon to'ome t'Co-op* means *nowt.*' There were folk in Miri to whom Shell meant *nowt*, and they were refreshing company.

After some months, news arrived that the man who was to have replaced me had been forced into resignation (he had dared to criticize the facilities and to recommend that a qualified anaesthetist be appointed), and the Chief Medical Officer made a special visit from Seria to offer me his post, which I accepted with alacrity. At last I had a first class job in the tropics with a delightful house attached. I spent every penny I had and all I could borrow on buying carpets and furniture, and even asked a girl to marry me and come out to share it. When everything was perfect (except the proposed wedding) a member of management got drunk at a party and blurted out 'Of course Crook only thinks he is staying here. Actually he is going to be posted to Indonesia.'

Indonesia under Sukarno was at that time the most unwanted posting in the world. The Shell operation there had always been entirely Dutch but the Indonesian Government had refused to allow it to continue unless it could show 'more tangible evidence of being an international rather than a Dutch company'. It is just possible that the operation could have succeeded if Dutch staff and management had been pulled out completely and replaced by British almost overnight; but this was not acceptable to the controlling interest which was almost completely in the hands of the Dutch Royal Family. On the contrary the intention was to retain the Dutch stranglehold on management and staff, while going through the motions of bringing in British personnel. The result was an unheard of rate of resignations among staff posted there, which was the reason for the lies which I had been told. It was felt that if I was given the longest possible time to integrate myself professionally and financially into the Shell machine, there was more hope that I would decide I could not afford to leave. Standards of housing, salary scales, leave entitlement, sanitation, and even medical care and welfare services, had always been far below those of the British side of the group, and it had always been policy that nobody from the Dutch side who had visited a British area should ever be allowed back in Indonesia to report what he had seen. The idea was strangely like the attitude of Stalin to Russians who had accidentally been allowed to see the true situation in the decadent bourgeois countries.

I did at least get the usual sea voyage back and wasted some months in the London office waiting for a visa. I was sent to Holland with about twenty others who were in much the same boat on what was called an 'Orientation Course' at the Tropical Institute in Amsterdam, to learn something of the language and the Dutch way of doing things. I knew there was no future in my trying to learn a language (although they did give me a diploma in 'Bahassa Indonesia') and on Rupert Scott's advice spent much of my time investigating conditions and way of doing things at various Dutch hospitals. I was not impressed. The Dutch doctors and surgeons were very polite and helpful, but I probably learned most from a young English anaesthetist who was the wife of one of the junior doctors and had set up what she claimed was the only modern anaesthetic unit in the country. There were some astonishing differences between their approach to surgical matters and our own. There was very little attempt to control haemorrhage during an operation but enormous care was taken over accurately measured blood replacement. Swabs would be taken by the handful from a drum, weighed before use, and then weighed again as soon as they had become soaked. I watched this procedure for some time, fascinated at the enormous amount of blood spilled and replaced in what with our technique could easily have been a bloodless operation, before it struck me that I could not see where and when all these swabs were being counted. I asked my English friend about this.

'They never count swabs' I was told.

'But do they never lose one in a patient?'

'Yes. Frequently.'

It was with great difficulty that I managed subsequently to get a Dutch theatre staff to introduce swab counting. It was something they had never done before and to demand it was seen as a reflection on the Dutch Empire. However they had never before met a man who lost things as I do; and when the Matron one morning had found and retrieved from different corners of the hospital my pipe, my tobacco pouch, my stethoscope, my pen, and my Rolex, she announced in the staff common room that she understood now why British surgeons needed their swabs counted. Everyone laughed and honour was satisfied.

The centre of the Shell operations in Southern (Indonesian) Borneo was a little town called Balikpapen. The town itself comprised some former Dutch colonial houses, now squalid and dilapidated, a large but ill-equipped Government Hospital with all-native staff, a substantial civil Government Office building, and an army base from which an entirely independent military administration was carried out. The main trouble with Indonesia at that time was that nobody could agree as to who was in charge. Officially there was a civil administration run through the Government Offices; but there was also a quite separate administration run by the police, who paid lip service only to Sukarno's Government. In addition the army considered it was in charge and the marshal law administrators paid lip service to nobody. We all had to carry no fewer than sixteen different residence and work permits issued by the various authorities, and entry and exit visas had to be obtained separately from the army, police, and civil administration. At times the situation became Gilbertian. The army set out by sea to make a raid on one of the five rebel armies on another part of the coast. Emigration solemnly checked them out (one needed emigration permits to visit other parts of Indonesia and the army were not exempt) and Customs immediately confiscated their ammunition as it had not been dutied on coming into the country. Immigration thereupon refused to re-admit them without the usual month-long formalities, and they were obliged to sail for rebel territory with guns but no bullets. I am told they left looking less confident of success than they had been.

The oil camp at Balikpapen was much the same as others but more shoddy. The houses were large as the overseas Dutch have large families though they seldom succeeded in raising many children in Indonesia. Sanitation was medieval with open sewers alongside every house and road and even within the hospital. There was a club and a cinema, subject to rules of protocol suggestive of feudal times. Every two weeks or so an official party was held at the club. Wet or fine all the members formed a queue outside and slowly paraded in to shake hands with the Manager and three or four of the lesser gods. The party lasted exactly for the stipulated time, after which the Manager would announce loudly that he was going, and everybody would stand up and bow. Until then nobody was allowed to leave but at that point everyone MUST leave, even if only to walk round the corner and then return for the usual drunken evening. I was working almost as hard as at Miri and my night round seldom took less than two hours. I was always sent for the next day and told that my absence had been 'Noted'.

Not all the customs which had been accepted in the Neder-lands' Indies from time immemorial found ready acceptance with the newly arrived English. The routine visit to see the Manager had more practical purposes than in other areas. In particular each newcomer would have impressed on him his exact social status, and be given a list of others in his own salary bracket whom he was permitted to know socially. To drink with an inferior was as much a company crime as to make a pleasant remark to a superior. An English under-manager had been appointed in the first few days of the British invasion, and a little later his chief came to him in great perplexity asking 'What does it mean when they say "Put it where zer monkey put zer nuts"?'

One of the endearing things about Indonesia is that they drive on the left of the road. Up to the fourteenth century people drove on whichever side they pleased or down the middle but in order to avoid traffic chaos in Rome during the first Holy Year of 1300, Pope Boniface VIII declared that all civilized men should drive on the left. Nobody questioned this until the age of revolution. The Americans then began to drive on the right to be anti-British and the French to be anti-clerical, and Napoleon carried the pernicious doctrine wherever he conquered, including Holland. In spite of the Dutch claiming they have ruled the Nederlands' Indies for four hundred years (and the Indonesians talking constantly of four centuries of Dutch misrule) the only time there has been anything like a civilized central government was during the British occupation. Sir Stanford Raffles told them that the only gentlemanly side to drive was the left: and it has remained the rule ever since even under Sukarno. Unfortunately in Raffles' day there were no road signs, and when they came in they were placed on the right as they are in Holland. It did not matter all that much with slow moving bullock carts on narrow roads, but it makes life a little difficult with fast moving motor traffic in Djkarta's six-lane double carriageway roads to have all the signs on the far side of the opposite carriageway.

Another traffic problem was that with three authorities each claiming to be running the country, not only Sukarno but the army commander and chief of police each claimed absolute priority. When one of them sounded his siren all other vehicles had to stop. An excitable Indian once described to me what happened when they all arrived simultaneously at a crossroads. 'Sheer bloody chaos man – they all got out, sat on the grass and cursed the Dutch.'

Like every oil camp in the world, Balikpapen was provided with a magnificent golf course. I know now that the Lord does not intend me to play golf, but at that time I still considered it my social duty to try to learn. I had made a half-hearted attempt at Miri with borrowed clubs and once broke a hundred (for nine holes). I never enjoyed the game. I didn't mind playing my second from behind the tee. It was regularly having to play my fourth from behind the tee that got me down. This time though I decided to treat the matter more seriously and before leaving had gone to the sports department at Austin Reed's to buy a bag and a complete set of clubs. I should have taken it as an omen that I laid out and almost killed their professional before I had actually got a club into my hands. The poor man selected for me a steel-shafted driver (a thing fortunately with a wooden head) and waggled it about in an expert manner. There was a sharp crack as the head shot up into the air and descended onto the back of his neck, laying him out cold. Had I taken the hint I would have abandoned the idea there and then, and much misery to the secretary at Balikpapen would have been avoided. Although it sounds improbable there were several witnesses to say that I had driven a ball between his ears. He was quite unhurt, but begged to be allowed to return my subscription if I would call the whole thing off. I readily agreed on condition that he would find someone to buy my clubs, which he did to the satisfaction and relief of all concerned. I did in fact win a trophy there in the annual championship (the booby prize of a set of snakes and ladders) and was only too pleased to be able to retire at the pinnacle of my fame.

It was at Balikpapen that I first met 'The Rev Bev' though he has since become a lifelong friend. Beverley Coleman was, before he heard the call, a tenor with D'Oyley Carte and almost certainly the only vicar in history who has had the courage to sing *The Ghost's High Noon* in the presence of his Bishop. (On another occasion, when there was a discussion on the correctness of Pectoral as against Ventral Crosses and the rather stout Bishop of Singapore expressed doubts as to which his was, Beverley said 'It is Pectoral when your Lordship is standing but becomes Ventral when your Lordship sits down.') He had been an army Padre in Malaya during the emergency when even non-combatants were required to carry side-arms. He gives a wonderful description of the scene in the officer's mess somewhere in Malaya when his automatic pistol slipped from his pocket and put a bullet through his knee joint behind the ligamentum patellae but without touching the bone, a miracle of the first magnitude in itself. The Sergeant Major stood at the door of the mess-tent and shouted 'Stretcher party . . . the Padre's shot himself.'

Beverley was at that time 'Vicar of Java with Sumatra'; his parish being the largest in the world and including Indonesian Borneo. He had ninety-two million parishioners, not all of them Church-going Christians. Nevertheless it is a vicar's duty to visit everybody in his parish regularly irrespective of whether he comes to Church. Had Beverley done so and talked to each for a mere ten minutes, one round of his parish would have taken him about 1,700 years working day and night and without allowing for eating, sleeping, or travelling time. Even so he managed to appear regularly everywhere services were wanted, and I came to know him even better when I went to Rumbai in Sumatra. I have recently visited him in retirement in South Wales where he thinks nothing of driving two hundred miles for a day's chalk-stream fishing.

A surgeon is in an immensely strong position in any isolated community and I was probably better treated by the Dutch as well as by the Indonesian authorities than any of the other British.

Even so Balikpapen was not a pleasant posting. I was neither wanted nor welcomed by the Dutch doctors: facilities were poor and many decades out of date: and all requests for improvements needed to be approved by the Medical Department in Holland. They were not. Anaesthesia was murderously old-fashioned, consisting of induction for adults as well as children with ethyl chloride poured onto an open mask, and then maintained with ether and air from a vaporizer. Modern major surgery is impossible in such conditions, and yet much major surgery was required. A request for the simplest of anaesthetic machines was turned down on the grounds that the CMO in the Hague (a man with no surgical or anaesthetic training even by Dutch standards) had once in his student days seen a death from the use of Laughing gas. He was of course senior to any of us in the company and his opinion had to be accepted without question; so that expatriates as well as locals even with appendicitis or a perforation had to submit to this barbarous, inadequate, and dangerous anaesthetic procedure, or die from want of surgery.

In their own country the Dutch, like the Irish and perhaps even the Australians, are charming and unbelievably courteous. You can stop a working man in the streets of Amsterdam to ask your way in English, and he will not only be delighted to tell you in your own language, but if the directions are at all complex will walk far out of his own way to guide you. In one of the many restaurants in Holland where six or more men sit at the same table, they will not speak first to you as they know that the English do not like being addressed by strangers; but as soon as you sit down they will stop conversing in their own language and talk to each other in English so that you will not feel left out. I can't imagine this happening anywhere else in the world, even among the Chinese.

The overseas Dutch are a different proposition however, and

202

in Indonesia for a very remarkable reason. In Holland every Dutchman considers that if all else fails, the Nederlands' Indies owes him a living. If he cannot even get a job as a labourer at home he goes there and is given one. Even in my time the Dutch manager in Djakarta employed two Dutch gardeners. Over a period of about four hundred years, the worst of each generation in Holland went out to what is now Indonesia, and the best few of each generation raised there returned to Holland. There was thus a process of Darwinian evolution in reverse, and the Indonesian 'Dutch' were the result of four hundred years of survival of the least fit. No similar process occurred in South Africa, and there was I think a further difference. Almost all Indonesian Dutch, like the Africanders, have the very pale blue eyes indicative of a slight admixture of Teutonic with 'Malay' blood, but that in Indonesia was essentially Javanese while in South Africa it is due to breeding with their truly Malay slaves who are a quite different race. (The Afrikaaners and the Cape Coloured are essentially the same people differing only in skin shade and hence presumably in amount of non-European blood. The very few South African Hollanders despise both equally.)

The Dutch doctors decided among themselves (they were the only so-called Dutchmen I have met who did not invariably speak English in my presence) that not only should I be on continuous call for surgery but that I should look after all expatriate outpatients and emergencies twenty-four hours a day, seven days a week. In fairness I suspect it had been forced upon them in respect of the British staff and their families and they felt I might as well do the Dutch as well. It soon became essential if I was not to have murder on my conscience for me to offer to take over the paediatric ward as well. The mortality there (which I was able to reduce by four-fifths) was quite appalling, due entirely to ignorance of the physiology of a sick child or a sick baby. The standard treatment for a child with fever, diarrhoea, and vomiting was to wrap it up in blankets and feed it with cold tea. By simply putting up a drip, stripping the child, and sponging with cold water, I was able to save every one that came my way. Even the nurses were impressed, but a Dutch doctor took it upon himself to bring me one of their textbooks to prove that all these children were suffering from a mythical condition called 'Toxicacie' and that my

203

treatment was entirely wrong and was certain to kill one before long. He was genuinely hurt when I pointed out that even if I killed the next twenty, my results over the three month period would be vastly better than when he was in charge of the ward.

I would certainly have resigned from Shell rather than go to Indonesia (as I made quite clear at the time) if I had not been given by Rupert Scott a written promise that if I went there for six months he would 'move heave and earth' to get me an overseas appointment where I 'would be THE surgeon'. In my innocence I assumed that as he was the departmental head and it was on Company paper the law would require that it be honoured by the company. After having given up my last chance of a consultantship in the Health Service and gone through something like hell for more than six months in Indonesia, I was advised by the solicitor to the Medical Defence Union that it was not worth the paper it was written on. I keep it by me all the same, for a variety of reasons.

For most of my time in Balikpapen I was the only Englishman in the Medical Department but I was joined for my last few months by Ronny Houston from the London Office, a very able and hard-working young physician whom I suspect found life there no easier than I did. His wife was a devout Roman Catholic and he would frequently come to Mass with both of us (I had strong inclinations in that direction in those days) even though he like me was not of that Church. Ronnie had been a regular full Colonial in the RAMC before joining Shell and on account of his rank was treated at the same time with the greatest respect and the greatest suspicion by the Indonesian authorities. He was loved though by the patients who in addition to getting a standard of medicine unknown to them in the past, were at last getting some degree of twentieth century obstetrics and child-care. He was somewhat embarrassed however by an announcement in the local press of the birth of a baby concluding 'With grateful thanks to Our Lady and St Jude; ably assisted by Dr Ronald Houston'. During his time in the army he had been a medical attache to the Court of Addis Ababa. The Emperor awarded him The Order of The Lion of Judah second class, which I always referred to as 'The Order of Chastity, second class'. (There really is a second class in the Order of Chastity. It makes my imagination boggle.)

By the time I left it was clear that all my efforts to introduce twentieth century British standards and methods had failed. The Dutch Chief Medical Officer came to see me off at Djakarta airport and we fell to talking about my efforts to introduce analgesia in childbirth which he described as 'a dangerous experiment'. As it was then more than a hundred years since it was used on Queen Victoria, I maintained that it could really be regarded as an established technique, but to no avail. It was fifteen years since Indonesia had become an independent nation, and four since the British began to be sent there to prove to the Indonesian Government that it was an international company, but his last words to me were 'We quite understand that your methods are different to ours, but we are not satisfied that they are any better; and you must always remember that this is a Dutch Company operating in the Nederlands Indies, and we have no intention of changing our ways.'

Although I escaped from Shell early in 1960 with no great love for the company or its management, I think my dislike was not so much for them as for the whole of really Big Business and the sort of people who run it. I am myself a successful capitalist, and I am able to distinguish between the system and the morality of those it employs and gives rise to. I have no hard feelings for Shell, and as a Christian try to forgive those whom I met among its management who did dirt to me (which I must forgive) and to others (which is harder). They are all dead now and either they have repented, or it is too late. 'When a man is at rest, let his remembrance rest.'

Even so Shell did me great service for which I am very grateful. I believe that every man is made for and called to a vocation: one special nitch in God's plan for the world for which he is required and to which he is guided. Men are called to that special place prepared for them in very different ways, probably because of the differing natures with which they have been created, each for a different purpose. I was guided to see and to follow the Shell notice on the medical school wall that afternoon in 1951 and everything that happened to me while with Shell was part of that plan, to carry out the duties assigned to me at that time, and to prepare and fit me for what was to come. When the time came for me to leave the company and follow the call elsewhere it was not for me to blame any of those who brought these things about. We should not blame

Judas Iscariot for taking the action without which Man's salvation could not have been brought about in the way it was, according to God's plan.

I left Shell with what amounted to a 'Golden Handshake' of three months salary over and above that for my leave entitlement, and more than a year later they made me a further substantial payment arising out of a retrospective large salary increase for those who remained on their payrole. This money, with a similar payment from another oil company, formed the basis of my very modest fortune which, suitably invested, enabled me to work for twenty years in a Government hospital for less than my expenses, and to retire to a non-stipendary job with the Church. Working for Shell gave me all this, plus the experience which made me a surgeon instead of just a theorist, and it saved me from finishing up as an unhappy third-rate consultant in the NHS. I am profoundly grateful.

☆ ☆ ☆

News travels fast on the oil company grape vine and I was approached almost simultaneously by Caltex, who wanted a surgeon in Sumatra, and by British Petroleum who wanted me to go back to Doha. Going back to Indonesia was one of the last things I would have fancied, without the added horror of working for and among Americans: but I had met the retiring CMO of that hospital on the ship returning from my last job, and had learned some things which made it sound very attractive. My meeting with him was not felicitous as I was at that moment ordering a round of drinks for my table and invited him to join us. While waiting for them to arrive I was telling the story of the midshipman in 'The Cruel Sea' who having come aboard drunk was asked by the Number One what he had been drinking and said 'Creme de Menthe Frape' (The Number One was disgusted and said 'That's a whore's drink', to which the boy replied 'Yes sir; She suggested it'). It was sheer bad luck that when I asked the good doctor's charming young wife who arrived a moment later what she would drink she replied 'Creme de Menthe Frape'.

Caltex welcomed me with open arms, even when on being asked to provide blood to enable them to do a Wasserman test for syphilis, I tactlessly suggested that there would be more point in doing it after my service in an American oil camp than before. They took it in good part and generously promised to do it again for me when I left. I was appointed at a salary nearly twice what I had been getting from Shell, and settled down to wait the inevitable three months for a new Indonesian visa. This just enabled me to comply with the request from British Petroleum.

BP was not directly involved in the problem. It was the surgeon at the magnificent new Government Hospital who was sick, having been invalided to London with very severe hepatitis from which it was known he would be incapacitated for three months. This meant that there was no surgical care nearer than Bahrain, not only for the Qataries, but for the staff of the Shell oil camp at Doha and at the BP camp on the other side of the peninsula. Shell accepted the situation with equanimity, but the local BP manager cabled their London office that a locum replacement had to be found, and they recruited me on behalf of the Government. I signed my contract with Caltex and flew off to Qatar once again.

This time it was winter and the climate in the Persian Gulf (which for a brief period, for reasons known only to their own good selves, HMG was calling 'The Arabian Gulf' although it had been the Persian Gulf or Sinus Persicus to everyone else since the time of Ptolomy) was cool but a good deal better than I should have had to endure in London. I lived in a very pleasant government rest house about a hundred yards from the hospital which had been designed to be better than the London Clinic and had certainly cost a great deal more. It was a magnificent building designed as usual by someone who had vast experience as an architect, but had never designed a hospital before. This is always the case because hospitals are always so badly designed that the man who has done it is never asked to design a hospital again. Actually architecturally it was the best modern hospital I have encountered. The few serious errors were obviously dictated by those who ordered the building or were those of the specialists employed to install whole units like the x-ray department and the operating theatres. When the vast majority of patients have never seen any form of plumbing nor a sheet of toilet paper, it is a mistake to provide nothing but one or two bedded wards, each with its western bathroom and sanitation. Every patient brought in with him a supply of stones with which to wipe himself, and if the loo was not completely blocked with these before he died or was discharged, his friends and relatives would bring him more.

The design of the operating theatres had been handed over lock, stock and barrel to the greatest of all London instrument makers. They had done magnificently, but with no regard to the day to day needs of a surgical team. It was in the days before 'disposable' sterile equipment (which often costs more than the old re-usable equipment which only needed to be washed and boiled) and there was nowhere within a hundred yards of the operating theatres where it was possible to boil up a catheter. It had to be done in the electric kettle of the sisters' office on the other side of the hospital, and brought to theatre wrapped in a sterile towel, rather like a waiter bringing a piece of hot toast wrapped in a napkin.

The whole of the top floor comprised a Royal Suite with the master sick-room provided with a spiral staircase behind the bed leading to a room below for ladies of the court. I am thankful to say that I never had to treat a patient so senior that he was nursed there. I fear he might have burst his stitches.

On the whole Arabs make good patients and, with good staff and superb equipment, the hospital was a pleasure to work in. What made this very short appointment memorable however was making a wonderful friend in my Registrar. Michael Fuad was an Egyptian Roman Catholic, and even after a lifetime of working with the Chinese and a few Indian doctors he still stands out as one of the very best, most friendly, and most loyal juniors I have had to work with me. Most Englishmen have the lowest opinion of the Egyptians but of the very few Egyptian doctors I have known (and all but he have been Coptic Christians) I have found none I did not like and trust, but Michael became a friend for many years. I have lost touch with him now but would imagine that he has become one of the leaders of the profession in the Middle East.

I can think of only one surgical incident worthy of mention during that period. I have no time for the modern custom of allowing mothers of child patients to hang round the hospital day and night, and even fathers can be a nuisance and a danger to themselves and others. I had operated on a baby with a complete double harelip, and as it was wheeled out of theatre we encountered father who had no right in the theatre suite at all. The sight of his son and heir for the first time not looking like a lobster-supper dream, but with a stitch through his nose secured by two small buttons, proved too much for him. There was a crash and father was lying unconscious in a rapidly widening pool of blood. Baby was easy to carry but father was not; so the nurse took the patient back to the ward in her arms, while we picked up father, put him on the trolley, and wheeled it back into theatre to stitch up his scalp.

King Saud of Arabia paid us a state visit at that time accompanied by a vast army of court officials and palace slaves. He also brought a gift of fifty Cadillacs, each driven by a slave in slow procession through the town. Minor expatriate staff were turned out of their houses at a few minutes notice to accommodate their guests, and my resthouse became uncomfortably congested.

On leaving I paid a farewell visit to one of the princesses who had been my patient for a very minor operation. As I said goodbye, a slave came in with two small boxes containing parting gifts. One was a pair of antique gold mounted ear pendants of Persian Gulf pearls, the other a gold watch. The Arabs are unbelievably generous in their gifts. All new staff are warned that they must never admire anything in the palaces or it will be given to them. It is not oil company policy that a junior member of the staff should suddenly find himself the owner of all the Persian carpets in the throne-room. There was one incident at Shell however which could not have been avoided.

A newly arrived junior engineer was driving his elderly second-hand Ford past the fort outside the town, when he became aware of six men strung across the road pointing guns at him. Not unnaturally he stopped. The Royal Cadillac was at the side of the road, and these were the Ruler's body-guard. The vizier came to him and said 'His Highness's car has broken down. You are to take him to the palace.' There was no room for argument, so the young man turned his car round and the Ruler and vizier got in, the others standing on the running board or lying on the roof. The Ruler did not look at him or say a word during the journey, but as he got out said something briefly to the vizier, who told their helper 'His Highness says you are to leave your car here. It will be returned to your quarters. You will take that one.' 'That one' was a new Rolls being taken out of its shipping case. A can of petrol was poured into it, and he drove it home.

The return of the sick surgeon was slightly delayed and I got back to Purley with only two days to go to the planned date of my departure for Sumatra, but Caltex very generously gave me nearly a week. I had a little shopping to do, but I had bought one of the very first precision four-track tape recorders and much of this time was spent on transcribing my opera recordings onto tape. I flew off as usual on the Sunday night flight to Singapore and arrived in Djakarta on 21 April to stay for three nights at the world famous Hotel des Indes. The Dutch will tell you that this is the finest hotel in the world and knocks spots off the Raffles. I found it a squalid huddle of hutments resembling the pictures of a Japanese prison camp. There was no air-conditioning, no bedclothes except a pillow and a 'Dutch wife', and no baths except a brick tank and a plastic saucepan to throw the water over one. Breakfasts consisted of tea and toast, but the bread was not delivered until after ten, so unless one was unbelievably late it was tea.

Rumbai camp was just like a Shell camp but with an American accent. There was the usual club, swimming pool and mess, the usual very comfortable bungalows, the offices, hospital, and the inevitable golf course. What served for the hotel was a small group of tiny luxurious two room flats across the road from the club building and mess, and it was into one of these that the CMO showed me on my arrival. I stood with my suitcases in my hands and remarked 'I trust this is not a permanent arrangement.'

He said 'Well it was intended to be: won't it do?'

'It might for a week or so, but if I am to do a two year contract I shall need a house' I replied, still holding my luggage. The matter might as well be settled there and then before the plane went back to Djakarta. He took it very well and it was at once agreed that I should have the first house available. From my previous experience in oil I did not really expect the first and saw this as the opening exchange in a long contest, but I did not know Caltex. I learned later that whatever the other defects of American Big Business (and they are many) an American Company does not tell lies or break promises. Also it knows to face facts when it requires a man's services and will not cut off its own nose to spite its face. In a later contretemps, a memorandum between Djakarta and New York which I should never have seen read 'If we have had the good fortune to recruit the best surgeon in South East Asia (their opinion not mine) we must allow him a certain degree of eccentricity.' Eccentricity is a good word. In this case it meant that they were prepared to concede that there might be method in my madness, rather than as had been suggested madness in my method.

Rumbai camp was situated about two miles from the large town of Pakenbaru, which I hardly saw in the three and a half years I lived there. I had on occasion to visit the Government offices and police station, but I never once saw the Government hospital although I was in daily touch with its doctors. Reports suggested that conditions there were terrible and certainly they suffered badly from shortage of drugs and supplies. At times, and quite without my knowledge, used swabs were being recovered from the floor of my theatre, washed, re-sterilized one hopes, and used at the other hospital. Their chief source of drugs appears to have been through the customs who quite openly seized a proportion of every consignment we imported as 'Samples'. I used to carry my own set of surgical instruments, which were properly customed on admission. On returning from my first leave, on which I used them on the ship, they tried to pretend that they were not the same and proposed that I should make a 'selection' of those I really required. I found later that the company had been forced to pay a bribe of over £3,000 to settle the matter. I hope it was spent on the instruments wanted for their hospital, but doubt it.

Our own hospital was small for the work it had to do, but as expected very well equipped and (as with the British Shell hospitals) if I wanted anything else I only had to ask for it. The entire company staff was American except for the Medical Department which except for one male nurse was entirely British. They had a great deal more sense than put an American at the top and then expect it to work with British staff. All oil company hospitals do a great deal of work ex-gratia for local people without any connection with the company, and here things were much the same as at Miri. The Government Hospital in the town had no proper surgical facilities and no staff trained in surgery except for what training was available at Djakarta. Non-company patients were only accepted with a referring letter from the other hospital, but well over half my new patients at every clinic were from them.

In the past there had been a tendency for all American staff needing surgery to be sent home, and large numbers of children to be sent elsewhere to have their tonsils out: but all this stopped when I got a regular surgical unit running. About my first month a departmental head was sent home to have a Nesbit prostatectomy from Nesbit himself. His deputy was an Indonesian who developed acute retention and was operated on by me on the same day as Nesbit operated on his chief. I have always used the very old-fashioned 'Harris' operation taught me by Vernon Pennell, modified by himself and slightly also by me. I still believe it to be the best. For some reason Nesbit sent his patient back in only three weeks, and not surprisingly the two men compared notes, particularly on such matters as how many naphthalene balls they could shift in the urinal and how long they could work at their desks without going there. My man won hands down; and thereafter it was impossible to get an American to go home for a prostatectomy. Americans are obsessed by surgical technique, and the word got round that Mr Crook was using a secret operation that nobody else in the world knew about. They were coming up from Djakarta for it as were children for tonsillectomy, and I strongly suspected that two American patients had no connection with the company until they were found to require surgery, when it was arranged that they should have.

Like most Englishmen I used to regard the American brat as the most unattractive thing the Lord ever made and didn't put a tail on; but I made there an astonishing discovery. Separate the creature from its parents and fellows and it becomes human. It was before the days of allowing parents to hang round the ward day and night, and very few Americans would allow their offspring to share a ward with non-white children, so the poor things had to be in a private room alone. I used to visit them whenever I passed during the day, and read to them on my night round (*Christopher Robin* for the smaller ones, otherwise *Treasure Island*). They were charming, polite, and very very grateful. They even used to call me 'Sir'. American children of course stay with their parents until they reach university age and simply make use of what schooling is available wherever their parents happen to be. There was a school of sorts in the camp for children of all ages and two 'Teachers' employed by the company. They struck me as the two most ignorant men in the camp.

It is difficult, and sometimes impossible, to throw off prejudice born of childhood experiences, and I fear my attitude to Americans and the American Way of Life is likely always to be coloured by the behaviour of American troops in England during my schooldays. In fairness it must be remembered, and I always try to remember, that these were not typical Americans. They were not volunteers and conscription although universal among the blacks was limited among the whites to those without money, influence, or in most cases anything but the lowest standard of state education. It was said that the white American soldiers in Europe had an average mental age of only nine years, and I see no reason to doubt it.

I was at school almost midway between two American army camps, one for whites and the other for blacks. Public houses and restaurants in the area were told they had to decide which they wanted to serve, and unless they were to elect to be 'Whites Only' (which meant banning a large number of our own troops and citizens) they would be put out of bounds to American whites, as almost all were. No apartheid was demanded on the buses however, though they maintained it themselves by brute force. If a white American private got on a bus and the blacks did not immediately scuttle off it, he would take them one at a time by the ear, drag them onto the platform, and kick them into the street. They took good care to make sure that the uniforms were their own of course.

Both the black and the white however were allowed to make free with the native women and children. There was no starvation, but luxuries which were obtainable by the ton for the Americans were unknown to the English. The village children would do anything (quite literally) for a tin of pears or a big bar of chocolate creams, and those at the village schools from the age of eight onwards were induced to prostitute

213

themselves for them to blacks and whites alike. I never heard of one being prosecuted, though in one particularly revolting case of the rape of a married woman in Combe Down, a negro private was courtmartialled and sentenced to death. Eisenhower however intervened and the man was released without penalty and returned to duty as a mechanic in the same area.

When I first arrived at Rumbai food and drink were freely available at the company commissary, but they were using up stock and after about a year there was nothing to buy there but flour and rice (of which one received a huge monthly ration as well as the right for one's servants to buy about three times what they could possibly eat, so that they demanded negligible wages), fresh vegetables, and meat from the company farm. Almost everybody imported food parcels from Hong Kong, but although I lived very well, meat and vegetables were about all I needed. I baked my own bread. In place of food parcels I imported wine and tobacco, and bought big tins of dried milk in the town. I considered myself virtuous in not taking advantage of my expatriate status to import food and in living the same way as the locals. It was then pointed out to me that the locals were starving and that by buying tinned milk I was depriving the local children. I therefore made a concession and ordered a whole parcel of tinned milk.

Unfortunately the very night the first consignment arrived, a young American dropped in for a drink and began talking about his household arrangements. He was used to catering for himself and admitted that his only servant (a girl said to be thirteen but who looked about eleven) was useless at housework and kept only as a mistress. Just to have something to say I asked what he paid her, and he replied 'Hell, I don't pay her. I buy her the rice ration and give her tins of milk powder for her baby brothers and sisters.' I gave up milk in my coffee and tea.

There were other Americans however whose sheer goodness took one's breath away. My next door neighbour, an old man but a very junior engineer who was one of the few Roman Catholics in the camp, should have retired four years before. His Amah gave birth to an illegitimate child (quite certainly not his) so he and his wife decided to adopt it and make it an American citizen. They had already raised a family of their own and calculated that to bring up an extra child and see him through school and high school or university would cost what they could save by doing two extra contracts. They therefore gave up the planned retirement and stayed on for another four years to provide for the child. They were neither of them in good health and I doubt very much that they will have lived long enough to see him grow up.

Impressive also was the tolerance shown to someone who however useful to them was by their own standards grossly abnormal. Americans all believe that they have a sense of humour although in reality they only have a sense of slapstick. The only American joke is the custard tart. They recognize that the English sense of humour exists but is incomprehensible; and as for some reason I got a reputation for being a humorist, every outrageous thing I said or did was regarded as being screamingly funny. When in desperation I said that Americans did not have an inferiority complex but just were inferior, this was not regarded as grounds for immediate dismissal but quoted all over the camp as an example of my wonderful sense of humour. I had a Sakai child bitten by some unidentified creature and was trying to discover through two interpreters (one Sakai-Malay and the other Malay-English) what had bitten him. The final answer was 'It was very likely a monkey but it hadn't got a tail.'

When I very indiscreetly remarked 'Oh, it must have been a young American', this too was quoted to everyone and greatly appreciated.

I think only once did I make the mistake of trying to make a joke to a group of them. In Balikpapen during the height of the nearest civil war (there were five of them going on at the time) the rebels had managed to recruit an American mercenary with a small bomber. He attacked Balikpapen one afternoon with four small bombs. With the first he hit a brand new tanker and blew it in two. The second scored a direct hit on the Government offices. Only the third was wasted as it blew up a tank in a tank farm which he was not know was disused and empty. He then went back to see how the tanker was getting on: and found that the Indonesian Navy, comprising one gunboat unhappily with Sukano's son on board, had put to sea to pick up survivors under the impression that the war was over. He put his last bomb literally down its funnel and then as an encore sprayed everybody in the installation and on the wharf with all the ammunition he had for his machine gun.

Some years later I was sitting in the bar at the Rumbai Club surrounded by Americans who were discussing a memorandum we had all received that morning from the New York office. Our own local civil war was still going on and there was shooting between minuscule Dutch and Indonesian forces over West Irian. Although we were a hundred and fifty miles from anywhere, some idiot in the States had ordered that we should dig air-raid shelters in our gardens. To my amazement they were all taking it seriously and having experienced Blitz conditions in London and Bath, I perhaps treated the matter with indiscreet levity. One man said 'Wal ah don't like it. We're in big trouble. We can be barmed by the Government, barmed by the rebels, and barmed by the Dutch.'

I replied 'Listen chum, the only man who has ever bombed me in Indonesia was an American.' I still think it was a very funny observation. I looked round for appreciation, and saw that one and all were looking at me with murder in their eyes. I finished my beer in one gulp and bolted.

A few years ago I was staying at a hotel in Cambridge where there was a telephone room with the instruments arranged around the walls and a large centre table piled high with reference books. At this was sitting an American struggling with the London telephone directory and not making much of a go of it. I had just decided to cut my visit short and drive up to Southport so I rang David Coombe's college to leave a message cancelling a dinner engagement. I caught the man's eye just as I was saying 'Is that Christ's.' He gave me a wild look, but nothing to that a few moments later when having rung my hotel in Southport I asked 'Is that the Prince of Wales.' His eyes protruded visibly for a moment, but when I had finished he produced the wittiest remark I have ever heard from one of his countrymen. He said 'Wal, you sure are moving down in society.'

I am afraid that my tactlessness sometimes amounted to what others called bloody-mindedness. Road safety is a thing that every Christian should support, and the Company had very rightly decided that all staff who wanted to drive a Company vehicle should pass a driving test conducted by their safety officer. Unfortunately Americans are the worst drivers in the world (because they are the most aggressive) and this officer was an American. Also I didn't want to drive any

216

vehicle. I never do and would always rather be driven. The Company required me to be on duty at all hours seven days a week, and if I generously agreed to do the driving for them instead of having a company driver always available (which would have meant four shifts) I was not going to have a young American deciding whether I was competent. I simply told them that I made no claim to be and that if they had misgivings they must either provide me with a driver, or let me walk to and from the hospital daily and do without my services outside working hours. Management accepted this as another example of my wonderful sense of humour, but the safety officer pestered me and the CMO continuously for years. As it happened I was the only person in history to have completed three years driving for the company without a crash, and he was ordered to give me a certificate to this effect when I left. He went sick, but they made him sign it and it was duly presented to me at my leaving party.

Actually drunken driving was a very serious problem, and the Manager once wrote a strongly worded circular on the subject which was sent to every department one evening too late to be distributed to the staff. Next morning there was a messenger waiting outside the office of every departmental head to collect them again before they could be seen. It transpired that the previous night on the way home from a party, the Manager had been run into by two separate stationary cars.

Safety officers are a strange breed. I knew one in another company, the nicest young man in the camp, but unlucky. One afternoon he was demonstrating to a group of recruits the dangers of a band-saw. He removed the safety guard to show how dangerous it looked without it and then, leaning across to switch it off, took his arm off at the shoulder. It was the finest and most persuasive safety demonstration in the Company's history.

Although Sumatra provided every bit as much exotic surgical material as Sarawak, there was just one fly in the ointment which prevented this being as satisfying and enjoyable a job. There simply were not enough beds, and for the first and last time in my life I acquired a waiting list. This is not to say that patients did not have to wait for operation in Sabah but I had learned my lesson and even if they had to wait eight or nine months (as many Thyroid cases did) they always had a firm date set for admission and operation. A waiting list is a diabolical thing and once started there is no escape but death or leaving the country. It simply grows and grows, and after a time one can assume that non-urgent cases such as varicose veins never will get done. Since 1964 when I went to Sabah I have made it a rule that once the decision is made to operate and the patient has agreed, his name, number, and proposed operation is entered on an operating list and he is told what date to come into hospital. This means having fixed operating days and planning one's leave dates a year or more in advance, but I have always been able to do this. Of course there is a small wastage from patients defaulting; but the space is readily filled up with emergencies and urgent cases already in the wards. A man who can have five or six operating lists a week can afford to book four or five hours work in each and if necessary extend it to eight or nine. It seldom is necessary. I used to book one Thyroidectomy every Wednesday and a cold Gastrectomy on Thursday whenever there was one to do. Thyroids were frequently being booked ten months in advance as I disliked doing more than one a week and if one booked two, one could be sure that there would be an urgent toxic one to do that week making three. However when the pressure became too intense I would book one on Friday as well.

In the western world, prostatectomy is almost always a planned cold operation. It is very common in the East especially among the Chinese, but I do not remember a single case in an Asian patient that did not come in as an emergency. This was not the result of patients putting it off for fear of surgery. Almost all would deny any previous symptoms, or at the most only the most trivial and over a period of two weeks or less. This did not mean that they all had emergency prostatectomy, an operation I dislike and only do if catheterization is impossible. Otherwise a catheter would be inserted and left in while all investigations were made, uraemia and/or anaemia and electrolyte imbalance dealt with, and plans made for an unhurried operation on the first convenient operating day. In this way I was able to achieve a zero mortality in some hundreds of cases.

Prostatism was not the only condition where the picture was totally different in Asian patients to what we see in Europeans. If I had my life again I think racial pathology is the subject to which I would devote it. (The only other major task which would tempt me would be a complete reappraisal of human nutrition and the potential of every area of the world for producing the essential food substances.) Hindus are of course Aryan and their incidence, symptomatology, and natural history of disease is very similar to ours. Among Mongoloid peoples however, although with few exceptions they suffer from the same diseases, the incidence, natural history of the disease, and response to treatment is often very different. All our usual forms of malignant disease are quite common, but the degree of malignancy, except in breast cancer, is enormously less and hence the 'Cure rate' very much better. In Europeans, perhaps three per cent of cases of cancer of the stomach can be saved, whereas of those Chinese reporting with the disease to the Queen Elizabeth Hospital (and very few would have seen a GP first) well over half would be alive and well five years later. Cancer of the Caecum (which oddly is the commonest bowel cancer there) showed a hundred per cent cure rate.

It is not fashionable to speak of 'Cure' of cancer and most surgeons concern themselves with a 'mean survival time' or survival for five years or ten years. I think this is wrong, and that it is quite proper to speak of 'Cure'. Everybody will die from something in due course (unless the Lord comes first) and if when he does his cancer (or any other condition you have treated) has not recurred, you have cured him. A patient of 104 with even a harmless mole on his chin can never be given a five year survival. If a patient has a cancer removed and lives to die from an unrelated cause (even if it be from slipping under a bus a week later) he has been cured. One of my Caecal carcinoma cases did in fact die of cancer eight years later, but it was proved at postmortem in London to have been cigarette smoker's cancer of the lung, and there was no recurrence of his bowel cancer which I had removed. This was not an 'Eight year survival' it was a cure.

Cancer of the breast is however the terrible exception. This tumour is in my experience horrendously malignant in the Chinese. Many cases were extremely early and had they been

219

Europeans seventy-five per cent of them should have been alive and well at five years. I think my operation was perfectly well done and several visiting surgeons have remarked that at the end I have achieved a result just like the pictures in the textbooks. Out of over 300 cases though, all but two were dead within a year, and all those I saw at six months were already riddled with the disease. It is well established that without treatment at all, such patients will on average live over two years. Far from doing any good then, I had killed them, and killed them horribly, in half the time the disease would have done without any intervention.

There are oddly two conditions very common in Britain which I never saw. In most hospitals, even with determined and dedicated physiotherapy, probably the commonest cause of death in all general surgical units in Britain is Pulmonary Embolism, a blood clot forming in the legs and travelling up to the lung. In thirty years I did not see a single case. 'Diverticulosis' and its complications is so common in the middle-aged and elderly in Europe as to be almost normal. Again I saw not one.

What was really fascinating though in Rumbai, but not in Borneo, was the normally very rare disease of Chorion-epithelioma. This tumour which arises from a pregnancy gone wrong is probably the most malignant and rapidly fatal known. An article in the *British Medical Journal* at that time remarked that as there were fewer than twelves cases in the whole of the United Kingdom in a year, it was impossible that any one Gynaecologist should have any adequate personal experience of the condition. I was seeing many more than twelve a year in my own little hospital in Sumatra. Today, because it grows so very rapidly, it is the most sensitive of all tumours to chemotherapy and is supremely curable, but at that time nobody had ever achieved a cure, and I certainly did not. Even if the chest x-ray was clear when the diagnosis was made, in spite of the most heroic measures there would be dozens or even hundreds of lung secondaries to be seen in days, and every patient would be dead in a very few weeks. Few indeed even left hospital alive.

Inevitably I have been brought into contact with non-medical healing. Just as we owe digitalis, and hence almost all our knowledge of cardiac action and functional pathology, to an old village woman who found that foxglove was good for the dropsy, it is not surprising that native healers (unkindly called 'witchdoctors') in Borneo should have empirical remedies for conditions which baffle medical science. I believe, as do all the locals, that there is a tree somewhere up the Baram river an infusion of whose bark will cure (not merely relieve) diabetes. I have seen a severe diabetic on a high dosage of insulin gradually improve until no insulin was necessary and his glucose tolerance curve had returned to normal. His Dyak wife had been giving him infusions of this drug, and had cured him. I wish that even with my limited knowledge of medicine and laboratory technique I could have got back to Sarawak to investigate it.

Acupuncture too is a science (yes a science) which interested me greatly even in the days when people in England regarded it with contempt. As I have said, our knowledge of cardiac physiology is almost entirely derived from investigation of an empirical remedy; but it is not always realized that the same is true of almost all the 'science' in 'scientific medicine'. What we have built up over little more than a hundred years is the accumulation and correlation of facts derived from clinical observations. A conscientious physiologist will admit that we probably know less than twenty per cent of what could be known of how the human body works. The Chinese have had a cultured civilization, with medical men held in much higher regard than our own, continuously for at least four thousand years with no interchange of discoveries or ideas between us. It would be perfectly possible for them to have a system of physiology also covering twenty per cent of what is knowable, without there being any overlap or points of contact between their science and ours.

To a greater extent than we would admit, our way of thinking, our concept of the 'scientific method', and our very way of expressing scientific facts, are based on the ideas and philosophies of the ancient Greeks, especially Plato and Aristotle; which are unknown to the Chinese. It is not surprising then that when an educated English-speaking Chinese tries to explain what he regards as the rational justification of Acupuncture, he finds it very difficult. I have even found this true of a very competent Edinburgh-qualified Chinese doctor who has given up Western medicine almost entirely. He certainly cured an Irish pathologist I knew of progressive spondylitis, though he could not explain in terms which that doctor or I understood either the nature of the lesion as he saw it or the mechanism of the cure.

I have seen a patient who had been tied up and whipped by the Gestapo put into a trance by an English hypnotherapist and made to re-live her experience. Rope marks appeared on her wrists and the marks of a flogging on her back. There is no possible anatomical pathway or physiological mechanism known to Western science by which this can be explained. It looks to me though to be closely related to the pathways and mechanisms claimed to be used by the acupuncturists. I have tried the simplest methods they described to relieve headache, particularly unilateral migrainous headache, and found them very effective although I cannot begin to explain how they work.

About the time I qualified, 'Fibrositis' was a popular and fashionable diagnosis, just as 'Focal sepsis' and 'Lane's kinks' were a generation earlier. We believed that if we tried hard enough we should find a 'fibrositic nodule' associated with every case of muscular pain and spasm, although often it was some distance away from the place where the pain was felt. Injection of procaine into these nodules was wonderfully successful; and I remember marvelling that the relief lasted weeks or months, even though the local anaesthetic effect of procaine wears off in a very few minutes. A young woman doctor published a diagram of where these nodules were commonly to be found, and the area of pain each was thought to produce, and said that good results could be obtained by injecting procaine in the right place even when the nodule was too small to be felt.

It was at least thirty years later that it was realized that her diagram corresponded almost exactly with that of the acupuncture points described by 'The Yellow Emperor' in about the year 700 BC. Although I had puzzled over the fact that the relief lasted so much longer than the effective action of the procaine; it never occurred to me or to anyone else to omit the procaine altogether and just stick in the needle. Had we done so we would have obtained results just as good, and probably realized that we were practising acupuncture.

In a different class though are 'Faith healing' (which must be recognized by anyone with any powers of observation at all) Divine healing (which should be acknowledged by every Christian) and just possibly 'Spirit healing' as something quite distinct from either.

Faith healing and hypnotic healing, which are almost certainly the same thing, the term used depending on whether one has trust in the healer or the remedy, are to be found daily in every branch of medical and quasi-medical practice. In every therapeutic experiment today, the cure rate obtained by the drug is measured against that found in patients receiving a placebo, a pill or injection which looks the same but contains no active ingredient. It is common to find that although dramatic results are obtained, the placebo is almost as effective as the drug. Cures for warts are legion, but results equal to those of the best drugs are obtained by rubbing with a family Bible, or washing in moon-beams in a silver bowl. HJs favourite method involved treating with Milton solution every night for exactly twenty-one nights. Once in outpatients when I was not feeling at my best he suddenly asked me 'How would you treat warts with Milton?'

When I replied 'Rub them with a copy of *Paradise Lost*' he agreed that this would probably be just as effective.

Divine healing is something quite different, and I am astonished that many Good Christians and even the Clergy often confuse the two terms. It is not common: dramatic miracles of any sort are not, but every doctor must have come across the occasional case where following devout prayer by the patient and/or relatives and friends an event follows which is completely outside the laws of nature as we understand them, and must be attributed to direct intervention by God. In a very real sense of course all healing is of God, and cannot occur unless God wills it or at the very least is aware of it and permits it. In these cases we are dealing though with a miracle as dramatic and obviously supernatural as the raising of Lazarus. I have described elsewhere two cases known to me personally, one of them being myself, where no other explanation is possible.

I am a little doubtful that 'Spirit healing' exists as an entity distinct from these other two classes. Undoubtedly most of the cures claimed by the Spiritualists and other 'Spirit healers' are cases of Faith healing; as very probably are many of the successes of orthodox medicine and surgery. If a dramatic result is obtained by a Christian practitioner after prayers to Our Lord, it is impossible to distinguish this from Divine healing. Also every Baptized Christian has some measure of the Gift of the Holy Spirit imposed upon him, and if he achieves a cure by prayer and the laying on of hands, one cannot say that this is not passing on the healing power of the Holy Spirit which is of God and indeed is God.

There remains a small group of cases though where the Holy Spirit is not evoked, and indeed where the techniques used are contrary to the law and teaching of the Church throughout the ages. Conan Doyle's book *Land of Mists* is an irreligious tract in praise of spiritualism published in the guise of a novel and found in all published collections of his fictional works, though he claims that all his facts are true. There are cases recorded (and Doyle was a doctor) where healing is attributed to Spiritual forces definitely not Divine. In one case a young doctor dying of Multiple Sclerosis is said to be cured by the spirit of a dead doctor of the Regency period using 'Spirit batteries', whatever they may be. I fear I cannot take these claims seriously, although I do not deny their possibility.

All this is not to say that I have any sympathy with the use or even toleration of unqualified medical practice. If a man knows of a method of treatment which he believes will be of benefit to patients in a western country and wishes to practice there, it is not unreasonable to required that he should obtain the minimum registrable qualification before he is allowed to do so. I think this should apply to acupuncturists like my friend the Edinburgh graduate; though now that we have just belatedly recognised its worth there would be a good case for the temporary suspension of the ethical regulation (which has the force of law) which prohibits the collaboration of a doctor with an unqualified practitioner. For a limited period it should be regarded as proper for a doctor to refer cases to such a man, in return for legislation that he in turn must refer cases to a doctor for his approval. Nobody should be allowed on his own to treat the sick unless he has been trained in modern diagnosis and pathology. Even the clergy who administer spiritual healing or unction in cases where they have any suspicion that there may be organic disease should insist on the patient consulting a doctor also. I would not extend this to mental disease as I think an experienced confessor, especially if he be a Roman Catholic, is at least as good at treating mental and spiritual disturbance as a psychiatrist.

Osteopaths certainly do a great deal of good, but also sometimes a great deal of harm in their ignorance of pathology, symptomatology, and systematic anatomy. Again I would make it legitimate for them to practice under, and only under, the supervision of a qualified practitioner; or else to obtain qualifications for themselves. The law against the use of secret remedies should apply to them also; and frankly I do not see why they cannot be rendered superfluous by teaching their theory and diagnostic methods to all doctors, and their methods of treatment to all physiotherapists.

I have never gone in for 'Heroic' surgery but there are times when it is forced upon one. One such case some years later at Kota Kinabalu was a woman in her seventies with a small carcinoma at the lower end of her stomach. Every operation has a 'point of no return', a point before which one can always abandon the operation, restore if necessary the previous anatomy, and come out. After that point whatever happens one has to go on and complete the operation. I was well beyond that point in this case when I made a terrifying discover. The Blood supply to all but the very top of the stomach had already been cut off and the Duodenum divided, closed, and buried. I turned up the freed stomach and found to my horror that there was a second tumour which had been missed on the x-rays starting in the stomach and extending along the oesophagus as high as I could feel up into the chest. The devitalized stomach had to be removed, but one cannot do an anastomosis by stitching through tumour. It was a nightmare-like situation. There was no way of completing the operation.

After several minutes thought, I turned to the Medical Assistant anaesthetist, a wonderfully able Kadazan named Florentius Epin, and asked him 'Can I open the chest.' The old woman had already had well over an hour of anaesthetic time, and the greatest anaesthetist in the world would have had misgivings. He understood the situation perfectly and said without hesitation 'Oh yes: she's very well Mr Crook.' I opened the chest carried the dissection up to the lung root, and having removed the lower oesophagus and entire stomach gave her a new one of sorts fashioned from a double loop of small bowel. The whole operation took nearly four hours.

It was a few days before Christmas, and when on Christmas morning my mother and I were making a special round giving presents to the patients I had nothing to give her. (It is not easy to think of a present for an old woman who has no stomach, does not smoke, and who has a drip up and a tube down.) I hung a little Father Christmas on her drip stand and she smiled. I then rummaged in the basket of small gifts for the children and found a wooden bead bracelet which I had got out of a very swagger cracker the previous evening. I adjusted it to fit her tiny wrist and as I put it on her she beamed with happiness.

Six years later when I had retired and was in Kota Kinabalu on holiday I heard a shout on the other side of the main street and a tiny old woman came weaving through the traffic towards me. She could see that I didn't know her, so she tore open her badjau to show the enormous thoraco-abdominal scar, and then pointed to the Christmas Cracker bracelet she was still wearing. It is incidents like this which make surgery worthwhile.

All this of course was nearly twenty years later than the time I am describing, but there was one such heroic case at Rumbai. An Indonesian had fought off a tiger with his bare hands in an unsuccessful attempt to save his two children. By the time the tiger gave up, the children were dead and he had a huge wound in his chest through which the heart projected. He made a twenty-four hour journey to me sitting up in a Land Rover with his heart hanging out of his chest. Now it is a basic principle of surgery that a wound more than eighteen hours old must never be operated on but only treated by antibiotics and dressings until the inevitable infection is under control, but this is a thing it is difficult to explain to a man who has his heart hanging out. I decided that the only possible answer was to forget the rule entirely and pretend it was a recent wound. Accordingly the wound was excised, the two missing ribs replaced by splitting two others, and the whole thing stitched up. It healed 'By first intention' with no fever, and without even going pink.

This case should be of some interest to the protagonists of the 'Save the Tiger' fund. I am afraid I had no photographs of the man's children either when they were alive and well or when the tiger had finished with them, but I would dearly have liked to introduce the man himself to the Duke of Edinburgh. I do not believe in saving the tiger, the malaria parasite, or the viruses of rabies or Aids. As far as I am concerned the only right place for a tiger is in a zoo, or better stuffed in the Natural History Museum. The rest should be shot by those who like this sort of sport, or failing that poisoned with strychnine or cyanide.

To the Christian I think this is an ethical and logical approach to all such problems. In an overpopulated underfed world the question should be not only whether a creature is a danger to mankind, but whether it is of any use. I attended a lecture some years ago by a rabid conservationist on the subject of the green turtle. He asked me afterwards whether I supported his efforts. I would have thought my reply 'Of course: it would be tragic if we had no more green turtle soup' should have pleased him but it didn't. If we believe what the Bible teaches, God gave us green turtles and whales, not because he made the world as much for them as for us and we should share it with them, but that he put them there for our benefit, comfort and use, and if we hunt them to extinction we shall be wickedly depriving future generations of a valuable gift of God.

For those scientists who are concerned with the threatened extinction of mammals of any reasonable size (I am not including sperm whales) there is an easy and cheap solution. If it is feared that zoo specimens might fail to survive (or nobody really wants to keep them there) one could, for a fraction of the cost of keeping a breeding pair for a single year, prepare a dozen or more deep-frozen embryos by in-vitro fertilization, and leave future generations, if they wish, to raise them with a surrogate mother of a similar class. [A friend has suggested that those who have no religious objection might even consider storing Aids-free human embryos the same way with computerized robots programmed to implant them in females of the orang-utan or other great apes a suitable time after the human race has become extinct from this cause. My only objection is that in the absence of religious belief it is difficult to see why anybody should think man any more worth preserving than the tiger.]

I spent more than four very happy years at Rumbai getting on well with both the Americans and the Indonesians, but it was too good to last. The establishment of the Dominion of Malaysia did no good to anyone but the Malays and much harm to many people, not least to those of us who were endeavouring to keep the flag flying and maintain the British reputation for service in Indonesia. Sukarno was an Imperialist (witness his seizure of West New Guinea in another continent, simply on the grounds that he was the successor to the Dutch Imperial power) and the sight of the oil-rich territories of British Borneo being cast adrift by the Crown excited his greed and murderous antagonism even to his fellow Muslims. Confrontation ('Confrontasie') was simply a military plan to seize a rich prize from a loyal part of the Empire which Britain no longer had the inclination, the guts, or just possibly even the ability to defend. He reckoned however without the courage of the Malaysian peoples and the loyalty of the Australians to the principles on which the Empire was built even if they now meant nothing to the Mother Country.

At first 'Confrontasie' cost us nothing more than having to put up with amusingly vituperative anti-British propaganda and minor irritating regulations (which were seldom obeyed) such as a ban on listening to Radio Singapore. (Incredibly London at first included Buddhist/Christian Singapore in this militantly Muslim dictatorship.)

Before long all the British were thrown out, but it was not unreasonably assumed that I should be among the last; and it was due to my own stupidity and lack of tact, or at least to my deep-seated stubbornness of character, that I was the very first. Sukarno gave orders that the envelopes of all government letters were to be stamped 'Ganjang Malaysia' (crush Malaysia). Working the greater part of my time on non-company patients, I received at every clinic several of these which quite unnecessarily I took as an insult to the British Empire as well as to myself. Each time I crossed out the offending inscription and before tearing up the envelope and throwing it into the waste paper basket, would substitute something so obscene that I would have thought it would be meaningless to anybody but a

228

medical student. Before I knew what was going on, some dozens had been collected by a government spy and stuck together as Jigsaw puzzles to make a file in the office of the Secret Police. I was charged with 'Opposition to the struggles of the Indonesian People' which I was told was a capital offence.

For the first day I was under House Arrest, which made the pleasantest and most restful day I spent during the whole of my service in Sumatra. I had two delightful guards with Tommy guns, who helped me to carry my two large loudspeakers onto the balcony overlooking the golf course round which the rest of the camp was built. I then connected these via my power amplifier to my Wurlitzer organ and played *Land of Hope and Glory* all over the camp, with the two guards standing stiffly to attention. Fortunately the fourteen year old son of the chief of Police perforated his appendix that night, and as I was the only surgeon in Sumatra at that time, they thereafter made it Camp Arrest so that I could get to and from the hospital. As apart from my leave I had not stepped outside the camp for nearly four years, this was not very trying. Even so it marked the end of my job with Caltex and also my career in the oil world, which again was not very unwelcome. I had done well in oil, but was beginning to feel like a sardine.

Caltex offered me a job in the Persian Gulf, but as I did not want it gave me another very generous 'golden handshake' comprising pay in lieu of notice and for my accumulated leave, one month's salary for every year worked, and the value of the passage home which I did not require. I was left in Singapore in November determined to find some work to do at least until the English spring, and after two weeks recuperating at the Raffles flew to Kuching to see if the DMS there could find me a temporary job. He couldn't but kindly telephoned Jesselton and the DMS of Sabah (formally Colony of North Borneo) said he had a job for me for a few weeks if I wanted it. I did, and was there for over nineteen years.

☆   ☆   ☆

Tawau is a small town at the extreme south east corner of British Borneo. It is on the coast of a wide estuary facing the island of Sibuku which is divided in two by the Sabah-

Indonesian border. Actually the border runs obliquely, so that we were within sight of Indonesia. Two ships of the Royal Navy patrolled the straits and every week or two lobbed a few shells up to the border to discourage the Indonesians from crossing it. There was a typical open-type Government Hospital with a staff of two Medical Officers and a Surgeon. The wards and offices were of wood and the operating theatre formed the only modern and brick-built part of the structure. A new, lavish, multi-storey steel and concrete hospital building was under construction across the road, but was only finished long after I left. I was there for some fifteen months before being transferred to Sandakan, and thence after only a few weeks due to quite unforeseen circumstances to Jesselton, the post-war Capital. Sandakan was the former Capital but, as has been remarked earlier, was almost totally destroyed by American bombing after the war was over, and the Government had to be transferred to Jesselton: although some large businesses still speak of Sandakan as the 'Commercial Capital' as Johannesburg is the commercial capital of South Africa.

Sabah itself, until the war the 'North Borneo protectorate' and made a Crown Colony in 1945, was one of the three countries which made up British North Borneo. The other two were the Colony of Sarawak (where I had served in Miri) and the tiny independent sheikdom of Brunei under British protection, where I had also worked for a few months in 1957. As recently as 1959 a half-page article appeared in *The Times* on the unbelievable loyalty and patriotism of the peoples of this region and the incredible fact that they most definitely did not want independence. In 1972 when the Queen visited Brunei, the streets were washed down with soap and water daily for a week before her visit, and a special Gold throne made for her. The situation was intolerable for a Labour Government and British agents were sent to both Sarawak and North Borneo with the unbelievable task of stirring up anti-British sentiment. In the latter, a notorious collaborator of the Japanese days was provided with a completely mythical war record as a 'Freedom Fighter' and schooled to lead a nationalist movement.

In the Federation there were some who genuinely wanted Dominion status, though they were all Malay Muslims and therefore in a minority. The Chinese and Indians, to say nothing of the native peoples of Borneo, dreaded nothing more than Malay rule, and the Constitution we had granted to the Federation and subsequently granted to Malaysia effectively guaranteed Malay control; just as the Constitution we granted to South Africa gave no political voice to the blacks. The two Borneo colonies were in fact to be worse off than any state in the Federation because the position of Head of State of Malaysia (Yang di Pertuan Agong) was to rotate among the rulers of the Malayan states, but the heads of state of Sabah and Sarawak were to be excluded, their citizens being subject peoples whose elected representatives could be over-ruled (and who are over-ruled) by the rulers of Malaya. Animism still exists among some of the Dyaks, and a relatively small number of the Chinese are still Buddhists, but Sarawak and Sabah were essentially Christian countries which HMG handed over with no protection whatever to a viciously militant Muslim dictatorship. The protection of the right of appeal to Her Majesty in Council was introduced into the constitution but immediately abolished when the Malay rulers asked that it should be. To retain it would have been as embarrassing (and onerous) as if Her Majesty had refused to sign away the rights of black South Africans to their privileges as Subjects of the Crown when a crowd of Cape Dutch had voted for a republic. A small party of enquirers were sent to spend a day or two in some of the larger towns and talk to a selected few 'representatives' of the people to find out if they wanted to be Malaysians and reported that they did, and the deed was done.

I arrived in Tawau on 22 December 1964 and for a week did not get a single surgical case. Then they started coming thick and fast and I stayed for seventeen months. I flew home for Bisley in 1965 and on my arrival back in Jesselton was offered the post in the Duchess of Kent Hospital Sandakan. It did not last long as within two months I had to fly to Jesselton to operate on Mr Krishna Metha the Senior Surgeon and, putting him off work got his job. It is not quite as bad as it sounds. Krishna was packing for his leave anyway and in the course of it put a PWD chair on a PWD table and climbed onto it. The result was a very nasty Colles' Fracture, which made him unfit to operate for a long time whatever I did. He went home to UK and stayed there. I moved into the Queen Elizabeth Hospital where I remained for the rest of my surgical career.

I had only been at the QEH a couple of days (leaving Tawau and Sandakan without a surgeon) when the fourteen year old son of a Sandakan millionaire ruptured his spleen. Father chartered an aircraft and at nine am on New Year's Day the DMS telephoned me to say the plane had just taken off from Jesselton and would be bringing me the patient in about four hours. I told him that if he put a child with a ruptured spleen into an unpressurized aircraft for two hours he might just as well cut its throat. I handed all the day's work to my MO (it was a holiday of course) arranged blood, anaesthetist, and theatre at Sandakan, had the aircraft turned round, and arrived at the airport just as it was landing.

A few minutes after taking off again for Sandakan I looked round the cabin of the Twin Piper and noticed a small boy on the rear seat. I asked what he was doing there and the pilot (who was a Scot) was strangely embarrassed. 'Well you see,' he began, 'last night was Hogmanay. I haven't actually been to bed all night, and nothing but a surgical emergency would have made me fly today. I brought him with me to keep me awake.'

I told him 'Set the radio compass to the Beacon at Sandakan, switch on George (the automatic pilot) and go to sleep. I'll wake you up when it's time to start the landing run.' He did so and in a few moments was dead to the world. The plane flew steadily on towards Mount Kinabalu.

Kinabalu is the highest mountain in South East Asia. It was dead ahead and over the next half hour got closer and closer and bigger and bigger. I banked the aircraft to port, and George promptly banked her to starboard. I went to starboard, and George politely but firmly put me back on a collision course. About a minute and a half before impact I shook my pilot awake.

'Wazermatter?' he asked somewhat crossly.

'Isn't that Mount Kinabalu ahead?' He gazed at it blearily, shook his head a few times and agreed.

'Yes, that's Mount Kinabalu.'

'Does George know about it?' He woke up with a jerk.

'My God, no.' He cranked up the altitude control of the automatic pilot and we shot straight up and over the top with several feet to spare.

The boy did very well and wrote to me some years later to

say that he was a regular officer in Fighter Command of the RAF.

The Queen Elizabeth Hospital was built by the British tax-payer and staffed with first class expatriate doctors and superb Chinese and Kadazan nurses and dressers. Equipment was good and we had an excellent Nurses' training school. There was a Physician, a Surgeon, an Ophthalmologist, and usually about six General Duties Medical Officers. For long periods I was the only Surgeon in the country and this had always been the situation until about two years before I arrived. Before I retired nearly nineteen years later, the surgical compliment had expanded to two General Surgeons, an Orthopaedic Surgeon, and a Gynaecologist, as well as the Ophthalmologist who remained there throughout. There were also a Surgeon and a Gynaecologist each at Tawau and Sandakan. Each of these had a full time Medical Officer attached to him who was a Registrar in all but name, and at the Queen Elizabeth a House Surgeon as well. The work that I had long been doing single handed, was thus spread among some twenty men.

In all fairness the situation was not really comparable. In the Colonial Medical Service days, which nominally came to an end two years before I arrived, the thirty-five GDMOs were all exceptional men selected most carefully to be able to take sole charge of an isolated hospital. Each would expect to do all his own routine surgery (hernias, haemorrhoids, hare-lips, ovarian cysts etc.) as well as all emergencies including head injuries, compound fractures, and Caesarean section. Only cold major cases such as Gastrectomies, Thyroids, Gall-bladders, Kidney stones and the like would be sent into the base hospital. Even long after the establishment of Malaysia such staff were being recruited in London by the Ministry of Technical Co-opera-tion (later known as 'The Ministry of Technical Incompe-tence'), and the greater part of the work at the QEH was still upon people in the town, or at least the immediate environs. From about the early seventies though, young doctors were being appointed who had only received training in Kuala Lumpur or even in some instances with foreign diplomas not recognized anywhere else in the Commonwealth and who had received no recognized training at all. The best of these very wisely sent even the most trivial cases into a base hospital, though there were occasional disasters from their trying to do things themselves. Two small boys had to have their right arms amputated within a few weeks of each other as a result of the same so-called doctor having applied an unpadded plaster and left it on until gangrene set in.

Unhappily this appears to have happened in every dependent country which has been granted independence. Scientific medicine and modern surgery are both British inventions and from the beginning all the best of both have emanated from Britain. Minor specialities such as ophthalmology and vascular surgery (and more recently transplant surgery) have indeed been developed in foreign countries but even there the basic methods applied have been learned directly from British teachers and are based on principles developed entirely in Scotland or England. The same applies of course to Parliamentary Government, economics, engineering, insurance, industrial management, and even the Limited Liability Company, without which modern commerce would be impossible. With few exceptions, training local staff and putting them in control of such operations to imitate the way the British do it has proved at the very least lacking in efficiency. Whether political theory justifies sacrificing so much in order to establish control by the local people does not concern me. In the field of Medical Services though, both the care of the sick and preventive medicine, I am concerned: and the results have everywhere been disastrous. Malaria was eliminated from Ceylon by expatriate workers under the WHO and for wholly political reasons control was then handed over to the local people with the result that the island is now the worst malarius area in the world and malaria their commonest cause of death. Even in South Africa the initiative in Heart and Heart/Lung transplant surgery was lost, not because Professor Barnard was not a local, but for the incredible reason that he was not a member of the political party in power, and his NAT colleagues ganged up to prevent him getting the necessary transplant material. Perhaps the fact that he was an FRCS was another reason.

At this one hospital I have assisted in the training of five local Medical Officers to become Surgeons and seen two others trained as Physicians. In each case they have obtained the FRCS (or in the case of the physicians the MRCP) at a cost to the British tax-payer of many tens of thousands of pounds each. Each has been given a Consultant appointment immediately on his return without waiting the normal minimum of five years post-specialist experience (one even refused to accept further training, of which he was in very great need) and every one left to go into private general practice within about five years or less.

Only one doctor who was there when I arrived remained until after I left. Richard Dingley was based on the QEH but was Ophthalmic Surgeon to the whole of Sabah (his predecessor was to the whole of British Borneo and it killed him) and spent about half his time travelling round the other hospitals. He and his wife Sylvia were devout Christians with a strong missionary vocation, and between them virtually ran one of the smaller Anglican Churches in Jesselton. Even so he was able to find time somehow for other activities including yacht racing and running the local very active St John Ambulance Brigade. As a member of the 'Sabah Society' he was interested in the amazing Orang-Utan sanctuary in the jungle about fifteen miles from Sandakan.

These creatures are classified as monkeys, although Le Gross Clarke wanted to put them in a supergenus 'Hominidae'. They do undoubtedly make tools, which by definition makes them human and should entitle them to a vote and representation at the United Nations, and have a fairly extensive language. I am not quite certain that they cannot count. The sanctuary is a clinic surrounded by a high fence which is not to keep them in but an attempt to keep the healthy ones out. It doesn't. They are admitted for treatment when they are ill and the females come in to have their babies. There are always a few youngsters about who have been orphaned. I myself only visited the place once, accompanied by Valerie's children when they were living with me. The Orang-Utan of all ages made them most welcome and I have photographs of David aged nine happily clutching a baby which he is quite unaware is one of the rarest animals in the world.

One middle-aged female with bilateral cataract was operated on by Richard. Somehow she understood perfectly how her sight had been restored, and on being re-admitted to have the second side done, lay down happily on the operating table and held out her arm for the pentothal. Thereafter she greeted him on every visit he made, and followed him about like a devoted dog. Unfortunately he did not realize that she was in love with him. One day he went there accompanied by his wife, and the Orang realized for the first time that she had a rival in love. She was normally the gentlest of creatures, but the green-eyed monster struck and Sylvia was very seriously mauled and bitten.

My first home in Jesselton was a long way out on the road to Penampang where my only two near neighbours were Bishops, one Anglican and the other Roman. They were both broad minded (for Bishops) and there was no fighting. The house itself was quite extraordinary. It was being rented by the Government from the estate of a rich Chinese doctor, and was always known as 'Dr Pang's House'. It was, externally, a quite enormous house that could have housed four of five families, as it had done in the good Doctor's time. Willing though he was to accommodate and support a large number of poor relatives, he did not want to have them cluttering up his own home. All the large rooms, and several of them were very large, therefore opened by their own front doors into hidden corners of the garden. The house proper had only a very few rooms and even they were minuscule. All the rest of the space was taken up by corridors. As is common in the East, bedrooms, dining room, kitchen and sitting room were on the first floor surrounded by a balcony, and entered by an outside staircase. After exploring the dark and dusty area below where the servants lived, I remarked one day that the rooms were much bigger down there and that I was thinking of giving them the house and living in the servants' quarters. It was only some weeks after I had moved out that it was discovered that I had been doing just that. Removal of a huge mass of tangled bush below the front veranda had disclosed a massive Victorian front door opening into an entrance hall blocked with debris, and it was the house itself that for years had been used for the servants.

By then I had moved to the hilltop which was to be my home for the rest of my life in Borneo. It was an unusual structure for that part of the world and in Africa would have been called a Kopje. There were just four houses on and around the summit and separated from each other and from the surrounding world by thick virgin jungle. It provided me with the complete isolation I wanted while only a mile from the hospital and little more from the town. With the house came a Sino-Kadazan Amah recently widowed with six children who together provided for all my wants. A few days after moving in I was given a full-sized Dachschund bitch by a returning expatriate and with my new Compton Organ delivered I had everything in the world I wanted, except of course a wife.

In April 1967 a cable arrived to say that Daddy had suffered a coronary thrombosis and two days later another to say he was gravely ill. I had an excellent Medical Officer and there was another Consultant at Tawau, so I was able to book an air passage and start for home within a few hours. I arrived to find him temporarily very much improved, but he had a recurrence ten days afterwards and died instantly. I cabled for an extra month's compassionate leave and was able to do most of the winding-up of the estate before I left. I also very fortunately extracted a promise from my mother that she would come out to spend Christmas with me in Borneo. She subsequently came out every year until my retirement. On all her later visits she came by air, but on this first occasion she sailed from Rotterdam on a cargo-passenger ship taking ten weeks and returned P & O from Hong Kong.

The Canal was closed at the time and I suggested that on her way home she leave the ship at Durban and carry on in about a fortnight by the *Union Castle*. Her plans were on her return to buy a house in Bath in which to spend her declining years. I thought (correctly) that she would do much better to settle in South Africa, and also (incorrectly) that she would meet a lot of the South African relatives in Durban and decide to make a home among them. Instead she made a bridge friend on the ship, carried on to Cape Town with her, and stayed there seventeen years.

Initially Mummy used to come to Borneo for Christmas and stay until about Easter, and I would visit her in South Africa on my way home or back every leave. After several years however it struck me that it was foolish for her to be wasting most of the South African summer and I going to Cape town in the very worst of the winter, so we changed it so that I went to Cape Town for Christmas and she came to me during the Cape Town winter. It reduced my visits to Bisley but enabled me to see a lot more of Mummy and South Africa. At first she stayed in a series of small private hotels but for the last dozen years she rented a small luxury flat in the southern suburb of Claremont with a magnificent view of Table Mountain. It was a lovely place to visit in the summer but for me at least quite impossible in the winter. The whole of my working life overseas I was able to return to England for every long leave by sea, and often towards the end to make part of the outward journey also by sea, taking the *Union Castle* Mailship as far as Cape Town and then flying on via either Australia or Hong Kong.

Our greatest friend in Jesselton was Archdeacon Archie Briggs of the Anglican Cathedral. Archie had been for many years a missionary in China but was thrown out by the Communists, and his ability to speak more than one Chinese language made him invaluable to the Church in Borneo. He was subsequently required to leave us when the Muslims became too militant and began imprisoning and expelling all expatriate priests and nuns. In his seventies he came to me in St Helena for a holiday at a time when we were a priest short, and did more work than any of us.

A curious aspect of my Government Service in Borneo was the regularity with which I resigned or was sacked. Throughout my overseas service I elected to have twenty-month contracts and seldom if ever were these actually renewed before I went on leave. Partly this was due to the absurd regulation that an officer was only entitled to a sea passage on retirement, so that in theory every contract had to be my last, but also to the unpleasant characters of a succession of Medical Directors. These men were always chosen on account of long service in junior (never specialist) jobs, or for racial, religious, or political reasons. There were three who were good, honest, and efficient. The rest were self seeking, untruthful and malicious; and included a drunk and an antichristian religious bigot. There was thus a game of double bluff; with my pretending I was probably not coming back, and the DMS pretending he didn't want me. This bluff however never proceeded to the point of packing up my house and paying off my servants or even stopping booking cases for my next contract, and I would always leave a steak or a chicken in the deep-freeze for the evening of my return. The only exception was when I came back unexpectedly from what was believed to be a mortal illness, and the DMS was so horrified to find me still alive that he refused to renew my contract. On this occasion his successor was made to, but not before I had put all my furniture in store and given up my house so that on my return I had to move to another on the same hilltop.

One such occasion was in 1969 when I prolonged my contract and sailed to Cape Town on *Iberia* to spend Christmas with Mummy. I bought a second-hand motor car and we set out together on a tour of South Africa and Rhodesia, driving two or three hundred miles a day and stopping off at Beaufort West, Bloemfontein, Johannesburg and Pretoria, and then spending six days in the Kruger National Park before going on to Rhodesia. The National Roads in South Africa are magnificent and over thousands of miles they are little if any inferior to our Motorways and with only a fraction of the traffic. There is an overall speed limit which varies from time to time and was then I think sixty. Over vast stretches there is no cover as far as the eye can see, but every six or eight miles there is one tree, and under that tree a speed-cop. Everybody slows down as soon as he sees the tree, and the cops have a very thin time.

On the first morning we stopped for coffee at a little pull-up in the Karoo run by an English couple, and overheard a rather sad conversation. The lady was talking to another motorist and said 'Yes, it does rain here. It was raining the day we came here twenty-eight years ago, but it hasn't rained since.' First impressions can be very misleading. I remember nothing of Beaufort West or Bloemfontein (they were only nightstops at 'Motels') and both Johannesburg and Pretoria were exactly what one would expect. The former is an ugly Dutch business centre, and Pretoria a spacious Garden City, but still with a Dutch accent.

There are two 'White' South Africa's. Natal and Cape Town (though not all of Cape Province) are English, while Pretoria and Johannesburg are Dutch. Cecil Rhodes spoke of them as 'The two nations', not including the Blacks in either. The Coloureds, although mainly living in Cape Town, belong properly to the Cape Dutch peoples, being of the same mixed race and differing only in skin shade. The Hollanders as well as the Indians (at least in Natal) belong definitely on the English side, being pure Aryans and for the most part intensely pro-British. In spite of recent troubles, the Cape Coloureds probably see themselves still as linked with the Afrikaaners, whose language they speak. They share with them the position of being committed to the country and, unlike the English, Indians, and Hollanders having nowhere else to run to. Those who know what happened in Indonesia in 1945 to the Eurasians there, have good reason to be afraid of any collapse of the Afrikaans Government and a Black take-over.

Things have changed now since Boetha's 'Rubicon' speech and the attacks on the Church; but during most of the period of Nat control the problem in South Africa was not (as the rest of the world believed) Apartheid, but Krugerism. To the Afrikaaner the Boer War was not over; and the country was not split between 'whites' and others, but between Dutch and English. Even now the vast majority of English South Africans have in their hearts no desire for racial equality and would welcome a return to the situation of George VI's day. However these people are, almost to a man, members of the Anglican or Roman Churches in common with almost all the Christian Blacks. To turn Cape Dutch conscripts onto breaking up Church Services with tear gas and rifle butts, to knock down Priests and Bishops outside St George's Cathedral with fire hoses, are the acts not of tyrants but of madmen. Such suicidal stupidity is the product of a national death-wish, and the Boer Nation has destroyed itself.

I was amused rather than horrified to see benches in the lovely gardens of Parliament House in Pretoria labelled 'Whites only'. Most examples of peti-apartheid were the same. In general the Blacks did not want to share in the shoddy facilities of the lower middle class whites. The 'Non-whites only' benches were empty not because they were offensive but because they were unwanted: and to see earnest Afrikaaners hurrying past them to find a bench at which they were permitted to sit, inspired not anger but ridicule and contempt. These things were childish and didn't matter. Then there was hope for South Africa. Now there is none; so they still don't matter.

I tried whenever possible to avoid driving in the towns so we left Pretoria at dawn, and again at nearly eleven in the height of the morning rush. The reason for the double departure was the family's weakness in matters of geography and in this instance of astronomy. I have never understood the Copernican theory, but I do know that the top of a map is North and that East and West are right and left respectively. My mother knew this too and never disputed the fact. It followed that on leaving Pretoria all we had to do to find the Kruger National

Park was to drive due east. There were signs at every corner showing the way to the National Road so that we reached it in a few minutes, but none indicating which was east and which west. After about ten miles I began to have horrible doubts and suggested we might be going the wrong way. Mummy was not always at her best in the early mornings and snapped back 'Nonsense. There's the sun rising behind you. Surely even you know that the sun rises in the west.' Actually until that moment I had never thought about the subject but forty-two years of experience of other things had taught me that Mummy was always right, so I drove on, put my foot down, and covered a very good distance in the next two hours. Mummy glowered for a time, then subsided into a thoughtful silence, and finally became very thoughtful indeed. I maintained a dutiful filial attitude of quiet, and the miles rolled by. Some time before we would have entered Angola, my mother said very quietly 'Just pull up at the side of the road for a moment while I think. I am not at all sure the sun does rise in the west.' I had no strong views on the subject and knew better than venture an opinion, so I did as I was asked until it was decided that we should turn round at the next entry point and go the other way. Fortunately this side road had a name on it corresponding to a little dorp on our map, so we were able to verify that, on this occasion at least, the sun had risen in the east. We reached Pretoria again in another couple of hours and, after weaving through some of the thickest and most ill-tempered traffic I have struck in South Africa, started off for the second time at about eleven.

The Kruger National Park was no disappointment even though I had been hearing stories of it all my life. It is not a Game Park as understood in other parts of the world, but a large chunk of Africa cut off from human interference and left essentially for the normal struggle for existence to go on as it has always done. The huge herds of buck, zebra, and giraffe look after themselves and provide food for the carnivores. Only if the balance of nature looks to be going seriously awry will the keepers interfere in any way. We saw and filmed in five days more varieties of Game than I have heard of anyone else seeing in three or four weeks. We were working to a fairly tight schedule as I was determined to see something of Free Rhodesia before the inevitable cable arrived calling me back to Borneo, and if the tryanical boasting of HMG was of any meaning at all (Wilson said he would destroy them in 'Days rather than weeks'), they might not remain free much longer. We left the park late one evening and drove to Rhodesia via Beit Bridge the next day.

The Colony of Southern Rhodesia was granted full internal self-government in 1924 by King George V without any provision for enfranchisement of the Blacks. The Government of Ian Smith was properly elected according to the constitution. I am getting a little worried at the way official lies in the New Elizabethan England are being persisted in long after they have served their purpose. Nobody today believes that Napoleon's troops ate captured children, or that the Pretender was smuggled into the Royal bedroom in a warming pan; yet they believe that Ian Smith's Government was illegal as much as they believe the even dirtier lie that Hong Kong does not belong to us but was only loaned to us by a treaty that expires in 1997. Britain's propaganda machine is enormously more efficient than anything Goebels achieved; and there is a very real danger that future historians will never know, because they will never suspect and investigate, the truth of the Suez War and the Biafran genocide. If there was any illegal authority involved, it was the British Government itself. The House of Commons has been of very doubtful legality ever since large numbers of overseas tax-payers and others were disenfranchised by the abolition of their rightful votes as university graduates. My sympathies were entirely with the loyal Government of Ian Smith as against the illegal Westminster regime under Wilson. The danger, the very great danger, is that if the truth of these things is discovered all together in a few hundred years, people will with these wicked falsehoods also discount the true stories of England's greatness in the past.

We entered Rhodesia by Beit Bridge across the 'Great grey-green greasy Limpopo River, all set about with fever-trees.' In front of us as we crossed was a large sign 'Thank you South Africa'. Ian Smith was one of the handful of fighter pilots who saved us in the Battle of Britain. Farming in Rhodesia was one of the recognized retirement jobs for Regular Army officers, and some hundreds of the settlers there were men who had given their all for their King and Empire throughout a lifetime of military service in conditions of toil and danger of which Wilson knew nothing. The leaders of South Africa were those

242

who had been locked up for treasonous sympathies and activities in one war and in some cases were the sons of known traitors and rebels of the previous two; yet they were the only loyal friends Rhodesia had, and were being thanked for it. Rhodesia and the notice have gone: but England's shame remains, as it will do for ever.

Salisbury was a beautiful little town with clean well kept public parks, in one of which was the War Memorial to Blacks and Whites alike, without any distinction thought of. It bore the simple inscription (which I have seen nowhere else) 'They died for their King'. On Sunday evening everybody was enjoying the very, very English custom of sitting round the bandstand listening to the same sort of music they would have heard at Southport. The children playing together were of both colours as were the parents sitting together. Any racialism was in the filthy minds of the people of England five thousand miles away. There were it is true two separate hospitals one called 'The African Hospital' and the other 'The European Hospital' and I visited both. As however I specially wanted to see the Radiotherapy and Kidney units which were not duplicated it happened that all the patients I saw in the European Hospital were Blacks and almost all I saw in the African Hospital were Europeans.

It was on leaving the 'European Hospital' that I had my most interesting experience in Rhodesia. I had telephoned for a taxi and when it arrived it was a Mercedes owned and run by its African driver. As he had picked me up outside the doctors' quarters, he turned to me after a few moments and asked 'You new doctor sah?' (This was an unusual word for an African who would normally have said 'Baas'.)

I said 'Well I am a doctor, but my hospital is about seven thousand miles away from here.'

'Is it as good as hospital as this?'

I wasn't going to stand for that so I said, 'Well, it's a very good hospital, but this is a very good hospital too.'

He was one of the downtrodden Blacks, and a successful Black capitalist too, who should have been counting the days before the oppressors were thrown out and he and his kind could run the country for the benefit of his people. Here was a golden opportunity to tell a visitor how they were suffering. He said, 'Sah, I have worked all over Africa. I have worked in Cairo, I have worked in Mombassa, I have worked in Lagos. There is no government in the whole of Africa that looks after the Black man as this Government does.'

We visited all the regular tourist sights including Fort Victoria and Cecil Rhodes' grave which I had been wanting to see since the film *Rhodes of Africa* in my prep-school days, and then drove on to Victoria Falls. The world famous 'Falls Hotel' was in a state of dilapidation not much better than the Hotel des Indes and after being shown a couple of rooms with brass bedsteads and crazily wired pre-1914 electric fans perched on wooden packing cases, we cancelled our booking and moved to the excellent 'Cassino Hotel'. It was here that disaster struck and Mummy went down with an attack of acute cholecystitis.

The Dutch, like most foreigners and today a lot of young British Surgeons as well, treat this condition by emergency operation. The mortality in good hands is of the order of five per cent, but the situation is made even worse by the greatly increased risk of disastrous surgical injuries to vital structures (as happened to Anthony Eden and cost us the British Empire when his liver went yellow on him at a vital moment) consequent on operating with the whole area inflamed and oedematous. I have always followed the traditional management of conservative treatment with drugs, starvation, and intravenous fluids. It is said that this works in all but one case in 200, but in the 200th case the gall-bladder ruptures and the resulting infected biliary peritonitis is almost always fatal. It is a risk I am very willing to take. I have treated almost exactly 400 cases this way and if I have another shall be quite prepared for a rupture and a fatal outcome. The law of averages caught up with me about my 200th case but after a horrendous operation and a very stormy convalescence she recovered. Most cases treated conservatively recover a normal gall bladder function and do not need operation. In those who do the mortality as a cold case is negligible. All my cases have lived whereas had I used the modern aggressive approach, twenty of them would be dead.

I could not of course treat my own mother, especially in a country where I was not registered and could not buy drugs. The only medical care available was from a charming young Hollander serving as a medical officer in the Rhodesian Air Force. He was somewhat overawed by my FRCS and was kind enough to ask my advice. Of course I recommended conservative management (the only alternative was an ambulance plane to Bulawayo and operation there) so he flew the drip solutions and streptomycin in, instead of flying the patient out, and the result was perfect. Had this been the 200th case I should of course have been guilty of matricide, but it wasn't. Gall bladder function did not return and my mother had a Cholecystectomy in excellent conditions in Cape Town the next year.

It was ten days before Mummy was fit to fly and we then flew back to Cape Town sending the car by rail. I still had nearly a month before the usual frantic cable arrived begging me to come back to Jesselton.

The only other time when my leave was prolonged as a result of a genuine possibility that I was not coming back was even more recently. On this occasion I was sailing on *Edinburgh Castle* to Durban with a possible view to getting a job at a mission hospital in Zululand, when my mother cabled to say she had received a telephone call from a doctor in Tasmania who wanted me to go there immediately to replace a dead surgeon in a group practice with its own hospital near Hobart. As a result of several long and expensive telephone calls it was agreed that I should go out as a locum for two months only to deal with a waiting list of urgent cases which was getting longer day by day. Incredibly, so gentlemanly was the whole negotiation, nothing was ever said about fees, remuneration or passage expenses. They trusted me, and I, mug that I was, trusted them.

I went to the Australian ambassador in Cape Town who assured me that there would be no difficulties, but that as there was no time for him to issue a visa then (I did not think to ask why) he would give me a letter saying that my visa application was approved and that it would be entered in my passport in Manila, which was the last stop before Australia.

After paying my own first class fare, I found that my arrival in the Australian embassy in Manila was the funniest thing that had happened in their country's history since they gave up poisoning the wells used by the black fellows. The entire embassy staff came down to see this Pommy Bastard who had travelled eight thousand miles at his own expense trusting in the word of their ambassador in South Africa. I was told that there was no question of my being allowed in just for a few weeks to save a few Australian lives, but that as a favour I would be allowed to apply for 'full immigrant status'. As however I was now in Manila I would have to come in under the 'Asian Quota' (Apartheid is a religion in Australia and this made me a yellow man) and it would be six weeks before I could have a medical examination to decide whether I was healthy enough even by those standards.

On telephoning my intended employer in Tasmania, a man who claimed to be a Scot, I naturally expected some sympathy and possibly assistance in recovering some of the enormous expense I had been put to in trying to help him and his patients; but I was met with complete indifference. Having arranged for all my mail to be sent to his address, and suspecting that he would not spend a penny on me now that I was not going to be a profit to him, I wrote to his secretary enclosing a cheque for five pounds for my mail to be returned by air mail. None was. A little did in fact reach me many months later by surface mail with my address scrawled across it but not re-stamped. The cheque was cashed.

Nothing much ever happened in Sabah but we did while I was there have visits from Prince Philip, the Queen and Princess Anne, Lord Louis Mountbatten, and the Archbishop of Canterbury, not to mention the President of the Royal College of Surgeons of Edinburgh.

The Duke's visit was while I was at Tawau where he was greeted by our almost globular, fair haired, smooth skinned, smiling, bouncing acting Chief Medical Officer, who in spite of all appearances was a very good doctor and administrator with a heart of gold. As he stepped ashore they exchanged a grossly overacted Masonic Handshake which could be recognized from a hundred yards away. His Royal Highness had obviously not considered that this apparently blown up advertisement for Cow and Gate baby food ('Baby Hicks . . . so does ours') could possibly be one of the brethren, so that when it was thrust upon him he was so astonished he could not remember whether to press first or tickle. He has a wonderful gift for concealing boredom, and when he flew off to Jesselton after a whole day with us, everybody felt he had been very interested in everything we showed him and had enjoyed every minute of it. The Queen does the same, but of course it is expected of her. Princess Anne spent all her time with us obviously brooding on her horse left behind in England, and I at least had every sympathy with her.

The Royal visit was to be in February 1972. These things are planned down to the minutest detail several months before, and I knew that I was to meet her three times. I only had one respectable suit and although I knew Her Majesty would neither notice nor care, the Duke would almost certainly say the third time 'I recognized you by your suit.' Accordingly I flew to Singapore for two nights to have two more made by Ah Chum. Even the most famous tailor in the city was able to do the whole job in that time, and would have done so in a day had there been need. The second night I was just going to bed when I ran into Lord Louis Mountbatten. It was fairly obvious that he was on his way to join us, so I spoke to him and we went together for a drink at the Long Bar. He told me that he was joining *Britannia* in the harbour the next day.

As soon as I got home I telephoned the new Director of Medical Services to tell him that Lord Louis was going to be one of the Royal Party, and that we must make special arrangements for him. To my surprise he refused to believe me and ridiculed the suggestion. He was in charge of the arrangements and had been given all the necessary information. My advice and ideas were definitely not required. Fortunately I had working for me at that time an Indian doctor named Radjapaxa, the daughter of their ambassador at the United Nations and former ambassador in Paris. She had been brought up at the Paris embassy and knew how to behave. Besides which she was a very pretty girl. I knew she would be a success and told her to be ready to accompany Lord Louis.

The great day came and we were all standing in line waiting for the Royal Rolls Royce to draw up, when the DMS came to me in a state of pure panic.

'I have just heard that Lord Louis Mountbatten is one of the party and that he is to be given Royal Honours. What on earth shall I do?'

'That's all right Sir' I replied 'I have told Dr Radjapaxa to look after him. She will know just what to do.'

247

He looked at me with angry astonishment.

'You knew he was coming, didn't you?'

'Yes Sir, I telephoned you on Tuesday to tell you.'

'How did you know?' he demanded with fury.

'He told me.' I replied very politely.

I have known him for many years since but he has never dared to ask in what possible circumstances Lord Louis could have told me this. There are advantages in staying at the Raffles.

Archbishop Michael Ramsey called on us on his way home from a tour of Australia, very largely I suspect to see Archie Briggs. He celebrated a pontifical High Mass at the Anglican Cathedral on the evening of his arrival. The service was marked by high drama and very nearly by stark tragedy. The acoustics of the Cathedral are not good, and the priest cannot be heard at all unless he wears a throat microphone which plugs into a socket in the pulpit. He changes to one with a longer cable when at the Altar as he has to be able to walk forward to communicate the other priests and those in the Sanctuary. Everything depends on his walking round the Altar the right way. Ramsey didn't. At the climatic moment when our own Bishop, the Archdeacon, and all our priests, were kneeling in a semicircle and he was advancing on them with the Sacrament in his hands, the cable tightened round his throat and he began to asphyxiate.

The situation was terrible. There was the Archbishop strangling before our very eyes, and we all on our knees unable to do a thing for him. The tension was more than we could bear, as fortunately it was for the cable. It parted with a musical note suggestive of a breaking violin string, sprang forward like a whiplash, and knocked over a very small kneeling acolyte, putting out his candle. All was well.

Ramsey was a man beloved of everyone, but he will always have a special place in my heart. I had to meet him several times and he could never remember my name and always had to address me as 'Sir'. No doubt it was a childish emotion but I got a tremendous kick out of being addressed as 'Sir' by the Archbishop of Canterbury.

I had frequently spoken of an early retirement, and though Mummy often pressed me to leave and go to live with her in Cape Town, I never really wanted to. Retiring age for

248

expatriates is fifty-five and although not many are invited to stay on after then, I knew with reasonable certainty that I should be. Mummy was getting no younger however, and it was clear that there would come a time when she was no longer able to visit me every year. Even in 1981 she was saying that it must be her last visit and I only persuaded her to come out the next year by promising that I would retire the following Christmas. Perhaps I did not really think she would hold me to it, but when the time came she had so obviously set her heart on it that I could not refuse in spite of firm pressure to remain. I am profoundly thankful that I did, as she had only another seven months to live and it would have been terrible if I had been in Borneo when she died.

It was obvious that we could not live for long in the little flat, and I had in fact almost bought a house in Bishop's Court on my last visit. I was becoming increasingly doubtful though whether South Africa was going to remain a good place to live so, after selling off much of my household effects and packing my organ and a few books (about 2,460 actually), put them in storage. I little thought that I should next see them on the island of St Helena, which if asked I should probably have said was a fortress somewhere in the Pacific Ocean.

7

A MISERABLE RETIREMENT

I had been planning and looking forward to my retirement since the summer of 1932 when I was five. I can well remember the afternoon before my first day at Kindergarten. Even in those days I was accustomed to think things out and make my plans with great care. It was clear to me that the Golden Age was over, and that for the next thirteen years or so I was going to have to work. Also I knew that after that I should have to work to earn my living, but also to save money for my retirement. It may sound absurd but I determined there and then to work hard and to find myself a job where I could make money as quickly as possible with a view to an early resumption of the life I had known up to then. Just possibly this attitude has dominated my working life to an unhealthy extent, except that I have been very lucky that the jobs I have wanted to do, and have felt called to do, have always been sufficiently well paid for me to have had no serious temptation to look elsewhere.

I think probably that on that afternoon at the very beginning, my ambitions were largely limited to retiring to live at home with Mummy and Daddy (a child of that age sees his parents as immortal), but I knew that when I grew up I should be supporting them from the money I had made (which idea pleased me) and also wrongly assumed that, as I was paying, I should be giving the orders (which pleased me even more). Over the years however I came more to terms with reality, and thought mainly of a large house (large enough for my needs but not a palace), with extensive grounds in which I could shoot my own game, and of course plenty of servants. I don't think at any time I was building castles in the air. I was only thinking of sufficient servants to attend to my needs, and enough garden and estate to keep me happy. I think that had I been shown the house, grounds, and staff I now have on St Helena, I would have been perfectly satisfied and not asked for more. Within a few years I was thinking in terms of a big library and a music room with a piano and an organ as big as Grandpa's, as well as the chance to travel round the world in luxury whenever I wanted, but I have got those too. It is astonishing that neither then or at any other time did a wife and family come into the picture. I always assumed I would have a wife (I thought everybody had), but I saw her essentially as someone who would supervise the servants: and the children as something entertaining who would come home in the school holidays and afterwards be making their own way in the world without interfering with my house, estate, and travelling. Over the years I added minor details, almost all being things I wanted to do and see on my travels.

All this I tried, and indeed accomplished, in the ten months between retiring and starting to train for a new career. It was absolute misery.

South Africa is too cold for a chronic asthmatic from May to September, and I sailed for UK to spend the summer there on the only ship still on the run, *RMS Centaur*. Mummy was to follow me on the next sailing in June. I don't think I was even aware that we had to stop at St Helena, and had given no thought to going ashore. I did so however on a bright hot day and fell in love with the place. The second day I spent the morning in the hospital examining all the facilities and equipment in detail, and came to the conclusion that St Helena might prove a very satisfactory place to set up a retirement home for Mummy where we could both stay all year long when necessary without always having to run away from the winter, as I at least had to do in Cape Town. My idea was to buy my own house and get an 'Honorary' type appointment at the hospital where there was just enough surgery to keep me happy, but not enough to make a full time appointment for a surgeon doing nothing else. A few days later, having thought the thing out in detail and having met Bishop Edward Cannan who sailed with us on leave from the island, I improved the scheme to include, if he would let me, studying part time under him with a view to possible Ordination in about five or six

251

years when I became too old for any more surgery. I said nothing about it to him. Everything depended after all on whether Mummy liked the place and the idea. She didn't.

I wrote and telephoned her as soon as I got to England, setting out the whole scheme and asked her to go ashore and take a taxi ride around the island to see how lovely it was. I had arranged with the Pursar for her to be put ashore in the special equipment used for the aged and infirm (she was eighty-six), carefully concealing from her that it was normally used for landing cattle. She would have none of it; and made her own way by small boat, swinging herself up the landing steps with a rope. She visited everywhere and saw everything, and decided it stank. Surprisingly she gave the matter a lot of thought overnight, and came to the generous conclusion that as I had liked it so much she must be missing something. Next day accordingly she repeated the performance, swinging herself up by the rope from an even rougher sea and seeing everything again. She decided it stank even worse; and rang me up to say so. That appeared to be the end of it. Of course neither of us thought for a moment that she had only three weeks to live.

Meanwhile I was trying to make a holiday in wintry conditions in England. As usual I made my base at the Arundell Arms at Lifton but seldom left the hotel except to drive to the various pubs at nearby villages for lunch. It was much too cold for fishing but I did once walk down to one of the beats to look at the water, and not for the first time fell in while doing so and was able to look at the water from below. I always find this annoying (as well as wet). I accept an occasional immersion while actually fishing as I am always paying more attention to my fish than to where I am putting my feet, but there is something unjust in falling in when one is just out for a look around. After a time I gave up and drove to Birmingham for a few days with the Porters and then as it was just as cold there, flew over to Amsterdam where it was warmer. On my return I got some fishing in passable weather, visited Monkton for Old Boys' day, and then moved to the Fernly Hotel at Bath where I was to stay with Mummy.

Quite illegally I was able to board *Centaur* at Avonmouth docks and have breakfast with Mummy before driving her to Bath. We had five days lovely holiday together and then set off for Yorkshire, stopping for two nights at the Prince of Wales

Hotel in Southport. Mummy was taken ill early on Saturday morning and died on Sunday in the Royal Infirmary. She had told me many times that she did not want to die in South Africa but to be buried with Daddy, and although it would have been terribly difficult to arrange I had always resolved when she was unwell in Borneo or Cape Town that I would do it. In the event she died within half a mile of her husband's grave.

Valerie heard from her mother whom I had asked to the funeral and telephoned me twice in the next week. The second time she mentioned that David was in Wales on a few days' holiday with his father who was over on business. Without a thought I said 'Ask Brian to bring him round to the Arundell Arms and I will give him a holiday and put him on a plane home next month.' I had not got the telephone back on its cradle before I was saying to myself 'You bloody fool! You are a nervous wreck and not fit to look after yourself let alone a small boy as well.' I need not have worried. I had overlooked the quantum difference between a twelve year old and a boy of sixteen. There was no question of my having to look after him. I signed the cheques, but he took complete charge of me and gave me a holiday in Lifton, Southport, London, Rome, and Sorento. Anything I had ever done for the Loosmore children was bread cast upon the waters and it was returned to me a thousand fold. He saved my sanity and looked after me for a whole month when I most needed it; without having to spank me once, which is more than I had ever managed with him.

Having packed David off to Canada I returned for a few more days at Lifton and then set off to visit Borneo. For some reason I had an attack of economy and booked on the amazingly cheap return flight to Brunei which is one sixth the price of the standard first class fare. It looked to be worthwhile to put up with two day's discomfort to save two and a half thousand pounds but it wasn't. British Airways had messed up my booking of a seat in the non-smoking cabin and had to upgrade me (without charge) to the new 'Business' class. I was taken out of the tiny eggcup like seat in the stern and put into one little better at the front. What the comfort and service would have been like in the cheap class I dare not think as it was unbearable in the Business Class. When I got to Kota Kinabalu I went to see my usual travel agent who had been booking me first class for twenty years and told them what I had done. I was prepared if necessary to tear up my return ticket but against all the rules they telephoned London and got special permission to give me a refund against a first class ticket provided I travelled with British Airways. They must have concluded, quite rightly, that I was not fully responsible for my own actions.

With Mummy dead my circumstances had altered completely, and I was hoping that as Sabah had been so anxious for me to stay only eight months before, that they would offer me another contract. Unfortunately their situation had changed too: and with a young Chinese in my job, everyone's attitude was 'How nice of the old boy to come back to see us all. Let's hope he lives long enough to do it again.' I flew back to England via Bangkok and booked on *Centaur* back to the flat at Cape Town. To my joy, the first person I saw on the ship was Bishop Cannan, also going home at the end of his leave. The Lord guided me to ask him whether it might be possible for me to study under him with a view to Ordination, and to my surprise he at once became very enthusiastic and even offered me a living in a few years if I wanted it. Fortunately I made it quite clear from the beginning that I should not.

I still had a lot to do winding up my old life and my mother's affairs. Some of the papers I had to go through showed that family estates had not been wound up properly this century and I was writing letters to the successors of long dead solicitors and company secretaries over wills that had been proved as long ago as 1892. One of these I have still not got cleared up. It was thus over six months before I got down to any serious studying and I did not get to St Helena until April 1985. It was from one of these papers, a writ issued against the Duke of Devonshire over some cottages, that I discovered that Grandpa described himself as 'I Frederick Arthur Crook, Fishmonger'. Presumably the Duke did not want to be seen in dispute with a fishmonger and the case appears to have been settled out of court.

I met the Bishop again in Cape Town where he was for the Provincial Synod and was given a lot of reading to get done, as well as a list of clerical clothing which I should need and which I had made by a local military tailor: but I still had business to settle in England so sailed back for the summer of 1984, took the opportunity for another visit to Borneo, and carried on round the world with a two week stop in Canada staying with the Loosmores. On my return I got down to very serious study, using my old technique of writing a long precis of the lectures and textbooks. I soon realized I was getting nowhere fast. On a visit to the local vicar he made a chance remark which changed everything. we were talking about changing times (and of course how much better everything was when we were young) and he said 'There is my boy upstairs doing his Theology on a computer.' I didn't know what a computer was, and still don't; but I went out and bought one and have never looked back. I wrote six thick volumes of notes in four months and now use it several times a day for all my household business, correspondence, stockmarket records, and above all for writing my sermons.

One's attitude to computers today should be the same as an intelligent man's was towards the early motor cars. They are no more reliable or indispensable than a car was in the early days of motoring, and at least as likely to break down or to injure one. No sane man would have regarded a motor car as a substitute for traditional forms of transport or have given up his horse and carriage because he had bought one of the new toys: nor would he have trusted to one for an important journey. A man who uses a computer to the exclusion of methods which have served for centuries and then blames it for his failures, deserves as little sympathy as one who failed to keep an important appointment because he was lying on his back in a muddy road tinkering with a primitive differential gear.

I sailed for St Helena on 20 April. My retirement was over.

8

OLD MAN, YOUNG PRIEST

'You can't make a silk purse out of a sow's ear.' This is a very old proverb, and people usually say that the words have become corrupted and that it was originally something quite different. Even so pig-skin is a very good material to make a purse out of; and in the days when a pig's head was cheap it must have been perfectly possible to empty out the ear of a sow and turn the skin into a very good purse. The point is that it would not be a silk purse. Those who have read this far must surely have said just that when I spoke of becoming a priest. It would be a very understandable thing to say; but if they said it they would have been forgetting something. You cannot make a silk purse out of a sow's ear, and neither can I, but God can. For with God all things are possible. I am going to try to tell you how he did it.

Men do not enter the ministry because they think it would be a pleasant life and a well paid job. When he is made Deacon (the first stage toward priesthood) a candidate is required to swear that he believes he is truly called by God, and I believe that everyone who does so is speaking the literal truth. I know I was.

The call comes in a number of very different ways. There are men (and women too) who have been called to the Religious life by hearing an audible voice speaking to them. In some cases a man is of such vital importance to the working out of God's plans, that if he will not co-operate, he has to be made to. Such a man was Saul of Tarsus. Another was Jonah. Fortunately for us God does not have to call everybody in such a dramatic fashion. To a few he does speak in an audible voice, as he spoke to the infant Samuel, and to Paul after he had been struck down but it is not given to everybody to hear God's voice speaking directly in this way. Possibly a fair number of boys and young men called to serve God in the Ministry of the Church, or of women called to the Religious Vocation do so; but certainly most do not. At Monkton, which in my time produced virtually nothing but Priests, Missionaries, and Doctors with a very strong sense of vocation, we were constantly exhorted to be prepared for God's call and to be ready to respond to it when it came. I believe some did receive the call in this way, sometimes while kneeling at prayer in the School Chapel; but the majority did not. The call came none the less, as a call to a vocation comes to everybody in God's own good time, and in the way he knows to be best. I certainly had no idea of becoming either a Doctor or a Priest when I arrived there, but I think I knew my destiny with a fair degree of certainty, long before I left school.

I am never happy about the expression so popular today of 'Born again Christian'. The term is not original, and in the sense in which 'Born again' was used by Our Lord is absurd. One cannot be a Christian at all unless one is born again of water and the Holy Spirit. I cannot remember a time when I had any doubts about the reality of the immanent presence of God, or the basic truths of the Faith. I have never been a particularly good or particularly demonstrative Christian, just an ordinary solid and stolid middle class believing fairly regular Church-goer. Perhaps, and only perhaps, I differed from some but not all, in that I have never made even a minor decision without murmuring a momentary prayer for guidance, and then being absolutely confident that what I have been guided to do is the will of God. In many ways it has made for a very easy life.

But what decided the matter (I cannot say precipitated because it took me so long to respond) was what happened in the summer of 1974. It was just a simple straightforward miracle. Sabah was at that time a militant Muslim dictatorship and people were going to Church in peril not merely of their jobs but even of their liberty. Large numbers of Christians were in detention without trial for no other reason than their Christian faith. The Church was of course flourishing as it always does under persecution. I don't know whether it is true to say that God listens to and answers prayers especially at such

257

times, I think he always does, but perhaps coming to Church at risk of suffering for it makes one pray especially devoutly and fervently, and strengthens ones faith, when of course God never lets you down.

I had to have a minor hernia operation which could perfectly well have been done by one of the Medical Officers. However it is a bad thing to let juniors operate on their chiefs (it makes promotion too easy), so I flew to Cambridge to have it done at Addenbrooke's Hospital. On the third post-operative day I had a stroke. I was only forty-eight and a spontaneous subarachnoid haemorrhage at that age carries a hundred per cent mortality. I made my own diagnosis, which impressed everybody though it was not difficult as before I sank into what was inevitably a terminal coma I was hemiparalysed. That is to say half my brain was in the state of that of Lazarus when he had lain four days in the grave. Three weeks later I woke up, without any disability.

For some days I was in doubt about my own sanity, or at least my clinical acumen and knowledge of pathology. Then I received a letter from Archie Briggs. Addenbrookes had cabled the Queen Elizabeth Hospital to say I was dying, and the persecuted people of Kota Kinabalu had been offering prayers of intercession for me at daily Mass in both the Roman and Anglican Cathedrals. As far as I am concerned it was as certain a case as the twenty authenticated miracles they have had at Loudres.

However there have been many other cases of much more deserving and useful people for whom God in his wisdom has not seen fit to provide a miracle of healing, and I had to ask myself 'Why me?' I still don't know the answer. At first I thought it possible that I was wanted as a 'Doctor Priest' for one of those places where priests are not admitted but where suitable men get in as Doctors and spend most of their time in the ministry, but in spite of much prayer and attempts to get myself accepted for training, things did not work out and I decided (and once more I stress that I know that after praying for guidance it was the right decision) that my vocation still lay in the job for which I had been trained. With that job gone things were vastly different and retirement having proved a flop there was no temptation to reject the very clear call to accept the Bishop's offer and go to St Helena.

I arrived in April 1985 to find that Bishop Cannan had either forgotten that I had originally asked for part-time training while I continued to do some surgery, or that he knew better what was good for me. I was given an unoccupied vicarage and precipitated into an intensive course of training that left me exhausted, but happier than I had been in years. The Cathedral Parish had been vacant for some months and the Bishop himself was as happy as a sandboy doing the work of a Parish Priest as well as his own; but there were plenty of non-sacramental services for me to take. He also had other amusements including servicing electrical equipment for the whole island. He was an expert instrument technician, having entered the RAF as an apprentice in 1937. With his gratuity at the end of the war he took his degree and Holy Orders and a little later returned to the air force rising to become their Assistant Chaplain in Chief before coming to the island as Bishop. It was a little frustrating for me because anyone else on the Island could count on his willing and enthusiastic help, but I as an ordinand could never being myself to call in my Bishop to repair my hoover or refrigerator.

The vicarage was a rambling house originally built for Sir Hudson Low the famous (or in some opinions infamous) Governor at the time of Napoloen's exile. It had at various times since been a school and the Bishop's residence. Its only endearing characteristic is its mice who own the place and know it. Only once in my life have I been able to sit by my very own fireside. I did so one cold night in the old schoolroom there which had a fireplace. The next day I had the fire re-laid but did not light it as the weather had turned warmer and I did not need one for a week. By that time the mice had moved in. I was just approaching with a match when I met face to face a very pregnant mouse who looked at me severely knowing that no gentleman would burn an expectant mother literally out of hearth and home. During the next few shivering weeks I comforted myself with the thought that I could have a fire again as soon as the family were grown up and able to fend for themselves. The children were delightful little things but when they were obviously adult I hardened my heart and went to shake them out of the now extensive dwelling to avoid incinerating any, only to find that they were now pregnant too. I never got another fire, but I grumbled about my misfortune to the Bishop and found afterwards that my reputation for spirituality (though not for sanity and worldly wisdom) had been enormously enhanced throughout the island.

St Helena is almost in the centre of the South Atlantic Ocean and the most isolated place on earth. Indeed it is the most isolated on this earth and in its immediate environs; it being much quicker to get to the moon and back. There is no airstrip, and the only communication with the outside world is by one small ship, *RMS St Helena*, which runs a shuttle service between Avonmouth and Cape Town six times a year. Once the ship has sailed north, there is no possible way of getting on or off the island for another six or seven weeks. It is only ten miles by six but has a quite unbelievable range of microclimates and distinct areas of vegetation.

The area around Jamestown (which holds about two thousand people and is the size of an English village but the only town on the island) is virgin desert. Driving a mile up the zigzag 'Ladder Hill Road' one comes to an are of Karoo indistinguishable from that in Cape Province. A mile further on approaching the Cathedral one turns a corner on the mountain side and comes upon rolling English downlands as far as the eye can see. One can then if one wishes turn right towards my present home, winding down a typical Devon lane to reach my Orange and Lemon orchard in what is still called 'Lemon Valley'. Otherwise one carries on down towards the far side of the island, through a small patch of tropical rain forest which could well be in Borneo, before reaching a half mile strip of barren rock along the southern coastline. St Helena has been described as 'A green emerald set in a ring of bronze' but the southern border of the ring is not the bronze of volcanic rock but the ivory of huge white boulders and shingle.

The schooling on the island has been good for two centuries (thanks to the Church which ran almost all the schools up to 1948 and provided Headmasters even to Government schools which sprang up from about 1815) and everyone can read and write; but there are many people, perhaps a hundred or more, who have lived on the island all their lives but have never travelled far enough to have seen the bright lights of Jamestown.

The people are Londoners and speak a form of Cockney not unlike that of Dickens' day with constant confusion of 'V' and

'W'. The island had few inhabitants before 1666, but after the Great Fire the East India Company provided passages to those left homeless in the Pudding Lane area, and they have been here ever since. Unfortunately, for the next century and a half they all had Malay slaves, which has turned their skins a little brown. This does not worry them but has had disastrous consequences in their relationship with the Mother Country. They have a charter guaranteeing them all the rights of citizens of England, in the name of King Charles II, his heirs and successors for ever. One would have thought this binding on any British sovereign, and that any attempt to sign an act purporting to deny them those rights would be void ab-initio as an act of abdication admitting that the signatory was no lawful successor to the Stuarts. Such would undoubtedly be the case if anything similar were attempted over the Falkland Islands or Gibraltar. The Colonies of St Helena and Hong Kong are different though. The people of the Falklands and Gibraltar have white skins.

In spite of this the 'Saints' remain intensely pro-British and almost pathologically devoted to the Queen and the Royal Family, whose photographs (as well as those of Queen Victoria and every Monarch since) adorn every house and cottage on the island. I once indiscreetly referred in a sermon to the divorce of an (unnamed) Royal Princess, and received an hysterical letter of rebuke from a devout parishioner who not only told me it was not for me to judge a member of the Royal Family, but implied that it was no concern of Our Lord's either.

In fairness it must be admitted that the island and its people are almost entirely maintained by the British taxpayer who in addition to major capital expenditure such as the ship, a new nineteen million pound school, power station, tank farm, etc., is paying a regular three and a half thousand pounds a year for every inhabitant, to be spent on providing largely nominal four day a week jobs and other ways of unostentaciously channelling the money to the people. They are not stupid or lazy however, and most of them would be much happier to be given work permits to compete in the Mother Country with the Germans, Italians, and others we admit so freely. They know full well that this is their inalienable right, and one doubts how long their loyalty will last if they continue to be treated as outcasts.

Their other outstanding characteristic is their Christian faith. The proportion of regular Churchgoers and Communicants must surely be higher than in any other country in the world except Vatican City. Probably also there is no other country (again except the Vatican which is a very special case) which supports more Priests than Doctors, and we are all working flat out. There are ten Anglican Churches on the island each with regular services and three secular buildings where Masses are celebrated at least once a month, as well as a House Church at Rupert's Valley where services are held and where a new Church is under construction. St James' Church in Jamestown is certainly the oldest protestant Church in the southern hemisphere and if it is not the oldest of any denomination as some claim, it only fails to be by a very few months. Actually both the vicar and congregation of St James' would strenuously deny that they are protestant. The whole Anglican Province of Southern Africa is extremely High Church and St Helena in general and St James' in particular are a good deal higher than the dome of St Peter's. The cloud of incense at the end of Mass there is such that one can barely see the congregation to give the blessing. I have two otherwise excellent stoles with holes burnt in them as a memento of an incendiary acolyte who plagued me in the days when I was a deacon there. Somehow I used to hypnotize him and the wretched child would get closer and closer with his candle until something went up.

Nearly ninety per cent of Christians on the island are Anglican but there are also two or three Baptist Churches in regular use, a Seventh Day Adventist Church, and Sundry Salvation Army halls and places of worship. There are also regrettably two, or possibly three quasi-Christian, Pagan, or downright antichristian sects and a Masonic Lodge, the size of whose membership is as usual unknown except to its members. All these have been imported from South Africa in the past century or so. Regrettably it appears to be the policy of the present South African Government to encourage people who oppose the Christian Church, and in recent years several groups have been sent over from there with travel permits and currency allowances which are frequently unobtainable by bona fide Christians. They are going round from door to door teaching the Muslim doctrine that Christ was not God and that he did not die on the Cross but that it was an Angel that appeared to do so, thus explaining the empty tomb. They deny the Holy Trinity and teach that the Church (which is Christ's body on earth) is of the devil. Having already committed the Sin against the Holy Ghost, these people are beyond the reach of the church and can do a lot of harm. While young Christians in South Africa are being given long prison sentences for refusing to join the army and break up church services with tear gas and rifle butts, these people are allowed to register as 'Conscientious Objectors' and make up almost all those who are accepted as such. The Devil knows well how to look after his own.

St Helena was discovered by the Portuguese Admiral Juan de Nova Castello on 21 May 1502 which the Church on the island always celebrates as St Helena's day, as apparently did the good Admiral. The Portuguese are Roman Catholics and should have celebrated the feast, as does all the rest of Western Christendom, on 18 August. Presumably de Nova Castello had a Greek or Russian Orthodox chaplain on board. They must have been badly off course for the Cape sea route, but the discovery of an island with fresh water and citrus nearly two thousand miles north of the Cape was so valuable that its existence was kept as a secret by the Portuguese Navy for some fifty years. The first Englishman to visit the island was probably Captain Thomas Cavendish in June 1588 although there is a legend that Sir Francis Drake came eight years earlier. Cavendish writes at length on the supply of oranges, lemons, figs, pomegranates, dates, parsley, sorrel, basil, fennel, aniseed, and radishes. Except for dates and perhaps aniseed, these are all to be found on the island today though hardly in profusion, and I suspect that pomegranates are now confined to my own garden. Parsley and fennel are prolific weeds and will grow anywhere (indeed do grow everywhere) except of course in the herb garden by my kitchen door where I simply cannot get them to take root. Cavendish writes in his journal for 8 June 1588:

> 'The same day about two or three o'clock in the afternoon we went on shore, where we found an exceeding fair and pleasant valley (which will be

where Jamestown now stands) wherein divers handsome buildings and houses were set up; and one particularly which was a Church, was tiled, and whitened on the outside very fair, and made with a porch, and within the Church at the upper end was set an altar, whereon stood a very large table, set in a frame, having on it the picture of our Saviour Christ upon the Cross, and the image of Our Lady praying, with divers other historics painted curiously on the same. The sides of the Church were hung round with stained cloths having many devices drawn on them.'

After sundry bickering disputes between the Portuguese and the Dutch, the island passed into British hands in 1659 and was administered until late in the last century by the East India Company. Officers of that company have of course provided many of the finest Colonial Governors the world has known, but few of the best came to St Helena. Their character can best be judged by the constant war they waged against the clergy. One of the worst of them, a Governor Johnson who reigned in 1720, had a drunken dispute with the vicar at matins in St James' Church as to what Sunday it was and, finding himself to be wrong, had the unfortunate priest dragged from his Church, imprisoned, and deported. On finding, as was not surprising, some difficulty in obtaining a replacement, the company's directors merely reprimanded the Governor instead of hanging him for sacrilege as the law demanded. It says much for the charity of the Reverend John Jones that on his return to England he did not have the directors indicted as accessories after the fact; but by all accounts he was rather fond of the bottle himself. Two so-called doctors who dared to report the truth in a letter to London were put in the pillory; but they may only have been surgeons. I doubt that even a drunken tyrannical Governor would have dared to treat a couple of physicians that way.

No one else to my knowledge has written about St Helena without a long account of the exile of Napoleon, Longwood House, the Briars Pavilion where he spent his first few weeks on the island, the empty grave where he was buried for nineteen years before being removed to an ugly stolen sarcophagus in the Invalides, and the supposed infamies of that excellent

Governor Sir Hudson Low whose claim to fame has nothing to do with his function as a gaoler but is that he put down slavery on the island. I have no interest in the fate of a defeated Corsican Brigand (apart from the fact that if we had hanged him as he richly deserved, we might have had less trouble with his successors Hitler and Mussolini) and the reader will have to look elsewhere for information on this topic.

I was made Deacon in St Paul's Cathedral on 1 September 1985 by Bishop Cannan (the first such ordination on the island since 1901) and priested there by our new Bishop James Johnson just over a year later on 7 September at the very hour that Desmond Tutu was being enthroned as our Archbishop in Capetown. Desmond was educated at Kings College London at about the same time that I was training at St Mary's. Bishop James once asked me at a luncheon party whether I had met him there and I replied in perfect innocence 'I don't know King's very well. I only went there once for the .22 shooting.' Our dear Bishop's cry of horror 'Tutu shooting?' created a sensation.

My first year in Orders was spent in a private hotel in Jamestown run by the wife of one of our Subdeacons. They gave me the best and largest room they had and furnished it as an office-bedroom where I could have my books and work sixteen hours a day with my computer. I was already negotiating to buy one of the finest houses on the island and expected to move there in a few months. In the event, Farm Lodge did not become vacant until December 1986. The climate of Jamestown, though not what one would expect in the tropics, is much better than on the rest of St Helena and it was not until I moved into the country that I found how cold it can be, though I began to have my suspicions as it was hardly warm at St Paul's vicarage and I was taking services in all the other Churches on the island. I thought though that a big stone-built house well down in Lemon Valley would be warmer. I was mistaken.

A few months after being made deacon I took a few weeks off at the flat at Cape Town. It was so inexpensive by then as a result of inflation of the Rand that I intended to keep it going as a holiday home, and by the time that I had realized South Africa was no longer for me, had left it too late to pack up and move my furniture. I wrote to a friend on my return:

'I have never been more thankful for a leave coming to an end, or more anxious to get back to work. It is quite incredible the change in South Africa in the last year. A year ago with all the talk of reform and peace talks with the neighbouring countries, everyone was cheerful and optimistic and most of them genuinely believed that everything was going to work out and SA was going to be a united, peaceful, prosperous multi-racial country. Now nobody appears to see any hope. The English speakers are going around with long faces wondering just when they will have to pull out. The Afrikaaners know that they have nowhere to run to and quite definitely all have the death-wish, and are no longer making any effort. Indeed one has the impression that many are deliberately striving to hasten the end. The coloureds are frankly terrified knowing what happened to the Eurasians in Indonesia. Even the blacks are depressed. The last thing they want is to see things go the way they have in Angola. The only remotely cheerful people I have met are two old ladies with cancer who think it will last them out. I don't think it will.'

As a result I had to go back the following December to pack up and ship my furniture. Perhaps it was a good thing as I was still not able to get into my new house although it was bought and paid for and I moved into Farm Lodge the day after my return. On the hall table was a letter from a mad American who had just decided he wanted it (it had been on the market over two years) and was offering forty per cent more than I had paid to get me out. I did not accept.

Farm Lodge is described in one of the guide books as 'The finest Gentleman's Residence on the Island'. It is a very nice house but does not compare with Government House, so presumably the author did not consider the Governor to be a gentleman. With it came about fifty acres of farmland and timber as well as a garden stocked with a collection of trees and plants most of which do not grow elsewhere on St Helena. I was able to get immediate permission to buy without waiting for the usual qualifying period of residence as the price was more than any St Helenian would possibly pay. I bought the house and whole estate for less than I would have had to pay for a fishing cottage in Devon.

One of the most important features of the house is the possession of a wine cellar. It surprises me that so few people in England consider a cellar necessary, even with wine drinking now being an important part of life to almost everybody. Stowing a few dozen bottles at the most in a cupboard under the stairs means not only that wine often has to be drunk almost as soon as bought, with no proper time for it to recover even from the journey from the local wine merchants; but that it is always bought at its most expensive, it being quite impossible to lay down wine when it is cheap and drink it when it has matured. A tiny cellar such as mine where I can bin a hundred cases means that I never have to open a bottle which has not lain there at least several months, and that I can have a few good wines maturing over a period of years.

The other thing I find odd about the prosperous middle classes in England today is their willingness to live without servants. Admittedly those brought up during the war and since may never have known any better, but for those who do servants are not unobtainable and one cook-general need cost no more than many a man spends on his golf and tennis. Even to have to give these up completely would surely be a very minor price to pay for not having to make his own morning tea, watch his wife do all the cooking and cleaning, bring in the coal and help with the washing up after every meal. Nobody who has difficulty recruiting staff needs to go without. Domestic service is the one thing for which St Helenians can always get work permits, and unless the demand should become enormous they are always available. Our present Bishop is not ashamed to admit that he first went to England as a butler and his wife as a housemaid.

The house was already fully furnished with a little very good solid Victorian pieces and a lot of interesting but not so good Regency furniture, which does not blend at all well with my own bought in Bath during the war. To an English dealer, all the Regency pieces found on St Helena would be classified as 'Country Chippendale' but I doubt very much that any of it came from England. After looking round a number of houses on the island I feel almost certain that an English craftsman came here some time about 1800 and with the aid probably of local apprentices made all this furniture on the island. One of these may later have taken on a Chinese assistant. I have one terribly ugly Victorian sideboard with two brackets supporting the top which could have come straight out of a late Ming Buddhist temple. They have Lotus Flowers as well as the Chinese variant of Key Pattern incorporated in the design. It also bears a crudely faked coat of arms exactly corresponding to the 'Pseudo-hallmarks' found on Chinese silver of the period. There were some hundreds of Chinese indented labourers on the island and a number of the more prosperous families have Chinese names and features, though they are all good Christians and except for a little of the local cooking, nothing else remains to tell of their presence except a 'China Lane' in Jamestown and a 'China Cottage' with a Chinese inscription in the stonework. Incredibly they have not even looked after the graves of their ancestors and no memorials remain in the two big Chinese Cemeteries. The last of the tombstones on 'Mount Eternity', the largest of them and which overlooks my house, were removed in the last ten years to provide stone for a bus shelter.

Fully furnished or not, I had to find somewhere for my own things from Borneo and the contents of my mother's flat in Cape Town. The latter already looked like an antique shop, having absorbed the better part of the contents of a large house in Purley and my grandfather's three storey house in Southport: and my own house in Jessselton had been larger than Farm Lodge. I had to fill a storeroom almost to the ceiling but I am still overfurnished. There is enough crockery, cutlery, table glass, decanters, tea pots, and soft furnishings to equip a hotel. Few men really need three dining tables or four writing bureaus and having regard to the regular duties of a parish priest I don't really think he needs more than two microscopes at the most. Four is excessive. Add to this five cameras, four projectors, two large computers with three printers, three wireless sets, two hi-fi outfits, two reel-to-reel tape recorders, two lounge suites, sixteen standard and table lamps, 2,600 books; and then remembering that the house was already fully furnished, things are congested. As nobody in my family has ever had the courage to throw anything away, I had a problem. I still have. I was forgetting the collections of stamps, silver, and Chinese porcelain. There is also an antique nursery dining table with six chairs, not to mention two grandfather clocks and three antique card tables.

The quantity of books is symptomatic of a family failing. Some years ago Lord Medway (he was then actually Viscount Cranbrook, having passed his junior title on to his son) came to dinner at my house in Borneo and being shown into the air-conditioned study and beholding some two thousand volumes in glass-fronted cases asked 'Do you collect books.' It seemed at first a singularly unintelligent question, even for a member of the House of Lords, but when I had thought about it for a moment I realized that it was a very good question and one I had not considered before. The answer is that I don't collect books, I accumulate them. If a book is worth reading at all (and few are) then it is worth reading more than once, and worth keeping by one for the rest of one's life to re-read from time to time. Hence the 2,600 which I have to carry round the world with me. I find that even with such massive works as the *Encyclopaedia Britannica* I need more than one edition. I have little use for the Americanized post-war revisions, but for almost everything except some recent scientific advances, the eleventh edition is easily the best and most complete. I think the fourteenth is also indispensable, but I frequently refer to the thirteenth three volume supplement as well. Similarly if one is concerned at all with mythology (and what clergyman can afford not to be), the single volume edition of Frazer's *Golden Bough* is quite inadequate; but undoubtedly thirteen volumes do take up a lot of shelf space.

I think the only substantial set of books I keep and never read, although I have made many efforts to do so, is Scott. My Father said he only wrote stories as 'pot boilers' as he considered himself a poet, whereas the public considers him to be a novelist. I am afraid I think they are both wrong. I do however read and re-read all my complete works of Dickens, Thackery, Kipling, Stevenson, Conan Doyle, Mary Reynolds, Jerome, Jacobs, Neville Shute, John Masters, and even Shaw and Barrie as well as Marlow, Shakespeare, Webster, and Massinger. I have a copy of *Mein Kamp* which I keep discreetly between *The Wealth of Nations* on one side and *Das Kapital* on the other so as not to suggest any political bias. There is almost always a volume of one of Churchill's works out being read, as

I fear there is of Agatha Christie and Wodehouse. My collection of apocryphal and downright heretical early Christian writings would shock my Bishop.

Possibly the white ants will solve the problem for me. We have every insect pest known to science and a few known only to ourselves including a giant earwig. The worst of them all though is the white ant brought in by an American slave ship. St Helena is not beloved of the Americans as we used it as a naval base to seize and burn their ships and liberate their kidnapped Africans. This one though was not burned in time and the pest inhabits every building on the island. On a recent visit by Prince Andrew, a magnificent party was given for him in the council chamber of the castle. The ancient stairway, up and down which some hundreds of guests had walked, collapsed a few days later into a cloud of dust and dead insects. This visit was memorable in another respect. Stepping forward to greet the Prince on his arrival, the Governor overestimated the length of the island by about nine inches and descended into the depths of the Atlantic Ocean; his white plumed helmet floating away in the direction of South America. When he had been fished out and dried somewhat, His Royal Highness merely remarked 'I was afraid he was going to float off and leave me.'

Prince Andrew is almost worshipped by the islanders and has graciously agreed to the new secondary school being named 'The Prince Andrew School'. It has already been provided with a staff of expatriates who have been promoted above the excellent local teachers and some of whom appear not to be Christian. They are going to teach the sciences up to A Level to children who now at least are Christian and who have no apparent hope of getting permits to leave the island and apply their learning in fair competition to earn a proper living elsewhere. I anticipate trouble. A programme of 'sex education' has been drawn up based on hedonistic principles and giving detailed information and even advice illustrated by posters and video tapes for the practice of perversions unknown to those of my generation who went to decent schools. I anticipate more trouble.

I think the 'Saints' must be the most pleasant, grateful, and undemanding people in the world to work for. When after a service I stand at the Church door to shake hands with them,

270

they all say 'Thank you' and obviously really mean it. All the same I sometimes wonder why God has called me to them. I have very little opportunity for saving souls as I am sure that all those I meet are saved already. I spend my time quite literally preaching to the converted. Actually until I arrived on the island I had given not a single thought to preaching. I have a lot of experience in lecturing and a little in after-dinner speaking. This does not help all that much, and can lead to trouble. Put me into a tight-fitting pulpit and I can usually produce a sermon of sorts. Standing up against a vicar's desk though, I have to be very careful not to deliver much the same prepared material as an after-dinner speech, interspersed with risque stories which have just occurred to me: and in a Church without either where I can (and do) walk up and down behind the Altar rails, I am very likely to forget myself completely and deliver a surgery lecture. This actually happened when I was trying to preach on the ethical problems presented by the Aids epidemic, and realized afterwards that I had lectured entirely on the clinical aspects of the disease.

I think, if I had thought the thing out at all, that I had always pictured myself as what the Romans call a 'Mass Priest', a man who spends all his time going round administering the Sacraments and leaving to them everything that can be done by lay workers and Subdeacons. Certainly I had never given a thought to preaching or even to Parish visiting or Communion rounds, yet of course these together make up by far the greater part of a Parish Priest's work. I have in my life, especially in my young life, listened to a quite unbelievable amount of really bad preaching. At least nine out of ten sermons I sat through in my schooldays (except those at school) were devoted entirely to trying, (very clumsily and unconvincingly) to prove to us the existence of God and the essential truth of the Christian Religion. It seemed never to have occurred to any of these worthy clergymen that if we were not already convinced of all that, much more strongly than they could possibly convince anyone, we should not be wasting our Sunday mornings in Church. I cannot accept the adulation that some people give to my completely untutored preaching, but if that sort of thing is their standard I can well understand. If I felt I could not preach better than they did I would abandon the Ministry at once and take up fretwork.

271

There is another aspect of preaching though where my views do not meet with universal acceptance. I think sermons and church services should be happy and cheerful. Many years ago I read a schoolboy story completely lacking in merit except for one incident. Two small boys were up before the Head Master for the terrible offence of having been seen smiling happily in Chapel. The Head said sternly to the first 'Smith minor, don't you think that your father the Bishop will be distressed to hear of what you have done?' to which Smith replied 'No sir, my father says God always likes us to be merry in his house, provided we are merry for the right reasons.' Taken down several pegs, the Head asked in a much more conciliatory tone 'And are you sure you were merry for the right reasons?' Smith admitted frankly 'Well I don't really remember it, but if I was merry in God's House, it must have been for the right reasons.' Totally defeated, as a last forlorn hope the Head turned to the other boy and asked 'And you Jones, are you sure you were merry for the right reasons?' To which Jones wisely replied 'Yes Sir. Quite sure', and there the matter rested. Exeunt two small boys leaving a sadly humbled Head Master.

If the reason we are put into this world is in any way a training period for the next, then surely God must wish us to be happy here. An unhappy life would be very poor training for an eternity of unalloyed happiness. Desmond Tutu (who is our Archbishop, as St Helena is in the province of Southern Africa) certainly takes this view and I have known him not only to enliven his sermons with jokes about niggers (he has a very Jewish sense of humour) but to invite his congregation to clap when he touches on a joyful subject of which they should approve.

Perhaps another unusual feature of my sermons is that I tend to quote from very unorthodox writings; though I try to avoid any which were condemned by the early Church as heretical and take care not to quote from the Koran at least when my Bishop is present. I certainly do not believe that God's revelation to mankind is to be found only between the covers of the Bible; and still less that his revelation was exclusively to the Jews and the Christians. There were no Jews before Abraham, and the earlier chapters of the Bible are concerned with God's revelation to mankind in general. Revelation actually antedates our own species. Neanderthal Man buried his dead with

272

provisions for a hereafter. Knowledge of a life after death is not the result of logical thought (nothing could be less logical), and if early man knew of it, only God could have told him. Neither is belief in eternal life a result of wishful thinking as some would have us believe. It is interesting that (as the result of conditioning in the two different cultures) while the highest ambition of Western Man is eternal individual survival, this is the one thing the Hindu or Buddhist strives against; and he devotes all his spiritual energy (supposedly through many incarnations) to escape from everlasting life and achieve individual extinction.

To go on living after death is not a thing which we could logically expect; and God revealed very early, not just to the Jews but to all mankind, that we should all survive death. It was only just before the time of Abraham though that God revealed to the Egyptians of all people that life after death could be a life with God in heaven, and that whether they got there, or to everlasting destruction, would depend on a weighing up of their Good Works on earth. The Jews were not ready for this revelation for another thousand years. Similarly before even the time of Abraham God had revealed to the Aryan peoples the nature of the Godhead as a Trinity, and this information was brought with them in the Vedas to India at the time of the last great Aryan migration. Again the Jews were not ready to be told this for another two thousand years: and even then the bulk of them did not accept it and still do not accept it. True, some knowledge of the Holy Spirit is displayed in the *Wisdom Literature* (notably in the Book *Ecclesiasticus*) but this is only from about 300 BC.

Nor were these pagan religions offering a fools paradise: information on a Salvation that their followers could never attain to. The Church from an incredibly early date has taught that Christ died for all men, not just those who know of him; and that those who are in a state of 'Invincible Ignorance', who have no knowledge of the Christian Gospel, will be saved if they but live according to what they believe to be right, according to the dictates of a man's own conscience, which is the voice of God to all men. There is one astonishing passage in Malachi which deserves notice:

'People from one end of the world to the other honour me. Everywhere they burn incense to me and

273

offer acceptable sacrifices.'

Malachi 1/11 (Good News Bible).

This incredible statement, written about 500 BC, that the prayers and sacrifices offered by the pagans to their gods are received by and accepted by Yahweh in preference to those of the Jews and their corrupt priests, is a true rendering of the Hebrew. The verbs are in the present tense and the mistranslation of them into the future tense which makes the passage look like a Christian prophecy, as is done in most other translations, is incorrect.

Although I have spoken disparagingly of those who preach sermons to prove the truth of Christianity to those who clearly already know it, this book is not a sermon and not all readers may be convinced Christians. In the absence of personal religious experience, there can be only one sound reason for choosing Christianity in preference to any other religion; that it has been proved to be true. Jesus of Nazareth stated unequivocally that he was God ('He who has seen me has seen the Father. I and the Father are One'), but why should we believe him? I think this is a question which can be answered without any shadow of doubt. It is not a question of faith; it is a question of assembling scientific evidence and establishing scientific facts.

The four accounts we have in the Gospels were all written by devout members of the early Christian Church in the last quarter of the first century. The Church had already existed for at least thirty years and probably nearer fifty. It is as though a patriotic and admiring Englishman today was writing in praise of Winston Churchill or almost even of Nurse Edith Cavell. To them the Disciples who had known and lived with Jesus, especially St Peter, were the most revered and holiest of men. It is inconceivable that they should invent discreditable lies about them, indeed one would expect that they would do everything possible to gloss over their failings and make them appear more heroic and Saintly than they really were.

Yet what do they tell us about them in the last few hours of Jesus's life? They tell us that with one accord they played the coward; that they ran away in terror of their lives. St Peter himself, the Rock on whose confession of Faith the Church was

274

to be built, declared three times and with an oath that he was not a follower of Jesus. Could the Evangelists have told this ugly story if it were not all too terribly true, showing as it does these supposedly Holy Men, the founders of their Church, to have lacked a hundredth part of the courage shown by the children in the Hitler Youth Movement when their leader was defeated and dead, or the even younger children making their last-ditch stand against Russian tanks in the Hungarian Revolution. Horrible as it is, it must be true.

And yet only three or four days later they were back, openly preaching Christ with complete indifference to their own safety: indeed inviting and even welcoming suffering and Martyrdom for his sake. It is absolutely certain that something quite extraordinary must have happened. Men do not die for a lie. Cowards, and these men were the most abject of cowards, do not die for a lie. Something extraordinary had happened, and that something must have been what they said happened.

However incredible, the only possible explanation is that what they declared, was true; that the betrayed, discredited, deserted Jesus who had died and been buried on the Friday, had been alive again on the Sunday.

What then does the whole story add up to? Jesus said that he was the Son of God and would prove it by dying and rising again from the dead. And quite simply he did prove it by rising from the dead and thereby also proved, it seems to me beyond any shadow of doubt, that all his claims and all his teachings are true. There is no other possible conclusion.

But even if we accept that everything Jesus taught and which appears in the Gospel is true, does that mean that we have to accept everything the Church teaches, from Monogamy to the Assumption of the Virgin Mary? Let us first consider what we mean by 'The Church'.

Jesus said to Peter after his great confession of faith 'Thou art Peter, and upon this rock I will build my church.' That is clear enough, and it is part of Christ's Gospel which I have suggested we have to accept as the truth because he proved it to be true by rising from the dead, the evidence for which is beyond rational question.

Christianity is a religion concerned passionately with the welfare and Salvation of the Individual. It is not however an institution of individual worship. Of course those who habitually murmur prayers many times a day are in a sense worshipping alone, though when Christians sit down alone to say Morning or Evening Prayer they can, and indeed should, think of themselves as at one with the millions of others throughout the world who are doing the same. Jesus said 'When two or three are gathered together in my name, there am I in the midst of them' and there is no need to feel alone if they are not within sight of those others who are doing the same thing. Jesus has said he is in the midst of them all, and close to each one of them – 'Closer than hands and feet'.

There can be no shadow of doubt that Jesus founded a church, and that it was to be a Universal Church, a 'Catholic' Church. In spite of the various meanings commonly ascribed to the word 'Catholic' today, (The Anglican Church commonly uses it quite incorrectly to describe anything which they hold in common with Rome, while others use it as a term of abuse for anything in the Roman Church of which they disapprove), 'Catholic' merely means 'all embracing' or 'universal'. Jesus founded his church on the Rock of Peter's confession of Faith and it was to be ruled over by the Apostles and those whom they appointed and consecrated as their successors. There was no provision for independent sectarian groups, indeed Jesus warned his followers against those who would seek to divide them and form such groups. The Church he founded was to be the 'One Holy Catholic and Apostolic Church'.

But whether we like it or not, the Church today is divided: and not all the fragments of the divided Church are teaching the same thing, even those who claim to be parts of the One Holy Catholic and Apostolic Church which Christ founded. Which of them are we to believe, and what exactly are we to believe? This is a very difficult question, and although I think I know the answer, not all who have followed me up to now will agree.

Jesus founded his Church on the Rock of Peter's Confession of faith and belief. I don't think this can reasonably be questioned. He said to him:

'Thou art Peter, and upon this rock I will build my church; and the gates of hell shall not prevail against it. And I will give unto thee the keys of the kingdom of heaven: and whatsoever thou shalt bind on earth

shall be bound in heaven: and whatsoever thou shalt
loose on earth shall be loosed in heaven.'

There surely can be little doubt that the ultimate authority
was thus given to Peter, but the risen Christ said to all the
Apostles, and by implication to the rest of his followers 'Lo, I
am with you always, even unto the end of the world.' This
presumably has some definite meaning. His presence alongside
us would be of no comfort unless we believed that he actually
does something. He has told us to pray, and amongst other
things that we obviously need to pray for, and for which he is
clearly there to help us, is that we 'Fall into no sin, neither run
into any kind of danger'. In other words he is there to guide his
sheep and to sustain and protect them. I have indicated before
that it is my belief and experience that there are two prayers
which are not only always answered (as all prayer is answered,
though not always in the way we expect or even perhaps wish)
but which are always answered just as we wish and have asked.
We are always given exactly what we have asked for. These are
the prayer for Faith, and the prayer for Guidance. We are
given what we have asked for. What use we make of it is up to
us. If we pray to God to guide us in what we should do, we
always are guided, and what we have then been guided to see
to be the right thing to do is what God wishes us to do, it is the
will of God and therefore by definition is right.

Jesus has said 'When he, the Spirit of Truth, is come he will
guide you into all truth' (John 16/13). Did we not believe this,
there would be little point in practising any religion, however
true we believed it to be. This leads us directly to the dogmatic
authority of the Church, and in particular to the alleged
Infallibility of the Pope.

It is necessary first though to distinguish very clearly between Papal infallibility and the truth of the teachings of the
Roman Church. The Church does not deny that it made very
serious errors in the condemnation of Gallileo and the burning
of St Joan; but does not consider its authority thereby discredited. No claim is made that the Church, its ministers, and its
Pope do not make mistakes and sometimes terrible mistakes.
The Church's teaching on contraception for example may be
hopelessly wrong (although I don't think it is) and can at any
time be reversed; in spite of having been reiterated in a solemn

Papal Encyclical. Infallibility is only claimed when the Pope formally and deliberately proclaims a dogma which his followers are required to believe as an article of faith. [This is really a very modest claim and one might have thought it could give rise to little trouble. Many devout and unassuming Christians would claim more for themselves. A Christian who prays to God to guide him in a difficult decision and then does what his conscience tells him is right, should have absolute confidence that he has been guided, and that what he has been guided to do is the will of God. No Pope has ever claimed more for himself; and one who publishes an Encyclical such as this without making it the subject of a Dogma is claiming less.]

The traditional justification for Papal Infallibility, the teaching of the Roman Church, rests entirely upon historical evidence which can be questioned, and which is questioned by many people. It is admitted that Christ founded his Church upon the Rock of Peter's confession of Faith and in the symbolism of 'The Keys of Heaven' entrusted him with custody of the faith and the power to 'Declare and pronounce to his people, being penitent, the absolution and remission of their sins'. That the ultimate responsibility for the care of the Church was to last through Peter's lifetime is made clear in the final charge to him in the last few verses of the Gospel according to St John where he is told 'Feed my lambs' and 'Feed my sheep'. [In passing, I cannot help feeling that something has been lost here from the Gospel as it was originally written. The climax of this story must surely have been a third answer which was not just a repetition of the second.]

It is less easy to provide chapter and verse to justify the method of handing on this authority since Peter's death. The only really valid reason for accepting this appears to me to be that no other means was provided, that this is the way it always has been done, that God obviously had to provide some means, and that nobody claims he has provided any other.

There appears to me though to be a much more convincing argument in favour of the Dogma, and one of which when I have put it to a number of RC priests I have been assured is sound although the Church has never used it. Essentially I have already stated it. If we accept that when any Christian prays for guidance he always is guided, can we believe that

278

when the Pope prays for guidance on behalf of all Christendom (firmly believing that he will be guided and that if he is guided to proclaim a Dogma it will be God's will that all men will accept it as the word of God) that this guidance on which he and three quarters of all Christians depend could possibly be withheld?

It must be appreciated that although this is an argument for belief in Papal Infallibility, it is not in itself grounds for belief in the dogmata which result from the alleged exercise of this power. It would only be so if we could be quite certain that the Pope has prayed for such guidance, and has in good faith done what he then saw to be right. It is not a theoretical impossibility that for example a Pope excessively devoted to the Blessed Virgin should proclaim a dogma about her without either soliciting or acting on divine guidance. I am not claiming that this has happened, but merely that it could happen. There were Popes in the past who were not even professing Christians and whose actions were as un-Christian as they could be. The official attitude of the Church is that even so, if and when they spoke '*Ex Cathedra*' they would be 'Protected' from error. This is in itself a dogma, and therefore an unconvincing way of justifying other dogmata. In some cases these Popes would not need or wish protection, and the only way their saying could be trusted would be if we could be quite certain that they were actively prevented from uttering deliberate falsehoods in this way. I think the Infallibility of a Pope who is acting in good faith can be substantiated by the above argument; but I would hate to have to do so for one who was not.

I have stated with conviction that Christ founded a united and all-embracing Church, warned his followers against the risk of divisions and against those who would seek to divide them, and that I believe that these divisions are 'Clearly not the will of God'. I think that the accelerating progress towards Church Union since the proclamation of Papal Infallibility in 1870, and the consequent assumption by the Popes of far greater power and authority than they have ever had before, shows that this is so. With the Pope and the Archbishop of Canterbury concelebrating Mass together in public, the divisions between these two Churches have surely largely disappeared except in the minds of the laity. The Pope and the Archbishop have tacitly recognized the validity of each other's

Orders, else a Concelebration would have been sacrilegious.

☆   ☆   ☆

A few days after I had first spoken to Bishop Cannan on the ship about my coming to St Helena to study under him and when the scheme was virtually decided upon, he came and sat next to me in the smoking room and suddenly asked me 'Tell me what is your attitude to prayer?' I am afraid I sat for a moment frozen with horror and astonishment. I had never given any thought to the matter and had certainly never foreseen that I should be asked such a question. I can remember, I think, exactly what I replied, and how totally inadequate it seemed.

I said 'I pray a lot, perhaps sometimes twenty times or more in a day, but often only a very few words. I have done so all my life, from very early childhood, and have always been aware that I could almost consciously press a switch and get a direct line to God.' I hastened to explain that it is a one way line. I have never heard an audible voice speaking from the other end as some undoubtedly have. Even so I have never had any shadow of doubt that I have got through, that there is someone listening at the other end of the wire, and that such prayers are always heard and answered. I went on to say 'But as regards liturgical prayers I am afraid things are different. I think such prayers are very valuable and important, but sometimes when I use them, when I have finished a long liturgical prayer; I suddenly realize that, – I just haven't pressed the switch.'

Feeling how totally inadequate my answer had been, I apologized and said 'I am sorry, I had never thought I might be asked such a question. I just had no answer ready.' Bishop Cannan smiled and said 'Never mind – you have answered it.'

As I indicated in my answer, prayer does play a major part in my life as it probably does in all our lives, and as it certainly should do, but possibly few of us would be able to give a better answer than I did to Bishop Cannan's question. But there is one aspect of prayer which continues to worry me as it plays, or is alleged to play, so large a part in the lives of the clergy and of many good Christians not in Holy Orders. I am thinking of meditation.

I find it difficult to write about this aspect or form of prayer (for it definitely is a form of prayer) as even now I am not quite sure that I really know what the word means. When I set out on my course of study, I had a number of very devout advisors who tried to impress on me the importance of meditation and of the 'Spiritual life' which I took to be, and still take to be, the way of life of those who use meditation extensively as their way of communication with, and communion with God, which after all is what all prayer is about.

There is a story of a man who did not know the meaning of the word 'Prose', and when it was explained to him that prose was any form of speech or writing which was not poetry, was astonished and delighted to realize that he had been speaking prose all his life without knowing it. After some years now of trying hard to find out what others really mean by meditation I have come to the conclusion that either I still know nothing of what it is about, or that I have been doing it all my life without knowing it. Although meditation is commonly associated with what is called 'The Spiritual Life' it is only a means towards, and only one means towards that end, and I would certainly not claim for a moment that even if I have practiced medita-tion, I am anywhere near having achieved the Spiritual Life, which is something very close to what Our Lord called 'The Kingdom of Heaven'.

If I am right about my interpretation of the word (and I don't want to be dogmatic because I am not sure that to many people more spiritual than I am it does not mean something quite different) then true meditation does not need to be spiritual at all or in any way related to religious belief. My own Ideas on such subjects as Communism, Apartheid, Cosmology, Field Sports, and a host of others, are only in part the result of what I have read or been taught. If I have any substantial views on these or any other subject, they are very largely the result of my settling myself down on a river bank, an armchair, on in the bath; anywhere comfortable in fact but most definitely NOT on my knees, and considering the thing in all its aspects without any extraneous interference. A lot of my views on Biblical and Religious matters have in fact been arrived at in exactly this way.

Perhaps religious and spiritual meditation is just a little different as we should always begin by praying God for guidance and to guide our thoughts in the direction he would wish them to go. But then I have said before that I personally have never made an important decision without praying to be guided to do the right thing and then thinking the thing out and doing what then appears right, in the certainty that I have been guided and that it therefore is right: so the distinction, if there is any, is a very fine one.

David Griffiths (one of the triumvirate of the King Edward's days and now an Archdeacon), when he heard that I was going to join him in taking Holy Orders, wrote to pass on the advice of one of his teachers (to be fair he did not himself recommend it literally) that if I didn't spend at least an hour and a half every day on my knees I would be wasting my time. Certainly if I did, I should be wasting not only my time but what little useful function I still retain in my legs and back. I have said already that I think God intends us to be happy in this world and wishes us to do so in his house: and I at least cannot be happy, relaxed, meditative, or ready to listen to what God may choose to say to me, if I am in the acute discomfort that even five minutes kneeling produces.

But even so it is worth it when we can, to go into Church and, after a brief prayer, to sit down in reasonable comfort and just use the quiet and peacefulness to be with God, and to listen to see what he has to say to us. Some people say one should make one's mind a complete blank to be able to listen the better. I don't think everybody can do this, or even that it is always very safe to do so even in Church, unless it be after very thorough prayerful preparation. The devil is always on the watch to accost us when we are unprepared and if we make our minds a complete blank it may not always be God who speaks to us. It is because many Spiritual people do in fact do this with benefit and no harm, that I still have doubts that I really understand what it is all about. It is also undoubtedly for this reason that other Churches encourage the use of the Rosary, so that our minds remain fixed on holy things and our lips are engaged in holy prayers.

But I think we all can with great benefit take such an opportunity to think deeply on Spiritual things, perhaps on one of the fifteen so-called Mysteries of the Rosary, or just as well on any other aspect of our Religious belief such as one of the sayings of Our Lord or the writings of St Paul, or even just on the wonder of God's Goodness towards us. As I understand it, this is meditation and a very valuable form of prayer. I am sure all of us should do it more often.

I had accepted that I should have to devote a lot of time to the study of Theology, although I had always regarded it very much as a pseudo-science smacking of sophistry. To my astonishment I found it fascinating. I had almost as much difficulty with Old Testament history as I had with History at school, but otherwise all my studies were straightforward and enjoyable. Writing my notes into the computer as a sort of electronic notebook and every few hours having a printout and retiring to a comfortable chair to read and revise what I had written, I covered a prodigious amount of work in the two years between starting serious study and being made Deacon. After that I continued even more intensely for another year, with the added problem of having many more services to take or assist at and a little parish visiting and Home Communions.

A further complication was provided by the Bishop himself taking over what was then my one and only computer. In addition to then doing two full time jobs as Bishop and Parish Priest, he managed during his six years on the island to write a very detailed history of the Diocese 'and its precursors' from 1502. I think solely from false modesty he decided (and nothing would make him change his mind) that it was not worth publishing in the usual way, and determined on a limited addition of about 120 copies produced by photocopying in the Government Printing Office. By the time I arrived and was installed in St Paul's Vicarage, this project was almost complete and a provisional typescript had been produced by a devoted and hard working churchwoman. Unfortunately the quality of the typewriter used was rather poor, and as soon as the Bishop saw one my business letters written by computer with smooth margins and electric printing, he asked to be allowed to duplicate the first page on my equipment and took it to the Government Printer for his opinion. Not surprisingly the opinion was 'There is no comparison', and our poor Bishop was faced with the monumental task of learning to use a complex word-processing programme and then typing out the whole work himself. This he accomplished in less than a month, working in my study six hours a day in addition to his work as a Bishop, Priest, and electrician. He took away with him the thick instruction book and mastered it over lunch, starting work the same afternoon. It provided me with some welcome rest during the day, but meant that I was often up after midnight writing up my essential notes, while getting up at five almost every morning for Matins and early Mass at the Cathedral.

Bishop Cannan was pushing me forward with positively indecent speed and I doubt that even he realized how little my spiritual development was keeping pace with my technical studies. I needed at the very least a year more time before I could possibly have been considered mature enough to be a priest, but I think I have possibly got there now. Fortunately (contrary to the teaching of the Donatists) the efficacy of the Sacraments does not depend in any way on the worthiness or even competence of the priest, and the only person who suffered was myself. I had bestowed upon me the Gift of the Holy Spirit to fulfil the function of a priest and I did so. When I took a wafer into my hands and spoke the words of consecration, it became the Body of Christ: and the absolutely certain fact paralysed me with terror. I have not yet got over the terror: but I am now a little more resigned to having the job to do and accept that I am not doing it myself, but that it is Our Lord doing it in my presence and in me and through me.

Apart from visits by Royalty, perhaps every forty years or so, and not always enlivened by the immersion of a Governor, nothing much really exciting happens on St Helena, so that my Ordination to the Priesthood was the event of years. To my disordered imagination it looked as though the whole Island turned up at the Cathedral and the Governor gave a luncheon party afterwards to celebrate. I fear I was barely conscious of what was going on.

9

ENVOI

15 May 1987 was my sixtieth birthday. I had a regular weekly appointment to conduct a brief service with an even briefer sermon at one of the local Junior Schools. This time I put on under my cassock a three piece suit, a white shirt, and a cloth-of-gold tie of more than oriental splendour, and astonished the children by removing the cassock for the sermon. I said to them:

'You can see that I am wearing a suit, a shirt, and a tie. It is the tie I want you to look at. It is a very special tie, and I only wear it on very special occasions. I bought it in India.

'Some years ago I was wearing it at the Royal College of Surgeons in London; and a young Indian doctor came up to me and asked very politely "Excuse me sir, but where did you buy that tie?" I said "In Bombay actually at the Taj Mahal Hotel". He said "I have one just like it – I bought mine in Bombay too". I added "Unfortunately my mother doesn't like it. She will only let me wear it on my birthday". He smiled with a sudden sympathy. "My wife, she is just the same".

'Which brings me to my point. This is my birthday. It is a very special birthday. It is my sixtieth birthday.

'Most of you have fathers in their thirties. When your father has his fortieth birthday he will tell you that "Life begins at forty". He probably believes it and wants you to believe it too. When his fiftieth birthday comes along he will tell you that fifty is still the prime of life. He will not really believe it, and he will not expect you to believe it. He says it in the forlorn hope of persuading himself that it is true. But when he turns sixty he will not be able to conceal from you, from himself, or from anybody else that he is now an old man.

285

'So one's sixtieth birthday is a very good time to stop for a moment looking forwards, and look back to see what one has made of life and whether or not things could have turned out better. When I look back on mine, I don't really think they could. I have spent all my working life as a Surgeon, and I am quite sure there is no other job which would have given me as much pleasure and satisfaction. I have retired now to this island in a lovely house and with a quite New Job which is the only other thing I have ever wanted to do. God has been very good to me.'

What have I really made of my life? Could I have done better? If given the chance to live my life again would I plan it differently? Perhaps not everybody has a chance to ask himself these questions and perhaps few would answer them as I do. To achieve, to have achieved, a worthwhile and satisfying life (satisfying in the retrospect that is: not of necessity satisfying all the time or even much of the time) depends, I am quite sure, on ones work rather than ones play. Few aged men must be able to look back with satisfaction on a life devoted to hedonism (the pursuit of happiness), however vigorously pursued or however much time, effort, and money they were able to devote to it. The dying thoughts of Edward Duke of Windsor must have been bleak, though no other man has thrown away so much in pursuit of selfish pleasure as he did. Whatever ones expectation of the hereafter, satisfaction in this life depends on what one has done for the world, not what one has done for oneself.

How then have I fared, and would I wish that it had been otherwise? On this basis, using ones work as the only important criterion, I could not have done better. I have had two unrelated careers, and if I were choosing again, those are the ones I should choose. There are other openings though in Surgery and in the Church than those I have followed. Would I, looking back now, rather have been a London Consultant rising perhaps to be PRCS, or to have entered the Church much younger to become a Bishop or Archbishop (or even Cardinal or Pope)? I can say with absolute honesty that the answer is no in both cases. God has been immensely generous to me in guiding me to, or putting me in, the two professions, and in those niches in each profession, which were to me the most rewarding any occupation could possibly be.

Now I have mentioned God however, I have at once

introduced an entirely new set of criteria of success and satisfaction. My previous remarks were based on entirely secular considerations. To the Christian, every man be he Christian, Pagan, Agnostic, or one in a state of 'Invincible Ignorance', has a vocation. Vocation means 'Calling' and I am quite certain that every man is created slightly different from any other, for one particular task, one little niche in God's plan for mankind; and having been made for that purpose, he is called to it very clearly. Being blessed (or cursed) with the gift of freewill, it is open to him to follow or reject that call, but if he rejects it I doubt very much that he will later be able to look back on his life with any degree of satisfaction. The fault lies not in our stars but in ourselves if we are failures. I have mentioned previously the very different ways in which God calls men to the priesthood, and probably there are as many differing ways in which he calls others to their vocations in medicine, nursing, train driving, grave digging, and all the other great and humble tasks which have to be done if his world is to go on as he plans; and to each of which he calls the man whom he has specially created for it. To one who thinks and lives as I have done, there is never any problem of knowing whether one is following one's vocation or not. If before making any decision one murmurs a brief prayer for guidance and then just goes ahead and does what appears to be right, it always is right. One can be absolutely certain one has been guided, that what one has been guided to do is the will of God (and therefore by definition must be right), and that one is on course along the road that God has planned; that one is following that vocation. The proof of the pudding is in the eating. My remarks on the perfect satisfaction I have obtained from my two vocations were unrelated to satisfaction at feeling I have done the will of God. They are evidence (because few others would feel the same) that I was made for exactly that life and in such a way that nothing else could satisfy me.

But what of those to whom this route is closed? Who cannot pray to God for guidance because they have no knowledge of a God who guides. I am sure God never does anything without a good reason, and he does not create a man to live in the Amazon jungle or the unexplored parts of New Guinea unless it be to fulfil some specific task in his plan for the world: and he will not do so without very clearly calling him to that task. He will speak to him through his conscience, which in all of us is the voice of God, and thereby indicate to him what is the right thing to do. The man will still have the freewill to do what he sees to be good or what he sees to be bad, and if he chooses the good he will (though he knows it not) be doing God's will as well as the best of us. Jesus died for all men; not just for those who know him or know of him; and the Church has taught from the earliest times that those in a state of 'Invincible Ignorance' who live their lives according to what they genuinely believe to be right will be saved even though they have never heard of Christ or his Gospel.

Have I then nothing to regret? Has my life been as I would wish it to have been in all possible respects? Unhappily the answer is no. There has been one terrible defect. I have no wife and no children. Perhaps as a Christian, constantly asking God's advice on what I should do and how I should proceed, I should accept it as the will of God and be resigned or even joyful: but I am afraid I don't. I cannot help feeling that the fault is mine. True, in the distant past I have prayed fervently that God would, if it were his will, aid my wooing; but I really cannot think that after knowing what I should do I have always done it.

To a man who has not always been a priest and seldom a very good Christian, this is not of course one problem but two. I have said in the past (Heaven help me) that it would have been so much better if I had followed the local custom, in Sarawak at least, and taken a Dyak mistress. The girls when young are charming, loving, and loyal; and the children of such liaisons turn out attractive and usually highly intelligent. Had I done so I would now have a couple of children who had been to good public schools, married English girls, and provided me with half a dozen grandchildren. In all probability I should ultimately have married the girl and now have a devoted ugly wife in her early fifties who would be everything in the world to me. It would have been living in mortal sin for a time at least but, though one hates to admit it, sin in the past loses some of its horror. I doubt that the most devout of patriotic English churchmen today really regret that William of Normandy debauched the tanner's daughter. We once had a deeply religious middle-aged cook whose charming elderly 'Aunt' lived in a little house by herself and came up twice a

288

week to have tea with her in the kitchen. I remember that even then I was shocked that the old woman was so poor that she had no wireless as she could not afford the ten shillings a year for a licence. It was twenty years later that I discovered that the maid was illegitimate and the 'Aunt' was her mother and was living off her. One moral lapse fifty years before had saved the old woman from the workhouse, given her someone to love and be loved by, provided us with a cook in wartime when they were almost unobtainable, and provided the Lord with a loyal, devout, and devoted servant. I still wish I had a couple of children.